Brig

for
Dark Days

Bright Words
for
Dark Days

*Meditations for Women
Who Get the Blues*

Caroline Adams Miller

BANTAM BOOKS
NEW YORK · TORONTO · LONDON · SYDNEY · AUCKLAND

BRIGHT WORDS FOR DARK DAYS

A Bantam Book / November 1994

Library of Congress Cataloging-in-Publication Data

Miller, Caroline Adams, 1961–
    Bright words for dark days : meditations for women who get
the blues / Caroline Adams Miller.
        p.   cm.
    ISBN 0-553-37181-9
    1. Depressed persons—Prayer-books and devotions—English.
2. Women—Prayer-books and devotions—English.
3. Devotional calendars. I. Title.
BL625.9.D45M55 1994
158'.12—dc20   94-15934
                                                          CIP

Published simultaneously in the United States and Canada

Bantam Books are published by Bantam Books, a division of Bantam
Doubleday Dell Publishing Group, Inc. Its trademark, consisting of the
words "Bantam Books" and the portrayal of a rooster, is Registered in
U.S. Patent and Trademark Office and in other countries. Marca
Registrada. Bantam Books, 1540 Broadway, New York, New York
10036.

PRINTED IN THE UNITED STATES OF AMERICA

FFG   0 9 8 7 6 5 4 3 2 1

*To my grandmother
Dorothy Roberts Benner
who has brought so much sunshine into my life*

Acknowledgments

Many thanks go to my agent, Vicky Bijur, who is a constant source of support and advice, and to my editors Maria Mack, whose cogent comments shaped the direction of this book, Alison Rivers, who coordinated all the details of publication, and Toni Burbank, who polished the final product.

My parents, Bill and Millicent Adams, babysat in a pinch so that I could have more time to write, and they contributed at least one inspirational quotation from their beloved game of baseball.

I'd also like to acknowledge my rambunctious daughter, Samantha, who arrived in the midst of this project and whose merry presence illuminated many days; and my husband, H. Haywood Miller III, and son, Haywood IV, who give me so much to be grateful for.

Author's Note

This book addresses the serious and increasingly recognized problem of depression, which strikes 25 percent of all women at some point in their lives, but primarily those between the ages of twenty-five and forty-four. Depression is often misunderstood and misdiagnosed, which helps explain why only a fraction of the people who need treatment ever seek it. But depression is one of the most treatable illnesses, and 80 percent of those who receive treatment improve dramatically within six months.

I wrote this book to help the millions of women who experience various forms of depression—from run-of-the-mill blahs, or "the blues," to chronic depression, to postpartum depression. All of the meditations are designed to provide advice and hope for days when your mood is dark and life seems meaningless. This book, however, is not meant to replace therapy or medication, which are necessary with some forms of depression. I strongly urge anyone who is experiencing the classic signs of depression—a change in sleeping or eating habits, lethargy, feelings of worthlessness, an inability to concentrate, or thoughts of suicide—to seek professional help immediately. These meditations will comfort you, but they cannot cure you.

If you don't know where you're going, you will probably end up somewhere else.

—LAURENCE JOHNSTON PETER

When I was a teenage competitive swimmer, I lost an important race one night to someone I wanted to beat. Despondant, I sat on my towel afterward, and my father came up and put his arm around my shoulders. "You'll be the champion one day if you put your mind to it," he promised. "Just plan your work and work your plan." Those words guided me as I set about improving my times, and by the end of the year I was, indeed, the faster swimmer.

All of us need to set goals if we are to be satisfied with our lives. One motivational expert says that people who set goals earn approximately 50 percent more than people who don't. To get where you want to go in life, he stresses, you have to have some idea where you want to go and what steps are required to help you get there. Once you know that, your life has a focus. By starting with small steps, or specific tasks that you need to accomplish, you will begin to feel purposeful as you go about your day.

Are you depressed because your life lacks direction or you're reluctantly following a path that someone else wants you to take? If so, think about where you want to be in a year and what you can do to achieve that goal. Break this down into manageable steps and then bolster yourself with positive thinking. If you can wake up with a clearly defined mission each morning, you'll discover the self-confidence and happiness that flow from having a vision and believing in your ability to reach your goal.

Today I'll know where I am going.

The day will happen whether you get up or not.
—JOHN CIARDI

There are days when I'm so down that I resolve to not get up and get my work done because "it doesn't matter" and "things won't improve anyway." When I'm in this kind of self-pitying, maudlin mood I'm not much good to myself or anyone else. I wear my depression clothes—black outfits or formless sweatsuits—and mope around, snapping at anyone who crosses my path. Usually I find my way back into bed, wasting whatever hours I have left in the day.

When we're feeling discouraged or angry about our lives, we can crumple or we can fight. And if we declare that the day is going to be a disaster before anything's even happened, we ensure that the next twenty-four hours will be worthless. If we wake up feeling depressed but resolve to make the best of it, however, we open ourselves up to the possibility that something good can occur to change our mood or situation.

Throwing the towel in before the day even happens is our choice if we want to stay depressed. But if we choose optimism, we acknowledge that life is unpredictable and out of our hands, and that the chances of the day improving is as good as the chances it won't. Try to get out of bed with hopefulness today and remember that a positive attitude can be a magnet for good things to come to you.

I expect positive things to happen to me today.

I think wholeness comes from living your life consciously during the day and then exploring your inner life or unconscious at night.

—MARGERY CUYLER

A well-known psychiatrist and healer who runs week-long workshops on how to find "your bliss" opens his seminars by asking the participants what they dreamed about during the previous night. After years as a therapist he has found that the answers to many people's problems are contained in their dreams, and that often we need only be shown how to decipher them in order to find contentment.

I became a believer in dream therapy when I flipped through some old journals of mine one day and was astonished to find that the dreams I'd jotted down several years earlier had actually contained seeds to solutions that had unexpectedly appeared later. My experience echos that of a time-management expert who says that busy women can simplify their lives by asking their subconscious for answers to problems before they go to bed and then writing down their dreams the moment they awaken. More often than not, she says, her clients report that they've become happier and more organized as a result of paying attention to their nighttime visions.

Try to sleep on something that's depressing you today. Buy a book on understanding your dreams so that you have some tools to help make sense of what your subconscious reveals. Once you learn how to decipher the answers, it's possible you'll find peacefulness.

I will use my subconscious mind to bring me comfort and solutions.

We should do everything both cautiously and confidently at the same time.

—EPICTETUS

One of the things we need to do cautiously if we're suffering from depression is take medication. Although antidepressant and anti-anxiety medications can positively tranform the quality of our lives when we're scared and sad, they all have side effects. Accordingly we must be vigilant about monitoring their impact on our bodies and minds, and we mustn't be afraid to speak up if we feel we aren't thriving on a certain type of drug.

An older friend of mine who found that therapy wasn't making a significant dent in her long-standing depression went on a serotonin-enhancing antidepressant on the advice of her doctor. Although the medication worked for many others, my friend found that it left her feeling groggy and lethargic. She finally mustered up the nerve to tell her doctor she didn't feel right, and he switched her to another type of medication that provided her with the clarity and peace she'd been seeking.

Be an educated consumer of medications and instead of just taking a doctor's advice, be sure to monitor your reactions carefully. For example, analyze whether your medication is effective during the premenstrual phase when depression often worsens for women, or be sure to speak up if you are concerned about a side effect you've noticed. Understanding medication and using it to enhance your life must be done cautiously, but when handled well, it can be used with confidence.

I will be an educated and assertive consumer of the medications I take for depression.

Nothing makes one feel so strong as a call for help.
—GEORGE MACDONALD

My parents taught me that working hard and solving my problems myself were the best ways to deal with life's vicissitudes. Asking for help, especially from a therapist, wasn't considered admirable or self-reliant.

I lived this way for many years until a crush of problems including low self-esteem, an eating disorder, and severe depression forced me into therapy. I can still remember how embarrassed I was while making my first appointment; on top of all my other dilemmas, I added feelings of "failure" because I couldn't solve my problems myself. In hindsight, I believe that calling a therapist may have saved my life. Through a very wise woman's guidance, I learned coping skills I doubt I could have discovered on my own.

Reaching out for help—whether it is to a professional, a friend, or a self-help group—is one of the smartest things we can do when we're depressed. For when we're discouraged and feeling hopeless, thinking clearly is not one of our strong suits. We'll also find that when we have the humility to admit that we don't have the answers to what ails us, we open our minds to new solutions to our problems.

Whenever I can ask for help, I am strengthened, not weakened.

The process of living is the process of reacting to stress.
—STANLEY J. SARNOFF

One of the places where Americans increasingly face stress is on the job. Partly as a result of corporate cutbacks and mergers, people are finding that their jobs are hazardous to their physical and emotional health because they're unsure of their job stability. In fact, one study showed that seven out of ten workers experienced health problems as a result of on-the-job stress, and that at least 34 percent of the people polled had considered quitting their jobs to eliminate stress in their lives.

One friend of mine experienced this problem when the large corporation she worked for began a wave of downsizing over a period of years. Every few months people would be eliminated, evoking her fear that she would be the next to go. Morale at the office plummeted and people found it hard to work. My friend said that her ulcer acted up and she gained weight as she sought to bury her anxiety and depression in food. Finally, she was let go in the final round of streamlining but found—to her surprise—that her depression lifted and she suddenly felt free to move ahead with her life.

Psychologists say that avoiding "doom and gloom" talk at work, refusing to be drawn into criticism of management, and striving to be a team player are all ways we can minimize job stress. And if these techniques can help stabilize us at the office, we'll likely carry that sense of satisfaction and happiness with us elsewhere, too.

I will practice at least one stress-reduction technique today.

It is only possible to live happily ever after on a day to day basis.

—Margaret Bonnano

After I had my second child I found that the pregnancy weight was harder to shed than it had been after having my first child and that my body wasn't snapping back into shape as quickly as it had before. After several weeks of avoiding the mirror, I finally took out some jeans that I'd worn before I got pregnant. To my great chagrin I could zip them up only with great difficulty and the mirror revealed a very out-of-shape, swollen body.

Immediately I entered a depression about my weight, not unlike the countless ones I'd experienced throughout my life. I vowed to eliminate most food groups from my diet and to be at my prepregnancy weight as soon as possible. Luckily, it wasn't long before I realized that my resolutions were extreme and that my unhappiness was a silly waste of time. It was going to take some time to lose the weight in a healthful way because it hadn't appeared overnight, and I saw that I could choose between being miserable or happy as I gradually worked my way back into shape.

If you're facing a task today that seems overwhelming and you're depressed about how long it will take to reach your goal, find the positives in your life to emphasize and just work on living through each day at a time. If you can divert yourself with other things that make you happy while being patient, you'll discover that whatever it is you are waiting for always arrives sooner than you think.

I will only seek happiness one day at a time.

Within you there is a stillness and a sanctuary to which you can retreat at anytime and be yourself.
—HERMANN HESSE

Each day we are continually surrounded by noises and interruptions of all kinds, from the telephone to the television to the sounds of traffic. Because of all the demands put on us, it's not easy to retreat within to a place of quiet and stillness. Yet it is this inner sanctuary that can give us the comfort we need when we're hurting.

In Eastern traditions, meditation is encouraged to get a person in touch with their inner stillness and Native Americans go on solitary retreats in the desert for the same purpose. Many of my friends say yoga is what comforts them when they feel out of sync, and others use long, quiet walks or jogs to achieve inner peace.

In a world that feels unsafe and scary at times, it's important to be comfortable with ourselves when we're alone and to know how to access a feeling of inner security when we need it. Although depression isn't always helped by isolating ourselves from others, learning how to go within in order to heal, not hurt, can bring us untold benefits and a quiet feeling of peacefulness.

I will ease my sadness by calling upon the strength of my inner core.

Love cures people, the ones who receive love and the ones who give it.

—KARL A. MENNINGER

New research shows that those who are depressed can help themselves enormously by focusing on someone else in need. The resultant "helper's high" often provides enough of an endorphin boost that we feel positive long after the good deed is done. The "helper's high" has been shown to increase physical well-being, foster greater feelings of spirituality, and provide a more positive outlook. Volunteering often maximizes the benefits we receive, and it's been demonstrated that not knowing the people we help can be an even bigger boost. Former First Lady Barbara Bush once said that getting involved in a local soup kitchen was the only thing that had saved her from a "terrible" depression that manifested when her husband took a position that required frequent travel away from home.

There are many ways to stimulate the "helper's high" if you need a boost. Check the newspapers for listings of organizations that need volunteers, such as literacy programs and meals for elderly shut-ins, and then try to commit some time on a regular basis. It doesn't matter whether you pick the "right" charity or not; it only matters that you get out and take some positive action to counteract your negative feelings.

When I give, I also receive.

Of all the peoples whom I have studied, from city dwellers to cliff dwellers, I always find that at least 50 percent would prefer to have at least one jungle between themselves and their mothers-in-law.

—MARGARET MEAD

One of my best friends, Sandra, has the worst mother-in-law imaginable. The woman wore black at Sandra's wedding, refused to pose in the pictures, and groaned loudly throughout the ceremony. In the subsequent ten years she has repeatedly insulted Sandra, disparaged her to family friends, and pointedly avoided sending her or her children birthday gifts.

Although she usually concedes that her mother-in-law is irrational, Sandra sometimes finds herself depressed about her predicament, wondering if there is anything she could have done differently to prevent the hostilities. She also finds herself occasionally doubting her skills as a wife, mother, and friend, wondering if her mother-in-law might accurately see something awful inside her.

Unfortunately, we aren't always going to get along with others, especially the members of the family into which we marry. Mothers-in-law, in particular, may *never* feel that someone is "good enough" for their sons, no matter how beautiful and charming the women are. Try inwardly repeating the phrase "dignity and distance" whenever you are caught in this kind of position. Also, frequently remind yourself that you married a specific person, not his entire family, and that making your own relationship strong is one of the most effective responses you can have to in-law troubles.

I will be mature and dignified around people who dislike me for irrational reasons.

Words are, of course, the most powerful drug used by mankind.

—RUDYARD KIPLING

Some words have the ability to affect me greatly, and even to provoke depression, no matter how innocuously they are used in conversation. For example, the word *girl* immediately reminds me of a man I once worked with who used it to let me know how young and stupid he thought I was. Since recognizing this connection I've been able to monitor my emotions whenever I hear it and remember that I'm reacting to a memory, and not necessarily to what is being said at the time.

Language experts say that such occurrences are not uncommon and that we all have words stored in our brains that can immediately make us happy or sad. One professor of neurology says that this is the reason why lullabies create feelings of calm and memories of warmth, while words like *divorce* or *defensive* can make our blood pressure soar and cause our moods to swing downward. Everyone has different "trigger words," and knowing what they are and how we respond to them can save us from overreacting when we hear them.

Assess your reactions to certain words and sounds today. Within a moment of hearing a certain phrase, do you feel a burst of euphoria or painful sadness? Does your heart race and your face get flushed? Humans are complex creatures with mysterious reflexes, so understanding the stimuli that trigger our feelings and using that knowledge to fight depression can be potent tools for us.

I will be aware of the power of words today.

Life is full and overflowing with the new. But it is necessary to empty out the old to make room for the new to enter.
—EILEEN CADDY

Janet is a talented, attractive, and vivacious woman who desperately wants to get married and settle down. She wants Mr. Right to come into her life but Mr. Not-Quite-Right is usually present. When her friends listen to her complaints about how deficient her boyfriends are and encourage her to get rid of him, she inevitably responds that she doesn't want to be alone at night and on weekends.

What my friend doesn't realize is that until she completely gives up the wrong man in her life, the right one won't appear. As long as we insist on clinging to people, behaviors, or situations that don't really suit us, we'll never attract what we really want and we'll stay miserable and needy. When we create a vacuum in our lives, however, we can't help but fill it with something new—and hopefully better.

Is there some stagnant area in your life that is making you depressed? Are you holding up change by hanging on to something that isn't right for you but that you're comfortable with? Try today to create a vacuum in one area that you want to change and visualize what you want filling its place. Remind yourself that you deserve to have what is best for you, so don't lower your standards and settle for less than what you truly want.

When I make room for what I want to enter into my life, I'm one step closer to receiving it.

Often the test of courage is not to die but to live.
— Vittorio Alfieri

I once heard a woman talking about how her weight had driven her to the brink of suicide. Overwhelmed with misery at being over three hundred pounds and tired of the various futile attempts to lose them, she had gone to the tenth floor of a building where she looked down at the traffic and contemplated whether she had the courage to kill herself. At this point in her story the woman laughed because the only thing that had kept her from jumping was the thought that her skirt would land over her knees and everyone would see how fat she was.

Anyone who has been depressed has probably thought about suicide at some point. It may seem very easy to end the pain by just checking out of life, but it is definitely not the right answer. People who have tried suicide and survived almost always say that they're glad they lived, discovering that in the end their problems were only temporary. They're often so surprised by these feelings that it only takes another few days or so for them to have a totally new perspective on life and to find the hope that was missing before.

Suicide is not the solution to any problem—no matter how severe. If you are having thoughts of killing yourself, you must talk to a professional who can counsel you and suggest appropriate treatment. With time and help, you'll recognize that killing yourself is not the answer, and you'll be grateful you had the courage to live through the doubts.

It takes more strength to live some days than it does to die.

Silence is the element in which great things fashion themselves.

—THOMAS CARLYLE

A well-known businessman was once ousted from the company he founded and built into greatness. The qualities that had served him well in being an entrepreneur hadn't been helpful in expanding and managing the company, so his colleagues and board members demanded his resignation. Depressed, the man left the company, retreating to a deserted island in the Pacific where he pondered what to do with the rest of his life.

Within a year he regained his optimism and returned home to start up a new company. He was interviewed by several reporters, curious about his return to the business world. What had helped him the most, he told them, were long solitary walks on the beach every morning during which he cleared his mind and allowed himself to ponder over what he wanted from life and how he wanted to spend his time. He had never been an introspective person, he noted, so he was surprised that silence had provided him with the answers.

Instead of seeing silence as something to be frightened of, we need to embrace it—especially when we're troubled about something. Unfettered by noise and unnecessary conversation, we may be surprised that the solutions we seek are readily available and that our inner voice is unerring when given the freedom and time to express itself.

I learn the most when I talk the least.

Any woman who has a career and a family automatically develops something in the way of two personalities, like two sides of a dollar bill, each different in design. . . . Her problem is to keep one from draining the life from the other.
—IVY BAKER PRIEST

For nine years I attended a top-notch women's prep school where all of my role models were strong women who repeatedly told us that there was nothing we couldn't accomplish if we put our minds to it. Consequently I found that I emerged from high school, and later college, with an idealistic view that I could be a world-class writer, superb mother, and nurturing wife all at the same time without feeling stress or guilt.

In the last ten years my ideal has been shattered repeatedly by my own experiences and those of women around me. The simple truth is that we cannot juggle a lot of balls in the air without dropping a few every now and then. There are going to be times when our careers or our children may take precedence over quiet time with our husbands or friends. There will also be times when we have uninterrupted hours to talk on the phone as well as weeks when we won't even be able to return a phone call.

If you are feeling depressed today because you're trying to perform many roles and you don't feel adequate in any of them, try to remember that Superwoman exists only in the comics. Do the best you can in a certain role at a certain time and then move on to the next one without regrets. Once we can learn that our best is good enough and that women with many balls in the air are happier than those who aren't juggling enough, we will probably find more contentment and fulfillment in our days.

My many roles energize me; they don't drain me.

Grow up as soon as you can. It pays. The only time you really live fully is from thirty to sixty.

—HERVEY ALLEN

Many women find themselves getting depressed when they reach ages they consider milestones—thirty, forty, fifty, or sixty—because it reminds them of how old they are and what they haven't yet accomplished. Women, more than men, also associate aging with becoming unattractive, undesirable, and over the hill.

There has been a growth of women's gatherings in recent years to help fight these negative stereotypes. In California a group of women meets every month on the full moon to celebrate being in the "full moon" of their lives. Every woman is required to discuss at least one positive thing that their age has brought them, whether it's freedom from children in diapers, perspective on how to cope with men, or just greater stature at work. One participant says that being forced to concentrate on the benefits of aging has made her more fully aware of how many good things have come with being over fifty, and as a result she's decided to stop dying her hair and to let it go gray.

In Japan, families are considered to have a gem in their midst when an older member lives with them. If we can adopt more of this philosophy and see ourselves as wonderful accumulations of experience, knowledge, and love the older we get, then we won't torture ourselves by trying to preserve youth when our mature years have so much to offer us.

The best years of my life are always ahead of me.

Sex ought to be a wholly satisfying link between two affectionate people from which they emerge unanxious, rewarded, and ready for more.

—ALEX COMFORT

Therapists say that there is now an epidemic of sexual problems among working couples, the most common of which is inhibited sexual desire—when the wife or husband has no desire for sex. Most often, the therapists say, it stems from the wife feeling angry about the inequitable distribution of housework and despite a fulltime job being overwhelmingly responsible for laundry, childcare, and housekeeping. This complaint has a basis in fact; only ten percent of households say there is equal sharing of chores.

A woman who shops, cooks, cleans, handles pediatrician appointments, and also works outside the home without significant help from her partner can't help but feel depressed about her predicament. When this type of situation occurs, sexual passion and respect for our partner is nearly impossible. Until the woman has a chance to air her frustrations and household responsibilities are readjusted, sexual problems will probably remain and could become long-term and even more difficult to treat.

Examine the division of household work. Be assertive about your feelings and try to work out a sharing schedule that frees up more of your energy and time. If possible, hire someone to help out once a week, too. Not only will pinpointing some of the causes of depression and stress and taking action to address them empower us, but it may return some light-heartedness and joy to our sex life, as well.

I will not deplete my energy and emotions by taking on work that can be shared.

If you wish to live, you must first attend your own funeral.
—KATHERINE MANSFIELD

I was talking to my neighbor one day about her seemingly unending search for a rewarding, well-paying job and how difficult it was for her to make ends meet. I asked how she was faring with the disappointments and financial fears, and she said that the only way she coped was to experience her anxieties and depression to their fullest. "I really wallow in it," she said. "I cry, scream, throw things at the walls, and just suffer for a few days. Then I get it out of my system and move on."

Some of us first need to acknowledge our depression and fully experience it before we can begin the healing process. To pretend we really aren't hurting, or to avoid completely breaking down because we don't think it's dignified, will just put off feeling the pain that is sure to come. Embracing it with open arms, crying in frustration, and breaking a few things may be the best first step in getting back on our feet.

The road back to happiness and contentment is sometimes long and difficult, and starting on that journey is always preceded by moments when we doubt that we'll ever feel whole or optimistic again. If you are at that point now, acknowledge your suffering and remind yourself that life can only get better from now on. While your "funeral" may not be a pleasant place to be, it can be the beginning of a path that brings you much more joy.

Suffering always precedes a flowering of life.

For the sense of smell, almost more than any other, has the power to recall memories and it is a pity that we use it so little.
—RACHEL CARSON

One of the fastest-growing natural health remedies in this country is aromatherapy. Aromatherapy uses certain essential oils to stimulate the body's healing reflexes and induce a positive mood. The oils can be used in a number of ways; for example, they can be used in the bath, as massage oils, in hair solutions, as perfumes, and as room fresheners. Certain smells have even been isolated as guaranteed pick-me-ups, aphrodisiacs, or energizers that work on everyone.

I never fail to be calmed by the scent of roses, honeysuckle, and orange blossoms, which remind me of extremely happy times when I was younger and more carefree. One friend of mine spritzes on the cologne of an ex-lover whenever she is down because it reminds her of a very passionate time in her life. Another friend loves the smell of mothballs because it reminds her of her childhood and her mother's spring cleaning rituals.

Use the power of scent to pick you up today. Whether it's visiting a store's perfume counter, using some carefully selected oils in your bath, buying a flowering plant, or putting potpourri in your bureau drawers, draw upon the properties of fragrance to take you into another world and give you a much-needed positive lift.

I will surround myself with wonderful smells today.

All cruel people describe themselves as paragons of frankness.
                                        —TENNESSEE WILLIAMS

Sometimes when we are down we don't want to hear that we need to keep a stiff upper lip, that other people are suffering more than we are, and that our problems aren't *that* bad. We want—and need—to feel self-pity and receive sympathy. We have the strong desire to be babied and told that we have every reason in the world to feel wounded.

I've learned that when I'm feeling this way I have to choose carefully the people to whom I talk. I avoid one friend in particular who is fun to be with when I'm feeling good, but who is huffy and angry when I'm not. Whenever I have the flu, she has a list of friends who are sicker; when I'm sad, she insists that her life is worse; and when I just need sympathy, she retorts that I'm not homeless and impoverished, therefore I "should" be okay.

Remember today that our friends are valuable in different ways when we are feeling depressed and alone, and that we need to solicit their support carefully when we are in need. Call the loving, compassionate ones who will sympathize with your pain when you're down, but save the brutally frank, somewhat insensitive ones for when you're really ready to roll up your sleeves and go to work on yourself.

Friends who validate my pain and nurture me in dark times are healing to my soul.

Why is life speeded up so? Why are things so terribly, unbearably precious that you can't enjoy them but can only wait breathless in dread of their going?

—ANNE MORROW LINDBERGH

Often I catch myself becoming depressed in the midst of a happy and wonderful period of my life because I'm worried about that joy leaving my life. It's only upon reflection that I realize how I diluted the happiness within my grasp by looking ahead to its loss rather than appreciating its presence in my life.

I find this to be most poignant around the aging of my children. For example, one night when my son was very young I went in to check on him and instead of being happy that he was resting peacefully, I became depressed that I couldn't stop his growth and keep him at that lovable, innocent stage. I continued to do this as he got older until I saw that I was throwing joy away with both hands by living in the past. Now I try to savor every moment of his and my daughter's lives, knowing that unless I enjoy happy moments as they occur, they'll be gone in a flash and I won't be able to call them back.

Sometimes we can be our own worst enemies when we turn happiness into depression because we're anticipating the other shoe dropping, or we're worrying that our good fortune will disappear. Try to enjoy what you have right now that gives you pleasure instead of tainting it with fear and negativity. Learning to live in the moment and to see happiness as our right, not something that is bound to slip away, can help us shed sadness and seize the joy we deserve.

I won't speed up my life today.

If one is lucky, a solitary fantasy can totally transform one million realities.

—MAYA ANGELOU

One day I was reading an article about how to cope with anxiety and depression, and I was interested to see that daydreaming scored high as a way to shake off cares and worries. The researchers noted that people who were able to lose themselves in thought and fantasize about being in a sun-drenched spot in the dead of winter, or at a happy gathering when they were sad, were better able to marshal their inner resources than those who couldn't be as creative.

Daydreaming can serve many purposes. For one, it can open our minds to solutions that we cannot access when we are in a rigid mindset. When we are trying to take a minibreak from work demands or the hassles of child care, a few minutes of thinking about being pampered or of being in an open, flower-filled meadow can work wonders. And, of course, many people use fantasy as a safe way to perk up a stagnant sex life when they're in a rut with their partners.

If your life is so busy that you have no time for reveries, you're impoverishing yourself. Try to carve out a few minutes each day in bed, in a bath, in a quiet car, or in a restroom just to mentally float above your cares. Not only does this form of meditation often work to restore our spirits, but it can provide a respite that enriches our inner life and helps us better cope with life's daily tasks.

I will daydream about being in a happy place today.

The feminine mystique has succeeded in burying millions of American women alive.

—BETTY FRIEDAN

When *The Feminine Mystique* was published in the 1950s, it was unusual for women to break out of their stay-at-home roles and be anything but wives, mothers, carpool drivers, Cub Scout leaders, and PTA members. This strait-jacket caused many women who didn't find fulfillment in these roles to go quietly crazy and become addicted to all kinds of self-destructive pursuits. Even several decades later "the feminine mystique" is still making some women miserable.

At a dinner party one evening I was seated next to a woman who was once slim, vibrant, and outgoing. To my surprise she was none of these things any longer; she confided that she was depressed and fatigued by her nonstop routine of caring for three children, cleaning the house until late at night, and making sure her husband was happy. Because she didn't have a paying job, she didn't think she "deserved" to hire a cleaning person or a babysitter. And because her husband wanted her home with the children "for their own good," she was afraid to tell him that she felt unfulfilled and angry about her life.

Being a full-time mother and housewife is a noble and wonderful profession, but if you only do this to please someone else, you're setting yourself up for emotional disaster. Take steps to diversify your life if you're stifled by this role by hiring help, returning to school, or getting a job —even if only part-time. While we may think that someone else's expectations are making us depressed, we are often our own worst enemies by acquiescing to their desires.

I will not allow myself to be buried alive at home today.

[Cigarettes are] killers that travel in packs.

—MARY S. OTT

In the health-conscious 1990s, to be a smoker is to be a leper. Restaurants, malls, airplanes, and offices now routinely ban smokers from their premises because of the harmful effects of second-hand smoke, but even these sanctions are often not enough to get someone to quit. Nicotine addiction is one of the toughest to break, and unless someone's health or well-being is affected, a person often won't undergo the emotional and physical rigors of quitting.

New studies have come up with at least one compelling reason why we shouldn't smoke, particularly if depression is a problem. Smokers are far more likely to experience major depression than nonsmokers, and the more cigarettes a person smokes, the greater their likelihood of experiencing depression. Genetic predisposition is responsible for this link, but researchers say that with therapy and environmental changes we can override our genes.

Be aware of the smoke you are inhaling directly or indirectly today. If you are a smoker, try to make a commitment to break your addiction, and if you're forced to be in a smoke-filled environment, try to be assertive about altering your surroundings. These little changes in our lives will not only improve our physical health, they will have a direct impact on our emotions.

I will have a smoke-free day.

I will have no locked cupboards in my life.

—GERTRUDE BELL

I know several people who waste a lot of time in therapy because they don't tell their therapists crucial information about what is really going on in their lives. For example, I know a bulimic woman who talks to her therapist about many things, but not about her obsession with food. Another friend is having an affair with a married man but she won't tell her therapist for fear of what he'll think of her.

Whenever we're trying to understand our feelings and moods, it's essential that we be forthright with ourselves and those who are trying to help us. If we avoid discussing major parts of our lives because we don't want to confront them or we're afraid of others' reactions, then we're just wasting our time and the time of those who care about us. Therapists need our complete honesty in order to do their jobs, and we owe it to them and to ourselves to give them the tools that will lead us to self-understanding and self-acceptance.

Do you shield parts of yourself from others because you're ashamed to appear imperfect and troubled? All of us have pieces inside that we would prefer that others not see, but if we're looking for solutions, we need to be honest with those from whom we seek advice. If we just persist in hiding because we think it's easier and less embarrassing, keep in mind that whatever we don't voluntarily reveal often eventually emerges of its own accord, anyway.

I will be honest with people who have my best interests at heart.

Better by far you should forget and smile
Than that you should remember and be sad.
—CHRISTINA ROSSETTI

June is normally a happy and outgoing woman who enjoys the blessings of a good marriage and a satisfying career. But every winter she has a "creepy sad" period when she gets depressed for no apparent reason. With the help of a therapist, she discovered that her yearly blues were due to an unconscious remembrance of a traumatic time in her childhood when her parents divorced and her grandmother died. Now she plans a pleasurable activity—like a weekend getaway—every year at that time to help her cope with this annual melancholy.

Therapists say that the "calendar blues" are not just limited to experiencing sadness on the anniversary of a friend or family member's death, but that certain periods of the year can evoke depression because they are anniversaries of other painful events such as the loss of a sum of money, a miscarriage, or a job termination. It isn't uncommon for the person to feel out of sorts, irritable, and sad without knowing why, and for the symptoms to clear up within weeks for no apparent reason.

If you are depressed but there doesn't appear to be a specific trigger, search your memory for a traumatic event that occurred around this time. Perhaps a favorite relative died, you moved to a location that made you unhappy, or you broke up with someone you loved. If a buried memory is causing you grief, it would be wise to acknowledge your pain and mark your calendar so that you'll be prepared for your emotions when this time rolls around next year.

My "calendar blues" will pass with time.

Time is a great traitor who teaches us to accept loss.
                    —ELIZABETH BORTON DE TREVINO

In the United States we have become accustomed to solving problems in the blink of an eye. People are often angry if they have to stand in any kind of line, and headache remedies usually promise instantaneous relief. I'm frequently amused by weight-loss gimmicks that claim you will effortlessly lose pounds overnight if you slide on some contraption or spread some substance on your body.

One of the most pragmatic things I ever read was about how one woman coped with the abrupt deaths of her children in an automobile accident. When she went to a therapist to try to find out how long she'd have sleepless nights, angry rages, and teary episodes, he said to her quite simply, "This thing is going to kick your butt for a long time." Just having that knowledge and not the illusion that she'd feel better soon helped this woman recognize ways she could rediscover some purpose in her life and be gentle with herself when her grieving dragged on.

Time may be the only thing we have to help us deal with a loss or some other sadness we face. Instead of thinking that pain can be instantly obliterated, we must deal with the fact that the blues can stretch out for the forseeable future, and that the only way to get through them is to experience them in their excruciating entirety. Although long solutions may be painful, we need to remember that quick fixes often don't work and may leave us vulnerable to future depressions.

I will not expect overnight solutions to my problems.

We are indeed much more than what we eat, but what we eat can nevertheless help us to be much more than what we are.
—ADELLE DAVIS

There is a well-known film star whose weight has ranged from slender to obese over several decades. Although she's emphatic that she is the same fine actress whether fat or thin, she says that when she's overweight she's much more unhappy. "I've tried to be a feminist about this and find other reasons for my depression," she insists, "but when I come right down to it, I feel emotionally and physically better when I'm thin than when I'm fat and uncomfortable."

Although one's weight alone is not necessarily a cause for depression, studies have shown that overweight women react more strongly to life's lows—depression, anxiety, tension, and daily hassles—than normal or underweight women. Why this is, no one is certain. But if it enhances our well-being to be fit, it behooves us to be as close to the weight that's healthiest for us as possible. Eating moderately and exercising regularly are two of the most important steps we can take toward achieving this important goal.

Try to foster a lifestyle that increases your odds of being at a normal weight today. Not only will you reap the physical rewards that come with a sound body, but you'll undoubtedly have a greater sense of control, raise your tolerance of stress, and help stabilize your emotions.

A sound body can give me a sound mind.

I always feel sorry for people who think more about a rainy day ahead than sunshine today.

—RAE FOLEY

One of the hallmarks of a depressed person is the amount of time she spends obsessively worrying about things that have already happened and things that might occur in the future. Once we're already down, it's easy for our minds to continue on a loop of self-defeating, bleak forecasts for ourselves. And if we ruminate on the negative long enough, our predictions for ourselves may become self-fulfilling, which will only fuel our despair.

If we are to manage depression, we must manage our worrying. Therapists cite a number of techniques that are successful in doing this. One of the most popular is a "worry box." A chronic worrier puts slips of paper with her worries into a box and is told to look at and consequently think about them only at a designated time. One therapist who uses this exercise says that patients often find that their worries revolve around one theme—such as fear of economic insecurity—and that identifying the core anxiety gives them a specific area to focus on.

If your incessant worrying is contributing to depression, try the worry-box solution. Self-help books and therapists can provide other ideas about how to stop the negative thoughts that are paralyzing you from acting decisively. Whatever methods you use to change your thinking, you'll probably find that if you can manage your worries, you'll effectively manage your depression.

I will put my worries into a box today.

I am never afraid of what I know.

—ANNA SEWELL

After Charlene was successfully treated for alcoholism, an unexpected—and unwelcome—side effect surfaced. While driving over a bridge on the way to a familiar vacation spot, she developed overwhelming feelings of panic and she had to grip the steering wheel so tight that her hands turned white. Since that time she hasn't been able to drive across a bridge herself without having a full-blown panic attack, and when others drive she has to lie under a blanket in the back seat. Charlene is often depressed about her condition but is too embarrassed to seek help.

Panic attacks are a very common and treatable problem that often accompany, or precede, depression. Sufferers are overcome with feelings of dread and their bodies go into the fight-or-flight response whenever the stressful situation occurs; being in enclosed spaces, speaking in public, and leaving the house are some well-known triggers. The treatment for panic attacks usually consists of antidepressants or tranquilizers and "panic control" sessions in which the patient induces the frightening sensations and then learns how to cope with them through relaxation and cognitive strategies. One expert says that "Know Thy Enemy" is his motto because once a patient knows how to accommodate the uncomfortable feelings of an attack, she discovers that the catastrophe she feared doesn't occur.

If you are depressed because of panic attacks, seek out professional help soon because progress is almost always made in the first three months of treatment. If you can understand and face what you fear most, you won't just conquer it, you'll probably conquer your depression, too.

When I understand something, it loses its power over me.

That's the truest sign of insanity—insane people are always sure they're just fine. It's only the sane people who are willing to admit they're crazy.

—NORA EPHRON

Nan is a chain-smoking, self-pitying woman who can't sustain a friendship with anyone. When someone suggests that she talk to a therapist to see if there are ways she can attain greater happiness in life, Nan brusquely refuses, saying haughtily that therapists are only for "crazy" people.

There are many people like Nan who are blind to their self-destructive behavior and who believe that everyone but them is insane. Ironically, it's often these types of people who could benefit the most from therapy. For example, a friend of mine whose mother is emotionally and verbally abusive invited the mother to a therapy session to discuss their difficult relationship. After the rocky therapy session the mother loudly announced to family members that she was "so glad" her daughter was getting help for "her problems."

If you're doubting your sanity because you're in therapy or you're considering getting help, try to take comfort in the fact that only strong people have the courage to look inward and attempt to understand themselves. Coming to a place of contentment and happiness often involves going through periods of intense self-doubt and pain, but it is exactly these emotions that prompt us to get there.

Feeling insane is often a sign of sanity.

My solitude grew more and more obese, like a pig.
—Yukio Mishima

When we are discouraged and don't feel that our lives are on track, it's very easy to isolate and refuse the sympathy of others. When I was once in a particularly bad funk, I practically reveled in how miserable I was and how unconnected I felt to other people. Even when I knew I ought to be reaching out to others, I took perverse pride in remaining sequestered and dwelling on my sorrows.

As much as we like to avoid people when we're down, one proven and infallible mood lifter is mingling with others. I know I've gone from black despair to good humor by being forced out into public, whether it was to the dentist's office or the grocery store. In spite of myself and my efforts to continue to focus on my woes, the simple act of talking to another human being seemed to be an effective method for temporarily forgetting about myself.

If it looks like today is going to be a day of self-imposed solitude because you just don't feel like facing the world, force yourself to plan at least one outing. Commit to yourself or someone else that you'll create a window of time when you will interact with others. If you can make yourself do this, there's an excellent chance that you'll feel far better tonight than you can possibly imagine feeling this morning.

An outing today can keep the blues at bay.

A critic is a man who prefers the indolence of opinion to the trials of action.

—JOHN MASON BROWN

There's a person I know whose presence used to drag me down every time I saw her because she never had anything positive or encouraging to say about what I was doing. Under the guise of wanting to "help" me she'd throw cold water on my dreams, criticize my appearance, and say disparaging things about my friends. If I was filled with enthusiasm when I saw her, it inevitably evaporated after a few minutes of conversation.

I've since learned not to let this person depress me. After much thought I realized that my vivaciousness only reminds her that she's never had the courage to follow her own dreams, and I see how threatening that is to her. I still value other aspects of our relationship, though, so I limit what I discuss with her and make a point of only visiting her occasionally.

Remember today that those who depress you are operating from a sense of inadequacy that has nothing to do with you, and that your job is to prevent them from affecting you. If a coworker, friend, or relative doesn't lift your spirits, be sure to avoid them when you need support and enthusiasm. Separate their behavior from its ability to affect you and remember that as critics, they will always be on the sidelines, whereas you'll be on the field of life.

Today I will not let criticism affect my mood or my plans.

It's been so long since I made love I can't even remember who gets tied up.

—JOAN RIVERS

One of the most universal—and unpopular—side-effects of being depressed is not wanting to have intimate relations with anyone. One friend of mine who went through a protracted period of depression said that she used to walk down the street and see couples nuzzling each other, only to wonder, "Why are they doing that to each other?" Others' sexual desires are dampened by antidepressants.

As long as you are feeling blue, don't push yourself to be a dynamo in the bedroom. If you go through the motions with your lover just to satisfy him or her, you will probably experience little enjoyment, which will eventually lead to resentment. And if you tell yourself that you "should" enjoy intimacy because every other couple is "doing it" twice a week, you'll only wind up feeling inadequate and miserable.

Be realistic about what you can handle when your enjoyment of life is low. Expect that your interest in sex will be minimal for a while and remind yourself that like many things in life, there are natural ebbs and flows to sensuality. If your misery goes on too long, however, seek the advice of a professional because intimacy is one of life's most special gifts and going too long without the pleasure of closeness to another human being can only deepen your sadness and keep those you love at a distance.

I will be forgiving of myself when I can't find the energy to feel passion in my life.

They intoxicate themselves with work so they won't see how they really are.

—ALDOUS HUXLEY

One friend of mine in her mid-thirties went to see a psychiatrist because she was feeling depressed all the time and didn't understand why. Anne thought she should be happy: after all she had a job that took her all over the country, she received a lot of positive strokes from her colleagues and superiors, and she was well-compensated for her efforts.

The psychiatrist surprised Anne by telling her that she was running away from herself by working so hard. Like many of the "working wounded" he treated, Anne defined her self-worth on how well she did her job. Her subconscious, however, was letting her know that her emotional needs weren't being met. His suggestions included cutting back on work hours, making a weekly volunteer commitment, and spending more time with her family and friends. Unless Anne pulled away from her job and developed the other areas of her life, he warned that she was a candidate for a nervous breakdown.

Examine how much you depend on your job for your self-esteem today. If your mood is based on what happens to you at work, how much money you make, and how many professional accolades you rack up, you're setting yourself up for depression. Feeling good about yourself is something you bring to your job, not necessarily something you derive from it. Although it's important to feel satisfied with your job performance, remember that how you value yourself ought to be based on your character, not your résumé.

I will intoxicate myself with life today, not just work.

We are shaped and fashioned by what we love.
—JOHANN WOLFGANG VON GOETHE

I know a young couple that is never happy with what they've acquired or achieved. Their chief goal in life, it seems, is to make more money and amass more possessions. No matter how big or well-furnished their house is or how much money they have in the bank, they're still not satisfied. In fact, the wife often complains about how depressed she is because she feels as if she hasn't "made it."

Talking to this couple is impossible. They have no interest in anyone's lives but their own, and never ask about others' children or jobs except to compare their own situations. It's not surprising that their best "friends" are other self-centered people who probably wouldn't be too supportive in a crisis.

When we place our affection on material things, we'll always be prone to depression and envy. Ask yourself today what you love and where you derive your pleasure. If the answer is money, status, and possessions, try to shift your focus to more lasting, valuable things. Get involved in something that engages your soul, such as volunteering to a good cause, developing close friendships, or nurturing your children. You'll discover that whenever your values are in the right place, you'll always have an outlet to help restore your equilibrium when you're down.

Today I will love only that which will enrich me spiritually and emotionally.

Sleep that knits up the raveled sleeve of care.
—WILLIAM SHAKESPEARE

One of the wonderful anacronyms in twelve-step programs is HALT, which stands for "Don't let yourself get too hungry, angry, lonely, or tired," four states that can lead to sickness, depression, and poor performance in all areas of our lives.

Women are particularly vulnerable to depriving themselves of sleep because so many of us play multiple roles and find the only way to get everything done is to sleep less. Whenever we consistently fail to get at least six to eight hours of sleep at night, however, we run a higher risk of developing cardiovascular problems, menstrual disorders, and gastrointestinal disruptions, in addition to the other well-known effects of sleep deprivation: moodiness, impatience, and an inability to react quickly or efficiently to various tasks.

If you're feeling depressed, ask yourself whether you're getting enough sleep to keep yourself operating at peak levels. If not, consider trying to schedule one or two catnaps into your day, or a twenty-minute session of meditation. Also try to get regular exercise, avoid stimulants like caffeine, and religiously go to bed at a sensible hour, regardless of how interesting the late-night shows are or how many items are still left on your to-do list. If you do some or all of these things, you might be surprised at how much more energetic, happy, and patient you can be.

My days are richer and calmer when my nights are restful.

The monsters of our childhood do not fade away, neither are they ever wholly monstrous.

—JOHN LE CARRÉ

I know a great many people who are tortured all their lives because of things their parents did or did not do in their childhoods. Some are enraged by memories of abuse, some are upset about being neglected, and others have been scarred by a parent's addiction. Unless properly addressed, these memories can cause a person to keep from achieving total happiness with their own lives and prevent them from being the parent or person they want to be.

Sometimes our memories of childhood are accurate; sometimes we have embellished them. To understand what truly happened to us and how we can cope with it, we need to try to be dispassionate about what really happened. Was every holiday awful or were there actually pockets of joyous celebration? Were our parents capable of being the kind of parents we wanted them to be, or did they suffer abuse themselves in their childhoods that prevented them from being loving and compassionate?

Maturity means learning to view our parents as people, not as gods. We also must move away from our childhoods and construct meaningful adult lives no matter what happened, and if we need help to do that, we owe it to ourselves to get it. Keep in mind, too, that parents rarely set out to hurt their own children and that almost everyone, including ourselves, does the best job they can at any particular time.

My memories of my childhood will not imprison me today.

*One can never pay in gratitude; one can only pay "in kind"
somewhere else in life.*

　　　　　　　　　　　—ANNE MORROW LINDBERGH

During one of my hardest periods in life I found my-self leaning on friends for all kinds of services and help that I couldn't afford but that I especially needed. Initially I felt angry that I was in such a humbling position, but because I felt better whenever I took advantage of their offers, I continued to be in their debt. It was never an issue with any of these remarkable people that I didn't have money to reimburse them; they simply asked me to do something similar for someone else when I was back on my feet.

Several years later I was in a position to help others. I found that I had been so deeply affected by being the one on the receiving end that I was very sensitive to the needs of others. If someone I cared about needed a friend, money, or emotional support, I was very quick to give it and I didn't give a thought to whether they would thank me or pay me back. I knew from my earlier experience that I was just continuing the chain of giving and that those I helped would undoubtedly help others when they, too, were ready.

Don't be embarrassed if you are on the receiving end for love and support today. Although it can feel awkward to be taking, it is good for the soul to learn how to accept love and other gifts from those who care about you. Soon enough the shoe will be on the other foot and you'll discover that you, too, have the ability to give to others and help them until they are strong enough to be self-sufficient.

I will accept the help that is offered to me today with gratitude.

Nothing is so soothing to our self-esteem as to find our bad traits in our forbears. It seems to absolve us.

—VAN WYCK BROOKS

Kara comes from a family with a long history of depression—her father, grandfather, and great-grandfather all suffered from it and her uncle committed suicide after his business failed. Kara's own mood swings led to alcohol and pill abuse, and it wasn't until she entered a treatment center that she learned that her family's history of depression gave her a genetic predisposition toward it as well as to addiction.

Although we can't blame all of our negative traits on our ancestors, it is often comforting to realize that a tendency toward depression isn't something we control. When Kara understood that her spells of sadness weren't her "fault," she embraced therapy, stopped medicating herself with drugs and alcohol, and agreed to take antidepressants, which made her life more manageable.

Does depression or mental illness run in your family? If you don't know, find out. Understanding the roots of your nature and forgiving yourself for possibly being created a certain way might be the nudge you need to see yourself and your family in a new light and permit you to get the assistance that can change your life.

I will work with, not against, the traits and tendencies with which I was born.

Hiding leads to nowhere but more hiding.
—MARGARET A. ROBINSON

Louise, a coordinator of graduate degree programs, suffers from chronic depression. When her mood swings are particularly intense she takes two-hour lunches or calls in sick because she's afraid to confide in her supervisor about her condition. Louise's erratic behavior has cost her two other jobs but she's unwilling to go to an employee assistance program for fear that it's not confidential, and she also doesn't take medication because she's afraid someone at work would find out and she'd be discriminated against for having "mental problems."

When we suffer from a depressive condition and try to hide it from others, this eventually leads to more problems than candor would create. If Louise sought appropriate and confidential help in the form of counseling or medication, her job wouldn't suffer so much every time the blues strike. By taking steps to manage an unmanageable condition she'd also probably discover the feelings of empowerment and self-confidence that hiding often strips away.

If you're hiding your depression because you're afraid of discrimination at work or the condemnation of others, ask yourself whether your energy would be better spent finding helpful solutions. Being honest with discreet people is a good first step in getting the care you need, and it can prevent you from sending out inaccurate messages about yourself. Also, take some time to examine if *you* have completely accepted your condition because the process of hiding from others usually means you're also hiding something from yourself.

I will be honest in all my affairs today.

Men look at themselves in mirrors. Women look for themselves.

—Elissa Melamed

For over seven years, starting when I was fifteen, I routinely binged and starved myself to try to fit into society's ideal of the thin, beautiful, and accomplished young woman. Like millions of others, I jeopardized my health and sanity by throwing up, compulsively exercising, and taking laxatives, never once stopping to think that *who* I was inside was far more important than *what* I looked like outside.

My long, steady recovery from bulimia has been difficult, yet rewarding. If I hadn't come face to face with the fact that I was slowly killing myself, I might never have stopped to see I was assigning too much importance to external conditions that had nothing to do with my worth as a person. During stressful times, however, I still have to remind myself that I'm wonderful even if I don't look like the models in magazines.

If you are depressed today because you don't like your appearance, ask yourself if you are imposing impossibly high standards of fitness or beauty on yourself. Do you truly believe that your looks equal your value as a person? If so, start looking in the mirror and practicing acceptance, no matter what you see. Eliminating the perception that flawless beauty is the key to happiness is a good way to bring more self-love and joy into your daily life.

When I look in the mirror, I love what I see.

One fire burns out another's burning;
One pain is lessen'd by another's anguish
                                   —WILLIAM SHAKESPEARE

In the 1980s the number of self-help groups in America rose dramatically. As research bore out the value of shared experience, groups sprang up for people suffering from such ailments as depression and compulsive debting as well as from the stress in caring for elderly parents or chronically sick children. I have never met anyone who's explored the value of group support who didn't say that it was a beneficial and healing experience.

The biggest problem we face when we're depressed about something, though, is finding the energy and willingness to mingle with others. And in many cases these people are strangers, which in itself can be frightening and intimidating. But what we dread and avoid most can be what brings us the most healing if we have the courage and energy to face it.

Whatever you are suffering from today, remember that there is probably a group that can help you. If you want to start small, subscribe to a newsletter that deals with the issue that concerns you; many publish personal stories and some match pen pals. Once you're feeling bolder, resolve to attend a self-help meeting because seeing and hearing other people will not just help you make new friends, it will let you see that you're not the only person grappling with a certain problem.

I am never alone in my anguish.

In times of suffering, when you feel abandoned, perhaps even annihilated, there is occurring—at levels deeper than our pain —the entry of the sacred, the possibility of redemption.
—JEAN HOUSTON

There is a well-known book written by a man whose belief in a fair God was severely tested by the early death of his son to an untreatable, rare disease. For years the man had lived a fairly ordinary life and followed the rules that he thought guaranteed him a pain-free existence: he was a good son as well as an excellent father and husband; he didn't lie or cheat; and he attended church faithfully. Then, out of the blue, his beloved son was diagnosed with a deadly illness, and doctors said he wouldn't live past his mid-teens. It was agony watching his son die a slow, painful death, and he raged at a God who would allow such suffering.

Ultimately the man came to grips with the fact that "bad things" sometimes happen to "good people." Despite the trauma of losing his son, he also saw that he and his family had been immeasurably enriched in many ways by the long ordeal. Other people who have endured tragedies that left them feeling abandoned and empty have also agreed that once the pain eased, they felt richer and wiser than before.

Remember today that pain often serves as a wake-up call about the unfairness of life and the necessity of coping with challenges that seem cruel and senseless. When this happens try to remain open to the God of your understanding and watch for a sense of the sacred to enter your soul.

My greatest growth spiritually often takes place amid my greatest pain.

If every man would mend a man, then all the world would be mended.

—Anonymous

One of the most striking characteristics of depression is that it is rarely discussed in an open way despite the fact that it's the nation's most prevalent mental health problem, and one-sixth of all Americans grapple with it at some point in their lives. Not only is it often kept under wraps, but only 26 percent of its victims ever seek mental health counseling. Among the most likely groups to experience depression are white people, people of low income, women, residents of urban areas, and those with histories of alcoholism or mood disorder in their family.

Given the stigma still attached to depression, it's important that we start to bring healing to others by talking candidly about this debilitating condition. Sometimes all it takes for someone to start the process of recovery is to hear that a friend or acquaintance has had the courage to get appropriate treatment. This has been the case in the addictions field for years. When former First Lady, Betty Ford, admitted to being an alcohol and substance abuser, she enabled countless other women to seek treatment without feeling self-conscious or weak.

If you are still trying to keep your depression a secret because of embarrassment, start opening up to others who you can trust. You may be surprised to discover that someone else has some insight or similar experiences to share with you. And if you are feeling strong, reach out and try to help "mend" someone else who hasn't had the courage to seek help yet. Once we can use our pain to help alleviate others', the world will be a happier place.

I will mend someone else today.

Prophecy, however honest, is generally a poor substitute for experience.

—JUSTICE BENJAMIN N. CARDOZO

A friend of mine has had several difficult experiences the last few years, including losing her job, losing her husband, and being sued by a former business partner. At first she tried to cope alone, but as her troubles continued to mount she began to rely on the advice of a fortune teller, to whom she entrusted all of her major decisions. Before long she was heeding no one but the fortune teller and avoided listening to sound advice from people who were experienced in the areas where she needed assistance.

When we're depressed it's easy to turn to people whom we think will make us feel better quickly and who can offer us a map to what the future might hold. In fact, during recessions and economic difficulties, astrologers, psychics, faith healers, tarot card readers, and the like experience booming business because people are confused and scared, and seek the company of those who predict a brighter future. Sometimes a visit to a psychic can be helpful or mood lifting, but we can get into big trouble if we abandon common sense and practical advice to trust the words of people who may or may not be honest and gifted.

Be very careful not to lose your judgment when you are down, because that's when you can make large and costly errors. If you have legal or financial difficulties, rely on the advice of professionals—not palm readers. Sensible people will serve you better in the long run than those who rely on methods that are hard to measure.

I need grounded people around me when I feel ungrounded.

You can sort of be married, you can sort of be divorced, you can sort of be living together, but you can't sort of have a baby.

—DAVID SHIRE

One of the most decisive emotional changes in a woman's life comes when she has a baby. It is a remarkable event in many ways as it marks the transition from young woman to adult and brings with it huge responsibilities, changes in priorities, and an unprecedented outflow of love and emotion. It can also bring, unfortunately, some unpleasant side effects.

One of the most common occurrences after the birth of a child is the "baby blues," which for many women can turn into full-scale depression and even psychotic episodes. For a new mother who is expecting to feel nothing but joy and relief, these dark times and crying spells can be an unwelcome shock. And because you may want to appear to be the perfect, loving mother, you may choose not to confide in anyone, afraid it will make you look bad or uncaring.

If you are trapped in the postpartum blues today, remember that they are more common than you might think. Talking with other new mothers, confiding in a professional, and educating yourself about your condition will go a long way toward helping you feel better. Having a child is a huge responsibility that entails endless work and countless sacrifices, but to be as effective as possible, we must remember that our first responsibility is to take care of ourselves and not assume that feeling depressed is a temporary condition that will go away if we just ignore it.

When I tend to my emotional needs diligently, I set a good example for my children.

Happiness is not a state to arrive at, but a manner of traveling.
—Margaret Lee Runbeck

As a schoolgirl I heard an inspirational sermon about the danger of trying to grasp the happiness that lies in the next relationship, job, or location. The priest cautioned us restless children to find joy each day in where we were and what we were doing. "If happiness is a destination," he said, "you'll always be on a journey."

Many years later I find this wise man's thoughts ringing in my ears often. Too frequently I've made the mistake of pinning happiness on being a specific dress size, living in a certain area, or solving a thorny problem. When I've gotten what I wanted I've inevitably found that the real joy came from setting the goal and taking steps to reach it, and that the victory was never as sweet as I'd thought it would be. Now I view happiness as something I can have every day if I choose, and that it is completely independent of what I own, what I look like, or how I'm perceived by others.

If you are depressed and you think that you'll only be happy once certain conditions are met, challenge yourself to change your expectations. Consider happiness a birthright that can be felt while taking a walk, riding a bus, cooking, or just reading a book. By incorporating joy into your daily tasks, you'll see that it is well within your reach.

I will travel in happiness today.

A psychiatrist has to be a person who commits himself to making a person better. Nothing should be too menial for a psychiatrist to do.

—WILLARD NAGLER

I am often appalled at the stories I hear about how unprofessional therapists can be. One college friend of mine who was suffering from depression and anorexia saw a therapist who sexually abused her, which caused my friend to become suicidal, take drugs, and spiral into a deep depression from which she's never fully recovered. Another person told me her therapist spent more time talking about his problems than hers during their sessions.

Despite these anecdotes most therapists are ethical. As well-trained specialists, they can help us sort out troubling issues and our time with them can be a valuable investment in becoming healthier, happier people. But we have to be careful about those in whom we put our trust. We should ask friends for recommendations, follow our gut instincts if we don't "click" with a person, and understand that a good therapist will evoke strong emotions in us, but that he or she should never violate our trust with inappropriate behavior.

If you are seeking someone to counsel you today, don't fall for the first person who impresses you, but by the same token, don't waste time looking for the "perfect" fit. The key to receiving good therapy is not just working with someone you trust but being willing to commit yourself to the process.

I will hold my therapist to the same high standards I hold for myself.

I never work better than when I am inspired by anger; for when I am angry, I can write, pray, and preach well, for then my whole temperament is quickened, my understanding sharpened, and all mundane vexations and temptations depart.

—MARTIN LUTHER

Most women are taught from a young age that displaying anger is unfeminine and unattractive, therefore most of us repress it. The problem with this is that repressed anger often leads to depression, as well as physical problems such as stomachaches, neckaches, backaches, and headaches. Experts now advise women to put their anger to a positive use. Anger can not only energize us to make important changes in our lives, but it can serve as a warning sign that something in our lives is amiss and needs to be addressed.

Frances is a good example of this. In the office where she works she found that her male colleagues were continually claiming her work and ideas as their own, and that she was paid just two-thirds of their earnings. Instead of blowing off steam in confrontations, she learned to channel her anger in a productive way. By accepting more speaking engagements and submitting articles to trade publications, she was able to increase her visibility and marketability.

Use your anger as a tool to help beat depression today. Instead of expending energy on confrontations that may create enemies, use your emotions to devise an action plan for change and then put it into motion. Once you can befriend your anger and use it to inspire and motivate you, you may be able to head off depression before it manifests.

I will put my anger to good use today.

*The value of marriage is not that adults produce children but
that children produce adults.*

—PETER DE VRIES

Shortly after I had my first child I ran into an older
woman, an acquaintance of mine, who gave me some advice about what lay in store for me. "You'll find out what
you're made of now," she lectured, wagging her finger at
me. "When you have children you really have a chance to
make something of yourself." Although I wasn't sure what
she meant, subsequent years have proved her right.

Having children is often thankless, tiring, and frustrating. On days when I can only manage to scan the newspaper before doing endless loads of laundry and cleaning up
countless juice spills, I wonder how I will ever survive until
tomorrow. But at the same time it's only through caring for
a sick baby, teaching a child the alphabet, and providing
the security of unconditional love that I've been able to
mature into an adult. Although I'm often too caught up in
the daily hustle of taking care of myself and my children to
see how I've been affected by becoming a mother, at odd
moments I realize with pride that I've become more patient
and caring than I once was, or that I've learned to be sleep-
deprived and also selfless.

Take heart today if you're a mother who is so hassled
that you can't see the forest for the trees. You are learning
valuable skills just by being a parent, and although you may
wish for lighter burdens at times, remember that your children are helping you become an "adult."

As I help others grow up, I grow up too.

From without, no wonderful effect is wrought within ourselves, unless some interior, responding wonder meets it.
—HERMAN MELVILLE

One of the many reasons women suffer from depression is because we don't believe in ourselves or have confidence in our ability to achieve our dreams. When we're this negative about ourselves and have trouble mustering the energy or desire to change, it's unlikely that we'll create the situations that will bring us more happiness. It's only when we have a spark of hope and self-esteem that we draw opportunities and people to us who can help us transform ourselves and our lives.

How do we create that inner spark of hope? One therapist says that despite the overwhelming bias toward showing women as victims in the media, some recent movies have featured strong female characters who can inspire others to believe in themselves. The principal characters in *Thelma and Louise,* for example, demonstrate how women can go after their dreams even when the men in their lives object. A depressed woman who saw this movie said it gave her the courage to return to college and get her degree, something that had bothered her for years.

If depression has sapped your self-confidence, try to reignite your belief in yourself by watching or reading about strong, self-confident women. These inspiring examples might give you the confidence you need to seek out the people and situations who can help you help yourself.

I will create inner conditions that help make external dreams happen.

People earnestly seek what they do not want, while they neglect the real blessings in their possession—I mean the innocent gratification of their senses, which is all we can properly call our own.

—MARY WORTLEY MONTAGU

When depressed, we are often so preoccupied that we forget how much pleasure can be derived from stimulating our senses. There are many different exercises for doing this—most of them free. Here are some ideas:

1. Take out an album with pictures of a happy time in your life and let the memories wash over you.

2. Go for a long, solitary drive in the country and roll your windows down so that you can hear the sounds of nature.

3. Spend time outside. The greatest predictor of happiness is the number of hours spent in the sunshine.

4. Go somewhere where the scents are wonderful—a bakery, a perfume counter, or even a hardware store if that evokes pleasant memories.

5. Listen to a favorite tape on a portable tape player with your eyes closed.

6. Treat yourself to a food that reminds you of a happy, contented time in your life.

7. Get a massage or a facial.

8. Go to the library and check out books that will transport you to a peaceful place. Picture books are good for this exercise.

Remember today that our hearing, touch, smell, taste, and sight are all designed to bring us joy and that the more we can stimulate them pleasurably, the happier we will feel.

I will use my senses to gratify me.

What doesn't kill me, makes me stronger.

—ALBERT CAMUS

One day I read the results of a study of Jews who'd survived the Holocaust. It compared this unique group with Jews who hadn't had the same brutal experiences. The surprising finding was that the majority of the Holocaust survivors had created more successful marriages, more stable lives, and enjoyed better emotional health than their peers.

The Holocaust survivors tended to marry other survivors, which ensured that they had a partner who would empathize with their experiences. They were more adaptable, they took initiative, they were stubbornly tenacious, they were gifted with a healthy dose of "street smarts," they tended to volunteer more than their peers, and lastly, they compartmentalized their Holocaust memories, refusing to let them influence their daily lives.

As this study shows, experiencing the worst of horrors doesn't have to destroy us emotionally. These Holocaust survivors prove that many of the techniques used to fight depression—talking to sympathetic friends or partners about our feelings, volunteering, being flexible, having persistence, and not allowing our setbacks to negatively affect our outlook on life—can be effective in helping us recover from the worst that the world has to offer.

I will become stronger through the difficulties I endure.

Happiness is not a possession to be prized, it is a quality of thought, a state of mind.

—DAPHNE DU MAURIER

A very small number of people are lucky enough to be born optimists. They are the ones who see tragedies as stepping-stones, they rarely permit themselves the luxury of negative thinking, and they often give thanks for their blessings. Most of us, though, are not this fortunate, and creating a positive mood is something we have to work on daily.

David G. Myers, author of *The Pursuit of Happiness,* says that one way to create happiness is to fake it. "Pretend self-esteem. Feign optimism. Simulate outgoingness," he counsels. "The phoniness gradually subsides. We notice it no longer feels forced." He adds that several other time-tested methods work to create a happy mood: filling your time with productive activity, getting a good night's sleep, meditating for ten minutes a day, taking a walk, and having a hobby that overrides a desire to watch television.

While severe cases of depression may not respond to these tips for fostering joy, there are many reasons to at least try them. For one, some forms of depression start with negative thinking that can be nipped in the bud through a deliberate effort to be active. Furthermore, optimists report fewer medical problems and faster recovery times, and injuries and poor health are two of the top contributors to depression. Overall it can't hurt to pretend to feel good or to simulate joy because anything we can do to change our routine and introduce healthy habits will contribute to a positive frame of mind.

I will take the steps necessary to create a good mood.

The practice of deception was so constant with her that it got to be a kind of truth.

—LOUISE ERDRICH

Anna and her husband take separate vacations every year, which Anna gaily proclaims is "wonderful" because then they both get to do what they like without boring the other. At work when people question her about how healthy this arrangement is, Anna always has an answer ready as she skillfully covers up the widening cracks in her marriage that she's afraid to examine, and that she certainly doesn't want others to notice.

Sometimes when we're depressed our main concern is covering it up. Parents often go to great lengths to conceal their children's addiction, although what they need more than anything are heart-to-heart chats with other parents in similar straits. And when our marriages are shaky or our relationship with our parents isn't wonderful, we're frequently prone to insist that everything is just fine because we don't want to appear defective or needy.

Are you in the habit of lying about something that is troubling you because you don't want the pity or scrutiny of others? Cover-ups can be harmful because they keep us from examining what is really bothering us, and our energy goes more toward maintaining a happy facade than letting others see our troubles. Try not to whitewash your life when it isn't wonderful because not only will your efforts probably fail, but you'll also miss out on the support and advice others can provide.

I won't try to appear perfect today.

The creative person is both more primitive and more culti-
vated, more destructive and more constructive, a lot madder
and a lot saner, than the average person.

—FRANK BARRON

Because I'm a writer and a creative person at heart, I
have a lot of friends who are artists, entrepreneurs and
challengers of the status quo in some way. Over the years
I've noticed that we all tend to share similar traits such as
mood swings, intensity, and perfectionism. During our euphoric times we are incredibly productive, accomplishing
much with little sleep, but when our low energy periods hit
we become convinced that we'll never be inventive or brilliant again.

Being very smart or very artistic can be a burden because these gifts often carry the problem of having crippling spells of depression with them. Many of the manic-
depressive artists I know don't like their mood swings, yet
find the "up" times to be so rewarding that they're reluctant to take medication that would remove this creative
"edge." And years of swinging back and forth can result in
boredom or restlessness if stability or peacefulness prevails
for any period of time.

If you can identify with this type of personality, it's
important to ask yourself how valuable and rewarding it is
to have euphoric highs if they are always followed by dis-
mal lows that leave you lethargic and depressed. Medication and therapy can help ease the pain of the swings, and
you might also be surprised to find that living a more stable
emotional life can lead to more productivity than the short-
lived "highs" ever did.

Being creative doesn't mean I have to live the life of a tortured
genius.

Each man is questioned by life; and he can only answer to life by answering for his own life; to life he can only respond by being responsible.

—VIKTOR E. FRANKL

Shannon is an adult woman who has many emotional problems stemming from her parents' divorce, her father's alcoholism, and her estrangement from her siblings. Although she dabbles in support groups like Adult Children of Alcoholics, Shannon prefers to complain endlessly about how unfair life has been to her and how little love and nurturing she received during the formative years of her life. As a result, Shannon is often depressed and angry that she is unable to experience peace.

Shannon, however, has never really tried to stop playing the role of the victim. At a certain point, regardless of what has happened to us during our lives, we must take responsibility for getting help for our problems. It is unnecessary to suffer because of childhood abuse or emotional abandonment any longer than we choose; excellent treatment is widely available at a reasonable cost, and a plethora of self-help books are available on any of these topics.

Part of becoming a mature, well-adjusted person is accepting responsibility for getting help so don't play the role of victim any longer than you have to. Although your depression may stem from long-standing problems, it's up to you to make your present life what you want it to be.

I will actively seek the solutions I need today.

I might have been born in a hovel, but I determined to travel with the wind and the stars.

—JACQUELINE COCHRAN

Despite being born in a New York housing project to a mother who worked several jobs just to put food on the table, a well-known African-American preacher was determined to make something of himself, so he followed the example of his role models: He worked hard and never lost sight of his dreams. Today this man is successful and well respected and serves as a role model for many young blacks who were born into the same difficult circumstances he was.

It's very easy to look around and see what's wrong with our lives and what strikes we have against us. When we submit to that kind of thinking, however, we're sure to suffer from depression and frustration and to envy those who seem to have an advantage in life. It's harder, but far better, to adopt the can-do attitude of the preacher and decide that we'll reach our goals no matter what our obstacles.

Decide today to focus on where you're going instead of what stands in the way of your getting there. Like any learned habit, this may feel awkward at first, but if you can overlook your limitations and see the finish line instead, you'll be more likely to reach your goal.

I will stay focused on where I want to go, not what stands in my way.

Alone, alone, oh! We have been warned about solitary vices. Have solitary pleasures ever been adequately praised? Do many people know that they exist?

—JESSAMYN WEST

When we don't have enough time to recharge our batteries in solitude, we experience something called privacy deprivation. Privacy deprivation is a type of stress that taxes the body, fatigues the immune system, and often results in depression, lethargy, and irritability.

A twelve-year study of twelve hundred men and women who attended night school in addition to the responsibilities of family and job during the day found that the ones who didn't take time for relaxation were most likely to get sick and suffer from depression. Those participants who consistently found time for themselves emphasized that taking care of privacy needs was a priority; they valued their own peace of mind and realized that others' well-being often relied on whether or not they got recharged. Different ways of experiencing solitude were reported: some read the newspaper in silence, some ate a meal out by themselves, and others just stared at the ceiling in a quiet room.

Scrutinize your schedule today to see where you can cut back and create a period of solitude. Use unexpected breaks—like the children being at a slumber party or a lull at work—to do something for yourself. If you can replenish yourself before trouble strikes, it will be easier to weather uncertainty and sadness when it occurs.

Solitude is a way of putting my emotional health at the top of my priority list.

People tell about two lies a day, or at least that is how many they will admit to.

—BELLA DePAULO

There is a retired executive currently lecturing this simple message to all who will listen: We are too accustomed to lying to ourselves and others and, as a result, we've become a country of people with low self-esteem and high rates of depression. This man is spending his golden years cautioning young schoolchildren not to get into the habit of lying because they'll feel better about themselves if they can be honest and trustworthy in all situations.

I found out firsthand how depressing lying can be when I suffered from bulimia many years ago. To cover up for my food binges I always made up stories about what had happened to missing food or why I didn't feel well. My depression mounted as I felt worse about myself and my double life and I despaired that I'd ever be an honest person again. It was only through participation in a self-help group for compulsive eaters that I learned that "rigorous honesty in all our affairs" was what would help me gain the self-esteem and self-confidence I would need to live a happy, productive life.

Do you make it a habit to lie about big and little things because it's easy or because it makes you look better? Try to tell the truth as often as possible today and to be "rigorously honest" in all your affairs because if you can learn to do this, chances are good that you'll have more positive feelings about yourself.

I will be truthful with myself and others today.

You are what you eat.

—PAMELA FIORI

I am often astonished at how little importance people place on what they eat. Because it is so easy to get highly processed, fattening food, and because it can taste so good, people often fall into a rut of dining on sugary cereals and doughnuts, fatty meats, caffeinated drinks, and rich desserts. When they complain about feeling run-down, lethargic, bloated, or tense, they fail to see that what they've eaten is probably responsible for many of their symptoms.

We must remember that food is a powerful substance that can provide the fuel to keep us going or pollute us with unnecessary chemicals. Whenever I consume too much caffeine and refined foods my behavior becomes erratic. I sleep poorly, suffer from headaches, and experience drastic mood swings. On the other hand when I nourish myself with a low-fat, fiber-rich diet and avoid caffeine and alcohol, I am happier, have more energy, and can handle stress better.

Pay attention to your diet today. If you are depressed, you'll only add to your woes by eating poorly and drinking caffeinated beverages. Talk to a nutritionist or read some books on healthy eating to learn more about what powers different foods have over you; for example, studies have shown that people who eat meat are often more depressed than people who don't. Keep in mind that having a healthy and positive outlook involves more than just thinking and acting differently; it also means having respect for what you put into your body.

When I eat well, I feel well.

*Whether you turn to the right or to the left, your ears will hear
a voice behind you, saying: "This is the way; walk in it."*
—ISAIAH 30:21

One morning during my senior year in college, my
roommate, Betty, felt moved to go to the university chapel
to pray for her father, who was battling a long, protracted
disease. As she sat in a back pew crying softly, a man silently entered and sat beside her. Gently, he reached over
and touched her arm, saying that her father was going to be
fine and that she should know that he would always be with
her. With that comment he stood and left as quickly as he
had come.

After a moment of surprise, my friend leapt up and
ran out of the church to find out who the man was and how
he'd known about her father. She didn't see a trace of the
man, and passersby said they hadn't seen anyone fitting the
description either. When my friend's father died later that
night, she decided that the man must have been an angel of
some kind who had come to gently prepare her for her
father's passing.

We all have "angels" who visit us in times of need,
whether through dreams, unexpected phone calls, or lucky
"coincidences." Look today for the angels in your life and
remember to give thanks when they appear or when you
feel their presence, because whenever we look carefully, we
always find them.

Our greatest comfort often comes in unexpected ways.

Mental health problems do not affect three or four out of every five persons but one out of one.

—WILLIAM MENNINGER

If we have never suffered from a serious depression before, the first time is bound to be extremely difficult. When I began to experience all of the symptoms of major depression in the months following the birth of my first child, I fought the thought that I might have a "mental health problem." I much preferred to think of myself as capable and optimistic, although I wasn't exhibiting those traits at the time.

Since coming through that dark period, I have found that the vast majority of my friends and acquaintances have also had similar episodes of despair and feelings of being overwhelmed with responsibilities, but they haven't openly talked about them with others. Statistics support this; only a fraction of people who are depressed ever seek help, preferring to "tough it out" themselves and confide in as few people as possible.

As isolated as you may feel in sadness today, you are certainly not alone. It's common to have periods of doubt, confusion, and depression from time to time, and acknowledging this is better than pretending your feelings don't exist. Take time to learn a bit about depression and how widespread it is, and ask friends who have weathered hard times what helped them the most. Isolation is one of the most common side effects of depression, but the more you can connect with others like yourself, the better are your chances of finding solutions to what is bothering you.

I am never alone in my sadness.

When you arrive at a fork in the road, take it.
—Yogi Berra

Change is difficult for many people. We usually prefer to set a course for ourselves and then stick to it, avoiding risky detours. As a result, if something occurs to knock us off the path and change our direction, our tendency is to fight it and return to our safe journey.

A friend of mine, Nancy, is a case in point. One night her husband looked at her over dinner and announced he was leaving her for a younger woman. Being forty-something and without a job, Nancy sunk into a six-month depression during which she barely had the energy to get out of bed. Her beloved daughter then chose to go live with her father, leaving Nancy utterly alone and terrified of the future.

Finally, with bills mounting, Nancy went to school to become a massage therapist. She waited on tables while she earned her certificate, seeing clients whenever she could fit them in. Within a few years Nancy had a strong word-of-mouth following, self-confidence, a steady boyfriend, and her daughter had returned to live with her. Although she admits that she never would have sought out these changes herself, Nancy is now delighted that she followed the path that once looked so scary and uncertain.

Try to keep in mind today that unexpected events don't have to usher in pessimism and misery. Sometimes the most tumultuous and terrifying passages of our lives are what cause us to take the fork in the road that leads to our greatest fulfillment.

I will allow the upheavals in my life to take me optimistically down uncharted paths.

Decision is a risk rooted in the courage of being free.
—PAUL TILLICH

For over a year my friend Martha struggled with the decision about whether or not to have a third child. Although she was very happy with her son and daughter, Martha wasn't sure her family was complete. For months she weighed the pros and cons, and her inability to make a decision left her depressed. When Martha was offered a challenging part-time job, she found she had to commit herself to one route or the other. One morning after another anguished night of discussions with her husband, she awakened with the certainty that another baby would create too much havoc in her life. "The weight it took from my shoulders was unimaginable," she said.

Sometimes we go through depressions because of an inability to commit to one course or another; conversely, we can be incapable of decision making because we are in the depths of a depression. Either way, wavering about what to do isn't healthy and eats up energy and time. Instead of setting out on a course with confidence and enthusiasm, we go nowhere, terrified of making the "wrong" choice.

Resolve today that you will make a decision about something that is nagging at you. Don't worry about making the perfect decision; just choose to take a risk and live with the consequences, whatever they are. The more you can act with this type of assertiveness, the easier it will be to view yourself as strong and capable, and the harder it will be to succumb to inertia and depression.

I will act today with confidence.

I will lay me down in peace, and take my rest.
—BOOK OF COMMON PRAYER, PSALM 4:9

Our dreams tell us a lot about our emotional health, so when they are tortured, they often signify tortured self-esteem. This is what some researchers in Chicago found when they asked divorcing couples to record their dreams. The men generally had noneventful dreams, but the women tended to have dreams in which they saw themselves as fat, ugly, weak, or damaged. This led the researchers to conclude that women blamed themselves for the break-up instead of seeing that the relationships themselves may have been flawed.

Too often we as women will blame ourselves for what's wrong in our lives. If our children aren't perfect, we may blame our mothering. If our marriages aren't smooth, it's because we're not pretty or sexy enough. Or if we don't like our boss at work, we search for the personality defect that has led to the friction. By always looking inside ourselves rather than outside for solutions to our problems we're sure to develop low self-esteem and depression, and decrease the chances of addressing the real problems that exist.

Are you having nightmares and troubling dreams in which you are always scared, weak, and flawed? If so, you may be taking on too much responsibility for the problems in your life and not seeing situations in a realistic light. Try to attack your depression by putting blame where it really belongs, and you might be surprised to find that in addition to feeling better about yourself, you'll also have sweeter dreams and more restful nights.

When I am at peace with myself, my nights are peaceful, as well.

We will learn to think of ourselves, our personalities, as an orchestra of chemical voices in our heads.
                                        —ARNOLD J. MANDELL

Every month like clockwork Jennifer becomes depressed when she ovulates. For the next two weeks she is overly emotional, irritable, and withdrawn. When her period comes, the symptoms disappear and Jennifer feels like a whole new person. Although she's never so down that she has to miss work, Jennifer's uneven moods prevent her from fully enjoying life.

Research has established that women who are premenstrual and menstruating are often more depressed and emotional than those who are in a different phase of their cycle. Sometimes it takes several years for a person to notice that her moods are tied to her menstrual cycle, and some women don't want to admit that their hormones contribute to their emotions for fear they'll be seen as "weak." But we must accept our particular female chemistry if we are to find solutions for its difficult side effects. Denying that they exist will only keep us miserable every time our hormones go through the normal monthly rise and fall.

I will work with my body to enhance my emotional well-being.

The only thing of value in a man is the soul. It is the soul that makes us human.

—INIKINILIK

In the Native American tradition it is considered imperative that people get past the demands of their ego to get in touch with their soul. This process is known as becoming a "hollow bone." Negative emotions, addictions, and bad habits are considered barriers to this enlightenment, and their elimination is achieved through sacrifice, solitude, and relentless self-scrutiny. Dreams, in particular, are critical in learning about the needs of the soul and how to go about finding one's path.

Many of these techniques are excellent ways to overcome depression because depression is a sign that we are out of touch with our soul. Our inner voice can't be heard if we're silencing it with negative thoughts or self-destructive actions, just as our bodies don't function properly if we're feeding it the wrong things. Our task, then, is to find ways to listen to our soul, whether it's through prayer, rituals, or therapy.

Strive to start down the path of making yourself a "hollow bone" today. Take some time in solitude to examine ways you might be standing in the way of your development or creating negativity, and note any clues that might appear in your dreams. The more attention you can give to the enrichment of your soul, the greater are your chances of achieving happiness.

I will try to eliminate a barrier that is keeping me from being in touch with my soul.

Anger dwells only in the bosom of fools.

—ALBERT EINSTEIN

When depressed, we tend to be more irritable and volatile than normal. As a result we are quick to start fights for no reason, we look for disagreements rather than compromises, and we may say things that hurt others in order to spread our pain. While at our core we may be primarily sad, our despair may surface through angry outbursts.

I remember during a particularly bad time that I became irrationally infuriated whenever I saw that my answering machine didn't have any messages for me. Silently I'd rail against the people who hadn't returned a call or even called to check on me, assuming things about them that had no basis in fact. When I finally did talk to some of these people, I'd find myself getting curt for no reason— still hanging on to irrational anger about their failure to call when *I* had wanted them to call.

Studies have shown that seven out of ten times we think we've been offended when we really haven't. Are you carrying some foolish anger around because you're assuming something that may not even be true? Be aware of how much time and energy you're devoting to anger and ask yourself if the expenditure is worthwhile. If it's not, consider extending the hand of friendship or forgiving someone who has hurt you. The inner warmth you'll receive will outweigh any of the benefits you think your anger is bringing you now.

I will assume the best about others today.

Happiness is having a large, loving, caring, close-knit family in another city.

—GEORGE BURNS

Sue is a young woman who married into a large family with so many relatives that the wedding reception was held at a local stadium. Because she came from a relatively small family she initially enjoyed constantly seeing her husband's relatives—at Sunday dinners, frequent baptisms, weekend get-togethers, and countless other gatherings. But before a year had passed she was miserable about the nonstop togetherness and begged her husband in vain to create some distance from his family. "When you married me, you married my family," he responded.

As wonderful as having a close-knit family is, it can also be strangling and depressing. To become mature and independent, we must undergo the process of separation from our family, which is impossible if we're constantly with them and trying to meet their expectations. In-laws can also cause us to lose our self-esteem if they're always dropping by unannounced or interfering in our lives, and these types of situations must be addressed forthrightly if we're to feel good about ourselves.

If your family's tentacles are too long and you feel stifled by them, make a point of standing up for your own privacy. Don't attend every single gathering out of obligation; go instead to the ones that will make you feel good. And if a parent calls you or wants to see you daily, try to explain gently that less togetherness might be valuable for both of you in the long run. The more you can carve out your own identity without interference, the less likely you'll be to suffer from depression when the family comes calling.

A well-functioning family is one that allows space and privacy.

I think if you have a career and you have a marriage and you have children and you try and be a ten in all the areas, you may have a nervous breakdown.

—SHERRY LANSING

As women, we have a variety of unique and important roles we play in others' lives. We are, among other things, daughters, wives, mothers, and coworkers. Each of these calls for special skills and tremendous energy, and unlike previous generations, ours is often asked to be all of these things at the same time. In fact, the present generation of women is considered to have a 300 percent greater likelihood of suffering from depression than women from our grandmothers' time.

Some women are dealing with their multiple roles by "sequencing"—concentrating on one area, such as motherhood, for several years and temporarily scaling back their expectations in other areas. Personally, I've found that to be an effective mother and businesswoman, I have to let other roles slide—such as being Julia Child in the kitchen. I'd rather have my children remember that in my free time I read them books or played with them and didn't prepare brownies from scratch or scrub the floor relentlessly.

Forget about being a "ten" today in every area of your life. "Having it all" doesn't necessarily mean having it all at the same time, and there's only so much we can do without driving ourselves to depression or getting sick. Being the best you can in whatever you attempt, getting help when possible, and keeping your priorities in order are the only sane choices to make in this busy and demanding modern world.

Scoring a perfect ten is reserved for extraordinary gymnastics feats, not the busy woman.

Trouble is a part of your life, and if you don't share it, you don't give the person who loves you enough chance to love you enough.

—DINAH SHORE

A friend of mine in her late thirties desperately wanted to have a child and went through unimaginable trouble to conceive. After months of fertility tests, shots, taking her temperature, and being probed and prodded every which way, she finally got pregnant. Thirteen weeks later, she sat sobbing in the bathroom as she miscarried. "My husband held me tighter and loved me with more intensity that day than he ever has before," she said.

Very often we try to deal with our problems ourselves, thinking that bothering other people will annoy or bore them. But I've found, as have others, that in times of trouble our friends and family members *want* to be needed the most. When we let them in on our pain, allow them to feel needed, and rely on them for strength and guidance, we communicate how important they are to us. To shut them out can be insulting and cruel, even though we may not intend it that way.

Share your depression with those closest to you today. Trying to shoulder your own burdens and pretend that everything's fine won't help you one iota, and certainly won't help your relationships with others. Accepting love and tenderness is hard for many of us, but once we've learned how to receive, giving becomes that much easier.

I will not suffer silently and alone.

I have measured out my life with coffee spoons.
—T. S. Eliot

One of the biggest addictions in America is the addiction to caffeine. Studies have shown that people who consume as few as two cups of coffee each day will suffer from withdrawal if they don't get their daily fix, the side effects of which include headaches, depression, lethargy, and irritability. If we depend on caffeine to get us up every morning and give us an emotional lift, we are only guaranteeing that we will eventually crash.

For well over a decade I seriously abused coffee as a way of making me alert, raising my mood, and increasing my productivity. One day I'd had so much that I started to tremble and feel faint. Frightened, I cut back and suffered the withdrawal symptoms for a week. To my great surprise and happiness I found that less caffeine not only gave me *more* energy but it made my emotions noticeably steadier.

If you rely on caffeine to provide energy and enthusiasm, consider cutting back or eliminating it from your diet. Gradually weaning yourself is better than going cold turkey, and natural remedies such as acupuncture and herbs can make the process more bearable. Although society tells us that coffee is an essential part of each day, remember that we all have varying tolerances for caffeine and that too much of any one thing is never beneficial to our mood or health.

I will stimulate myself with activity, not caffeine.

If it seems a childish thing to do, do it in remembrance that you are a child.

—FREDERICK BUECHNER

A friend of mine who was being treated for depression was ordered by her therapist to go to a concert of a pop music artist she liked and to act like a music-crazed teenager there. What this meant was that she had to dance when the crowd danced, sing along with her favorite songs, and generally lose herself in the spirit of the evening. This assignment terrified my very proper friend who constantly tries to act so mature and together that she's completely lost touch with the youthful, playful part of herself.

Being serious and earnest about some things is important if we are to behave as responsible adults. But if we carry this to an extreme we may find that we act as if the weight of the world were on our shoulders. We rarely laugh, we turn every upsetting situation into a major disaster, and we worry endlessly about things that might happen sometime in the future but probably never will.

Do something childlike today. Watch an inane television show from your youth, put on a record and pretend you're a recording star, or go to a park and swing as high as you can. By recapturing the lightheartedness of childhood, you'll probably find your emotional load considerably lightened today, too.

I can be childlike without being childish.

The only time a woman wishes she were a year older is when she is expecting a baby.

—MARY MARSH

Like many women I find pregnancy to be a difficult, draining experience. I've heard all the clichés about how a woman is never more beautiful than when she is expecting and how lovely the pregnancy "glow" is, but the reality is that we're often more tired, nauseated, tense, and moody while carrying a baby than when we're not.

I do have friends who have sailed through pregnancy without a pang of nausea, whose skin has become rosy and translucent, and whose bodies snapped back into shape within days after having their baby. But for most of us, the nine months are filled with fears of birth complications and painful labor, as well as backaches, sleepless nights, strange food cravings, and water retention. And when we're balancing other children and a job, pregnancy can feel like the biggest burden we could possibly have been asked to shoulder.

Sometimes the only thing we can do to get through childbearing with a minimum of discomfort is to remind ourselves that our condition is temporary, not permanent. Our moods, diets, bodies, and sleep habits will return to normal before too long. In the meantime, try to remember that carrying a baby can be a very healing time in which we learn to slow down, nourish ourselves, and reflect on what values we'd like to instill in our children. And keep in mind, too, that as much as we want to rush through painful situations like childbirth, pain is usually the birth of something exciting in our lives.

Sometimes the conditions that are most difficult to bear can bring the most rewards.

It is not easy to find happiness in ourselves and it is not possible to find it elsewhere.

—AGNES REPPLIER

Sometimes when we're sad we look at the happy, care-free people around us and assume that they have come by their well-being naturally. And some probably have, a pre-disposition to optimism does, indeed, run in some families. But for most of us, having a happy life requires work, and often finding happiness means learning how to create it.

Studies have shown that happy people can not only identify what brings them pleasure, but they also regularly build time into their days to do that activity. One man re-ported that fly-fishing brought him happiness and tranquil-lity, so he scheduled an outing once a month and won't let anything stand in his way. Another woman said that gar-dening made her happy, so she spent as much time out-doors as possible and also occasionally worked at a florist. Both said that indulging themselves this way made them feel better about themselves and helped them to be hap-pier in other areas of their lives.

Identify what brings you pleasure today and make a commitment to include those activities regularly in your life. It may feel like work to schedule joy into your day, but the more pleasurable activities you schedule, such as play-ing with animals or having lunch with a friend, the more likely it is that you, too, will say you have a happy life.

My happiness is largely determined by my willingness to seek it out.

To love oneself is the beginning of a lifelong romance.

—OSCAR WILDE

As women, we too often dislike ourselves, especially our bodies. Numerous surveys have shown that the majority of women are unhappy with their figures and would dearly love to lose weight and reshape specific body parts— whether it be their legs, breasts, hips, or waists. When we tie our feelings of self-worth to our figures, however, and compare ourselves to the silicone-implanted, airbrushed models we see in magazines, we're bound to always feel insecure and disappointed.

It's important that we women understand how closely depression correlates with unhappiness with our bodies. Studies have shown that 80 percent of fourth grade girls are on diets, and by the age of seventeen one in five has a serious eating disorder. During this same period, girls become depressed twice as often as boys, frequently citing low self-esteem based on their looks as a determining factor. Furthermore, it's been shown that the younger a girl begins to experiment with cosmetics, the higher her chances of experiencing depression as an adult. We'd even rather die than be fat; in a national survey women overwhelmingly stated they'd rather be hit by a truck than gain 100 pounds!

Instead of castigating ourselves for not measuring up to some unnatural ideal that is foisted upon us, we must learn to love ourselves for who we are as people. It's hard to overcome years of being judged worthy based on our looks, but until we stop allowing ourselves to be victims of this mentality, we'll never have a "lifelong romance" with ourselves.

My outward appearance is a pale reflection of my inner worth.

A divorce is like an amputation; you survive, but there's less of you.

—MARGARET ATWOOD

With the divorce rate as high as it is, we all know of someone who has been divorced. There is no easy or painless way to end a marriage, particularly if you are the one who has been left. Friends of mine whose husbands have left them for another woman have told me that the waves of rage, depression, sadness, loneliness, and hopelessness are overwhelming at times, and that it is especially depressing to feel like a "failure" in such an important institution as marriage.

Therapists say that women often fall into the trap of thinking that if only they had been "better" in some way—sexually or emotionally—the divorce wouldn't have occurred. Marriages, however, usually break down because of incompatibility or lack of communication. And when we berate ourselves with statements that we "ought" to have complained less or cooked more, we're absolving the man of his responsibilities in the relationship and putting an unfair burden on ourselves.

Surviving a divorce—or the end of any important relationship—isn't easy. There will be a piece of you that will forever be missing, but new aspects of ourselves can be developed to compensate for this loss. Although it's very difficult to do, the sooner you can look at your new beginning as an exciting opportunity, the greater will be your chances of creating the life you want.

Whenever I feel broken, a stronger part of me is sure to emerge.

Nothing fails like success because we don't learn from it. We learn only from failure.

—KENNETH BOULDING

When Bill Clinton was in his early thirties he was elected Governor of Arkansas. Several years later the voters, angered by his cockiness and unresponsiveness to their concerns, cast their ballots for his opponent. Depressed by his loss, Clinton mended his ways and ran again, this time to win and go on to govern with acclaim. Then, just ten years later, he was elected President of the United States after surviving a bruising and difficult campaign.

Even if you don't like Bill Clinton or agree with his principles, it's hard not to admire his persistence. In moments of failure and rejection, he vigorously fought back to reach his goals. For him, failure became a way to learn from his mistakes and change course. Instead of allowing it to defeat him, he used failure to improve himself.

Although experiencing a personal failure can be devastating, remind yourself that most successful people have experienced failure and rebounded. As down as you might be, study your setbacks to see where you can learn something helpful. And remind yourself that without your failures, you'd never be learning and finding ways to improve yourself.

I will not see failure as a reflection of my personal worth.

That we are not sicker and much madder than we are is due exclusively to that most blessed and blessing of all natural graces, sleep.

—ALDOUS HUXLEY

A friend of mine who is training to be a doctor is one of the most sleep-deprived women I know. Every third night she is awakened with emergencies, and she often has 36-hour shifts at the hospital. Not surprisingly she is moody and irritable, and little annoyances of daily life have the ability to derail her day. It's only when she's on vacation or not on call that she gets enough sleep for her emotions to level out.

You don't have to be a doctor to suffer from the ill effects of sleep deprivation. Studies show that women consistently get less sleep than they need—usually between five and six hours a night—despite the fact that seven to eight hours is optimal. One therapist recommends that her depressed and tired patients institute a "Sleep Exchange" system in which they list all their activities between 5 P.M. and bedtime and then get rid of at least one of them. The therapist has found that many women who do this discover that they can easily delegate or eliminate one unnecessary task, giving them some extra time for rest.

Examine your nightly activities to see if there is something that can be taken out of your routine. For example, some paperwork, phone calls, or food preparation could probably be done at a different time. Also, ask your family to shoulder some of the nightly burden. By simplifying your life, you'll be doing both your physical and your emotional health a favor.

I will streamline my evening hours so I can have more rest.

Arranging a bowl of flowers in the morning can give a sense of quiet in a crowded day, like writing a poem, or saying a prayer. What matters is that we be for a time inwardly attentive.

—ANNE MORROW LINDBERGH

When my life is chaotic and my emotions threaten to spiral out of control, I find a sure way to calm myself that doesn't cost any money: I pull out the ironing board and attack a stack of clothes with a can of heavy-duty starch. For some reason the idea of creating fresh-smelling, wrinkle-free clothes coupled with the mindless rhythm of dragging an iron back and forth across an ironing board lulls me into a sense of calm that returns my missing sanity.

If our lives feel out of control, but there's one tiny area we can put in order—especially in the morning—we can start our days with a feeling of satisfaction. Friends of mine say that some of the mindless activities they find soothing are going for a walk, needlepointing, writing in a journal, cleaning a closet, writing a letter, or organizing coupons. The only rules for these exercises are that we do them in silence and finish whatever we start.

If you feel unconnected and frazzled, set aside some time in the morning to start and complete a small task. Whether it's arranging flowers or lining up your shoes, take comfort in the fact that you've cleaned one corner of your life and use it to remind yourself that any problem facing you can be broken up into manageable units and conquered in the same way.

I will create some contemplation and order in my day.

Where's my blanket?

—LINUS, IN THE COMIC STRIP *PEANUTS*

Ever since he was a baby my son has had a weakness for a certain stuffed animal named Floppy, whose tail he rubs between his fingers in an almost-meditative trance. As he has gotten older he needs Floppy less and less, but Floppy is always essential after a distressing occurrence or if he has to be soothed to sleep.

My son is not unusual; he is just doing something that comes naturally to most human beings. The touch of certain fabrics has the power to affect our moods and either soothe or irritate us. For example, babies placed in cribs with soft padding gain more weight, fuss less, and sleep more than those placed in cribs without padding. For me, I tend to get very uncomfortable in scratchy, lacy fabrics, but when I'm in an old terrycloth bathrobe that has been washed to death, I'm calmer and happier.

What clothes do you gravitate toward when you are feeling depressed? Is it cotton sweatshirts and baggy pants, or sheer, lightweight clothes? Learning which fabrics soothe us and which ones unsettle us is important because if we can learn to control our environments to benefit our moods, we can lessen our chances of becoming depressed and increase our ability to soothe ourselves when we're down.

When I dress for comfort, I dress for happiness.

The road of excess leads to the palace of wisdom.
—WILLIAM BLAKE

Treatment centers and therapists' offices are filled with people who are miserable because they've been excessive in some way. Some have been driven by addictions to food, drugs, or alcohol; some have pursued work to the detriment of their family and friends; and some have indulged in overwhelming amounts of negative thinking or greed.

Whatever has driven us to seek help in feeling better about ourselves, it's important that we respect the role our excesses have played in our lives. When the pendulum swings too far in one direction, it's healthy to feel the sting and seek to make a correction. Our guilt, shame, or depression is what awakens us to the fact that a change needs to be made.

The wisest people are those who have been excessive at some point in their lives, but who have used their experiences to better themselves. Don't waste time berating yourself for what you've done wrong or inadequately in the past. Focus instead on how that can be turned to your advantage in crafting behavior you *do* like. When you can convert your pain into your teacher, the road of excess can only lead to a palace of wisdom.

I will learn from my excesses and not berate myself for them.

Eighty percent of success in life comes from showing up.
—Woody Allen

Andrea has had trouble supporting herself ever since her husband unexpectedly died several years ago, leaving her with a mountain of debts. Although she has done exceptionally well in picking up the pieces and moving ahead with her life, she also has had periods of darkness in which she feels she has been dealt an unfair blow and that she'll never have a "normal" or fulfilling life again.

At times like this she and I talk about how hard life is and how far she's come against formidable odds. I remind her that she's kept her sense of humor, been a good mother, and managed to pay her bills on time, regardless of whether there's been any money to spare at the end of the month. We also reminisce about when she's been happy and optimistic. By the end of our conversations Andrea can usually acknowledge that she's a fighter and a survivor, and that although she hasn't done everything perfectly, she's at least shown up for the battles in her life and survived them.

When we're depressed, the last thing we want to do is summon up energy and enthusiasm to go through the motions of our days. But we need to try to remember that showing up for life doesn't require perfection and that just making the effort to be present when we don't want to be is a triumph that will help see us through to when we are feeling stronger and better about ourselves.

I will show up for life today.

The one absolutely unselfish friend that man can have in this selfish world, the one that never deserts him, the one that never proves ungrateful or treacherous, is his dog.
—GEORGE GRAHAM VEST

Although it's very valuable to have a friend to turn to for support and comfort when times are hard, research has shown that a pet can be a better aid in reducing stress than a friend. In a study of forty-five women, researchers found that the women who tried to solve anxiety-provoking problems with dogs in the room perspired less and had lower blood pressure than did the women who had friends in the room while they did the tasks. The former group said that the dogs gave them a sense of comfort and love, which increased their feelings of security and ease.

The powerful feeling of unconditional acceptance that emanates from pets is well known in nursing homes, where there are regular "pet days" during which people bring pets to visit the residents. Even the crankiest and most miserable men and women cheer up when a dog or cat bounds into their lap, and their happiness reportedly lasts for hours.

Your depression may be eased if you can spend time today with an animal. If you have your own pet, be aware of how soothing they can be and use that to your advantage. Whether it's goldfish, dogs, horses, cats, hamsters, or birds, having an animal around that wants nothing from you but your presence can be a powerful dose of medicine for a heavy heart.

I will seek happiness in the company of animals today.

Some people approach every problem with an open mouth.
—ADLAI STEVENSON

When I was in seventh grade my science teacher made a comment I never forgot: "Whenever you're talking, you're not learning." I have since found this to be true, particularly when I'm coping with an emotional problem; although there is a great deal to be gained by venting my feelings in a supportive atmosphere, unless I can stay quiet long enough to hear the advice and suggestions of my friends, I won't learn anything that might help me with my problem.

I have an acquaintance who would be well advised to take my teacher's advice in her search for peace and happiness. She's always talking and giving her opinion when she most needs to listen. For example, I was astonished to see her running a support group one evening and telling others what to do when I knew how depressed she was about the same issues in her own life. By creating the illusion of strength and control, she was preventing herself from receiving the compassion, advice, and support she needed.

Be aware today of how much talking and listening you do when you're looking for help. Airing your feelings is a crucial step toward becoming well balanced and happy, but if you don't take an equal amount of time to absorb others' wisdom and the knowledge you can glean from silent contemplation, you'll never have the resources to combat depression effectively.

I was given two ears and just one mouth for a reason.

The one with the primary responsibility to the individual's future is that individual.

—DORCAS HARDY

One of the hardest lessons to learn is that we are completely responsible for what we do, for how we behave, and for the choices we make in our lives. It's a common tendency to blame others for what happens to us or to expect them to make us feel better when we're down. But leaning that heavily on any one person or institution is bound to end in disappointment.

For example, Maria has become dependent on her astrologer to give her answers to her problems. Whenever she is depressed she visits this woman and expects that answers to her troubles will magically appear. Another friend of mine looks to her husband to be her rock when she feels adrift, but her constant neediness and inability to find other sources of support has put a strain on their relationship.

Although it's very important to consult wise people for counsel when we're troubled and to reach out for help when we need it, we must understand that we alone are responsible for taking the steps that lead to happiness. The longer we persist in viewing a parent, therapist, priest, or friend as the key to happiness, the less likely we'll find it in ourselves.

I am in charge of my destiny.

Of my two "handicaps," being female has put many more obstacles in my path than being black.
—SHIRLEY CHISHOLM

One of the things that is most depressing to professional women is the lack of opportunities many of us face because of our sex. Despite several decades of doors opening to working women, it's been difficult for us to reach the pinnacle of our chosen profession without surmounting overwhelming odds and needing to be twice as competent as the men around us. Women's careers are still derailed because they take time off to have children or they're not considered for certain jobs because traditionally such posts have been held by men.

In the course of my professional career not only have I been sexually harassed, but I've listened to tasteless jokes about female hormones as well. I'm also frequently asked who ghostwrote my books, presumably because some men believe that being attractive and smart are mutually exclusive. It's not surprising that we've become disillusioned and depressed by our female "handicaps," but we also need to recognize that this isn't a reflection on us, it's a result of centuries of stereotypical thinking and actions.

Try to take comfort in the fact that you're not alone in feeling victimized. Support groups can provide solidarity by helping you negotiate professional minefields, and therapy can also assist you in learning skills and behaviors that can increase your odds of success. Sexual harassment and the "glass ceiling" may still hinder advancement, but with humor, persistence, and support you may be able to keep these stumbling blocks from derailing your happiness.

I will not allow discrimination to determine how I feel about myself.

I have had enough.

—GOLDA MEIR

I have a close friend who successfully overcame compulsive eating and spending but whose sadness and sense of hopelessness refused to abate. To combat these she attended weekend workshops, took up new hobbies, and treated herself to annual vacations, but the paralyzing feelings of depression continued to dog her. Finally, after years of emotional pain, she took her therapist's advice and started on antidepressants, which beneficially changed her life. Now she is sorry that she waited so long to try medication but says that she had to hit her own bottom before she could take that important and life-saving step.

When we struggle with depression, it's imperative to reach a point where we throw up our hands and admit that we've had enough and that we'll do anything to change. Studies have shown that at least 25 percent of all women suffer from a serious depression but, sadly, only one in five will ever seek help. What's especially frustrating to mental health professionals is that depression is one of the most treatable illnesses.

If you've been fighting depression for a long time but you haven't done much to address it, please make today the day that you take the important step of reaching out for help. Call a therapist, talk to your doctor or minister, or read some literature to help you understand what you're experiencing. Depression can feel overwhelming and frightening, but by facing it, you'll find an abundance of resources.

When I ask for help my prospects brighten.

Nothing is so good as it seems beforehand.

—GEORGE ELIOT

Although Cynthia has been in and out of countless weight-loss organizations over the years, she's always been successful at reaching her goal weight. Her life, however, has not been transformed as she'd hoped and the weight returns. It isn't long before she's on another diet, believing that if she is slim and attractive again she won't have anything to be depressed about.

Anyone who anticipates that an external event like weight loss is going to be the ticket to happiness is bound to be disappointed. Twelve-step support groups call changing the externals while ignoring what really needs to be addressed inside "doing the geographical cure." Whenever we move to another city, change our appearance, or modify our surroundings in an attempt to eliminate negative self-image, we're bound to be disappointed because what really needs to be changed—our behavior or outlook—goes right along with us.

If you are focusing on being in a certain relationship or looking a certain way because you think it will lead to contentment, it's time to challenge your assumptions. What was the last thing you worked to attain that you were sure would make you happy? Chances are the satisfaction was short-lived and you set your sights on another goal you thought might be more fulfilling. If this describes you, try not to create unrealistic expectations for future events and look instead to today to produce the small events that create lasting joy.

I will look to today, not the future, to bring me happiness.

Maybe [alcohol] picks you up a little bit, but it sure lets you down in a hurry.

—BETTY FORD

Quite often people say that when they're down they "drown their sorrows" in alcohol. The problem with drinking to help yourself cope with depression, however, is that while it may initially provide a lift, alcohol is ultimately a depressant. Also, people with a history of depression in their family are more likely to turn to alcohol and become addicted than people with a different genetic background. So not only is drinking a poor short-term idea for managing depression, it also has the potential to foster another damaging problem.

Substances like alcohol and cocaine stimulate the neurotransmitter dopamine in the brain, producing the artificial "feel good" response, which is why it is so tempting to have a glass of wine or a martini at the end of a trying day or when we want to escape temporarily from our problems. But we must realize that stimulating these pleasant responses in ourselves can be accomplished through other methods, such as meditation, exercise, and small amounts of carbohydrates.

Be conscious of how often you drink when depressed and of what the motivation is. If you've tried to quit but failed, you may have an addiction that is contributing to the depression. Look into Alcoholics Anonymous for support if your drinking seems compulsive and see if a few sober days don't help your depression. While alcohol may not be your whole problem, eliminating it as a contributing factor to your negative outlook is a wise step to take.

I will not tranquilize my emotions with alcohol.

In order to be irreplaceable one must always be different.
—COCO CHANEL

One of the chief desires of most adolescents is to "fit in" and not stand out from their peers in any noticeable way. If we happen to be heavier, from a different country, particularly smart, or very tall, it can separate us from others and lead to feelings of depression that are only ameliorated when we become comfortable with our special qualities and appreciative of the uniqueness that we possess.

As adults, we may suffer from these same feelings of isolation and depression if we make lifestyle or career choices that set us in the minority. For example, lesbians are prone to depression because of the discrimination they frequently face when their sexual preference is known. A friend of mine who announced her lesbianism to her family and became an active proponent of gay rights not only lost the love and support of her family, but her coworkers shunned her, as well. After extensive counseling to deal with her depression, my friend learned to be comfortable with her choices and to accept that veering from society's norms often makes others very defensive and uncomfortable.

Strive to cultivate your uniqueness today instead of allowing the differences to depress you. It takes strength and self-confidence to stand out in some way, so instead of castigating yourself, learn that being who you were meant to be and not what others want you to be is the only way to be happy.

I will not hide my light under a bushel.

I could not say I believe. I know! I have had the experience of being gripped by something that is stronger than myself, something that people call God.

—CARL JUNG

I once spoke with a friend about her faith in God and how she'd formed her beliefs. She freely admitted that she'd done very little to foster her spirituality: "I was just born knowing that there is a loving God who will always be there for me, no matter what." I marvel at such people who have unshakable convictions because I've certainly had to struggle to find a framework for the beliefs that now sustain me.

The times when I've made the most headway in understanding the power I call God have occurred when I've been in the most despair. When I first began to recover from several addictions in early adulthood, I felt so small and defenseless that I relied on what I called a higher power to sustain me during moments of self-doubt and sadness. Years later, in the grips of a deep depression, I occasionally felt the undeniable presence of a loving God whom I believe kept me from giving up. It's impossible to describe the feelings of warmth and hope generated by these occurrences, but they've helped me to stay focused when I've felt shaky and down.

No matter how sad you are, try to hold on to the slim belief that you're not alone in this vast universe. Once you can comprehend that important fact and find enough strength to pray for courage and hope, you'll always have the inner strength to withstand your setbacks.

My darkest moments bring my most illuminating encounters with God.

Compassion for myself is the most powerful healer of them all.

—THEODORE ISAAC RUBIN

There has been so much talk in recent years about the "inner child" and "dysfunctional" families that the terms have almost become meaningless and trite. But the beliefs that started this movement have some validity for millions of women: If we were raised in families where our emotional needs were not met, we need to acknowledge inwardly that there is a young, vulnerable version of ourselves inside that needs to be comforted and reassured about not being abandoned in tough times.

A number of my friends have rituals that access their inner child when they are feeling frightened, angry, or depressed. One has a special stuffed animal that she hugs at night, while she affirms, "I love you and will protect you no matter what." Another friend displays pictures of herself as a child on her bureau so that she is frequently reminded of how lovable and bubbly she once was. Yet another friend meditates on images of herself as a child and inwardly avows, "You are a beautiful, special being and you didn't deserve what happened to you."

If you are carrying around the residue of an unhappy childhood, have compassion for that small child within who didn't get what she needed to feel loved, honored, and accepted. Although reparenting ourselves takes dedication and unlimited compassion, we are worthy of any effort that fosters self-love and happiness.

I will love the child within me who didn't get the emotional support she needed.

It isn't the great big pleasures that count the most; it's making a great deal out of the little ones.

—JEAN WEBSTER

A therapist in New York City conducts seminars called "Personal Pleasures" that attempt to reintroduce participants to the little pleasures that bring the most joy. With the average employed woman spending eighty hours a week on work, errands, and childcare, and only sixteen hours on leisure, it's important to maximize the happiness those few hours can bring by learning what gives us pleasure and how to best create it.

One of the assignments this therapist gives the participants is to write lists of the 100 things that make them happiest, that they're grateful for, that they'd like to do before dying, that they'd do to nurture themselves, and that they'd like to own. Most people get stuck around thirty, she says, so pushing beyond that limit is important. Another assignment is to plan and then experience a two-hour adventure that will bring joy, such as visiting a museum or trying on wildly expensive clothes.

If you're missing pleasure in your life, try one of these exercises. All of us have the capacity to create joy, but we don't always give it the same priority as buying groceries or doing laundry. Learn to turn your free time into pleasure time and you'll not only create oases of peace and happiness in your day, you'll undoubtedly find many ways to ensure that depression doesn't have a chance to take root.

I will make pleasure a top priority today.

Women are like tea bags. They both get stronger in hot water.
—ELEANOR ROOSEVELT

There is a well-known organization in the United States that helps people attain their dream of owning houses even though they have little money. In exchange for contributing "sweat equity"—hard work in the construction or rehabilitation of a home—a person can qualify for a low-rate mortgage. Members of the organization assist the person in building the house, teaching them self-sufficiency skills as they go along.

A newspaper reporter who profiled the organization discovered that the vast majority of people who were endeavoring to build and own their own homes were women. Time and again he was told that women were the ones who persevered in fighting against living in poverty, and that they were the ones holding the families together, trying to create a brighter future for themselves and their children.

We women are special and we're often tougher than we think we are. Whatever hot water you are in today, remember that it can strengthen and empower you, not just cause you to disintegrate and wallow in depression. Remind yourself of your strengths and find other women to talk to who have become more resourceful despite adversity. Although depression often makes us lose sight of how resilient we are, with the help of family and friends, and perhaps a therapist, we can develop a new appreciation for who we are and how far we've come.

I will let hot fires forge me into a strong piece of metal.

All sunshine makes a desert.

—EASTERN PROVERB

When things are going wrong in our lives it's hard to imagine that we'll ever feel happy or content again. For example, whenever I'm in despair, I tend to think that the bleak stretch will never come to an end. Realistically I know that my depressions usually have a beginning and an end, but when I'm in the middle of one, I'm hard-pressed to remember times of joy and laughter.

Life is composed of a series of ebbs and flows in our emotions and fortunes, and it's impossible to sustain one particular state forever—nor should we want to. As much as we may desire a life devoid of problems and filled with unremitting happiness, it wouldn't be helpful to us. Just as spells of sickness remind us how valuable good health is, bouts of depression and anxiety provide the insight and gratitude necessary to treasure happiness when we have it.

Even though no one really enjoys dark times, remember today that having a life only of sunshine isn't just unrealistic, it wouldn't make for an emotionally rich and varied life. Depression does feel like an endless desert at times, but oases of joy do come for all of us if we maintain our hopefulness and remember that exploring the dark side of life is occasionally very good for the soul.

Only by experiencing sadness at times can I learn to appreciate real joy.

*Don't burn bridges. You'll be surprised how many times you
have to cross the same river.*

—H. Jackson Brown

Several years ago a person I trusted hurt me very
deeply, costing me a lot of money and time. I wanted more
than anything to pick up the phone and let her know how
her actions had adversely affected me. For some reason I
never did this and instead suffered silently, inwardly fum-
ing about what had happened to me.

Three years later I got a call from the same person
who admitted her fault in our altercation and then asked
me to help her do something. Although I was reluctant to
work with her again, I agreed because I felt I'd profit from
the experience. The interaction proved to be mutually beneficial and I was grateful that I had been able to hold my
tongue and not burn my bridges when I wanted to.

Lashing out at people who have hurt us is a normal,
human desire, particularly when we're depressed and our
thinking isn't clear. But we mustn't let the pain push us to
say or do something harmful just because we want the satisfaction of getting back at someone. Life is long and has
many unforseeable twists and turns, so we'd be well advised
to avoid burning bridges when we're down and instead to
channel our anger into more productive pursuits that can't
come back to haunt us.

Burning bridges burns me the most.

Literature is mostly about having sex and not much about having children. Life is the other way around.

—DAVID LODGE

A friend of mine called one day to say that she was depressed about her and her husband's lack of an interesting sex life. With two children under the age of five she was frequently exhausted by the end of the day and uninterested in making love. "Everyone else has a great sex life!" she moaned. "What's wrong with me?"

The torrid sex scenes and exotic intimacy we read about in books and see in the movies can be depressing if we are foolish enough to think they represent the norm. The truth of the matter is that in long-lasting relationships sex can become boring, and small children can contribute to a logistical nightmare. Literature is a chance to escape and fantasize; to make the mistake that it represents average, everyday life is harmful to ourselves and our self-esteem.

If your lack of sexual sizzle is upsetting you, remember that children aren't young forever and that good relationships have ebbs and flows in passion. Try some creative solutions like arranging a weekend getaway or asking a friend to watch your children for an afternoon. While our sexual gymnastics may never match those in fiction, with tenacity and inventiveness we can rekindle that which brings us enjoyment and passion.

It isn't realistic or helpful to compare my life to the latest best-seller.

The man who treasures his friends is usually solid gold himself.

—MARJORIE HOLMES

There was a time in my life when I was so busy with motherhood and work that I lost touch with many of my friends. My schedule became so tight that having something as simple as a lunch or leisurely phone call was an impossibility, and instead of fighting harder to preserve my friendships, I simply let them drift. Not too long thereafter, I entered a very dark period when I felt alone and scared, and because I had let many of my relationships lapse, I found fighting the blues that much harder.

Research has consistently shown that maintaining a strong circle of friends is one of the best predictors of health and happiness. People who don't have families or social ties tend to have weaker immune systems, higher levels of cancer, more depression, and die sooner than those who reach out and share their lives. Having even one friend in whom you can confide—not just a large circle of superficial acquaintances—can significantly affect your mental and physical health.

Periodically assess your friendships to see if they are the types of relationships that are beneficial to you. A good friend is someone who doesn't drain you and whose input is sound and compassionate. A friend will also not be put off by your depression and will continue to support you and try to reach you, even when you try to isolate yourself. Making sure you have several high-quality friendships before you really need them can be one of the smartest investments you make in your health.

I will treasure my friends today.

How dry eyes can get when they are not allowed to cry!
—MARIA AUGUSTA TRAPP

When I was growing up my family placed a great premium on taking our losses stoically and not crying, no matter how devastated we felt. To cry was to be weak, and we'd be ignored or laughed at if we gave in to our emotions. As a result I stuffed my feelings down with food and other self-destructive activities which made me miserable and sick, and left me unable to express myself appropriately when it would have been very healing to do so.

Tears supposedly contain poisonous chemicals that, when flushed from our system during a good cry, cause us to feel relief. Not only is it biologically helpful to shed tears, it's often an emotional catharsis. Friends of mine who say they've held off from crying about something because they felt it was inappropriate or silly have found that inevitably they've gotten sick or unusually moody, and until they allowed themselves to grieve they felt physically and emotionally awful.

If you are depressed and suppressing tears because you think you will be considered weak or viewed as a "hysterical female," find a time to let go and have a good, heaving sob session. You may want to pound pillows, scream, or throw things as well, but whatever you do, allow the torrent of tears to cleanse your soul and restore some balance to your mind and body.

Crying strengthens me emotionally and physically.

Tea quenches tears and thirst.
                    —JEANINE LARMOTH AND CHARLOTTE TURGEON

Whenever a certain friend of mine is going through a difficult time, she takes a "cuppa" break to restore her equilibrium and regain perspective on her life. Her cuppa time is something her therapist recommended as a way of pampering herself when she's weary or sad; she makes a cup of her favorite tea, finds a quiet room with a comfortable chair, and then sips the tea slowly in silence. Inevitably, my friend says, cuppa time deliberately removes her from an upsetting environment, gives her a task to accomplish, and makes her feel soothed and calmed.

In Japan the process of making tea is so intricate that it takes years to master all of the nuances of this important ritual. The tea maker must concentrate completely on every movement and complete all of the steps in silence, which devotees say is akin to doing yoga. Although we probably won't ever learn the Japanese tea ritual, by taking the time to make something warming like tea, and then focusing on enjoying it in silence, we can create the same feelings of contemplation and serenity that this ancient ceremony evokes.

Try the cuppa solution if you are feeling stressed today. Invest in a nice mug and some high-quality tea and then take the time to nurture yourself. While socializing with others is always enjoyable, sometimes it's good for our emotional health to throw a tea party just for ourselves.

I will have some cuppa time today.

I don't know the key to success, but the key to failure is trying to please everybody.

—BILL COSBY

I never thought there was such a thing as being too nice until I read about a study done on women who had life-threatening illnesses such as cancer. One of the conclusions was that women who make an effort to repress their anger, be pleasant at all times, and defer to others' wishes are at higher risk of dying than are women who are assertive, headstrong, and even a little "bitchy."

I know a woman who is the quintessential "Stepford Wife." Although she sailed through college with high honors and was one of the first women admitted to a prestigious law school, she followed the trend of the 1950s and chose to give up her career aspirations to get married and have children. In an effort to have the "perfect" home, she defers to her husband's every wish, keeps her mouth shut instead of expressing her opinions, and accepts the blame for whatever goes wrong in the family. Only a few people know that beneath the well-groomed exterior lie enormous amounts of anger, depression, and low self-esteem, which are the result of trying to please everyone rather than be true to herself.

Don't think that making others happy will always make you happy, because it won't. Instead of trying to be demure and selfless all the time, allow yourself to be outrageous, outspoken, and even contrary from time to time. You might be surprised to find that not only will you preserve your physical health in the long run but you may also save your sanity.

Today I will please myself.

The mother-child relationship is paradoxical and, in a sense, tragic. It requires the most intense love on the mother's side, yet this very love must help the child grow away from the mother and to become fully independent.

—ERICH FROMM

One day a friend of mine called in tears, barely able to speak. When she finally calmed down I was able to ask what had happened. Sobbing, she said, "I just dropped Josh off at daycare. He's only one! I feel like the worst mother in the world!" In fact, she was so distraught about going back to work for the first time since his birth that she stayed home and cried all day, curled in the fetal postion.

There are many painful and depressing phases of motherhood, with the return to work after having a child being one of the hardest. However, it is just the beginning of learning that despite how much love we pour into our children, we must gradually entrust them to the world in order for them to be shaped into responsible, self-sufficient adults. This type of depression is sharp, but it's something most mothers must live through if their children are eventually to thrive on their own.

If you're depressed about separating from your child —for the first time or because they're beginning to rely more on their peers than on you—make your time together special and meaningful. Do activities you both enjoy, listen to their concerns and thoughts without judgment, and let them know how much you love them. If you can let them go with the knowledge that you'll always be there for them, they'll never truly be separated from you.

Whatever I love unconditionally is always with me in my heart.

The tendency to identify manhood with a capacity for physical violence has a long history in America.
—MARSHALL FISHWICK

One day I was watching a TV show about domestic violence and I learned the shocking fact that half of all homicides are committed within families—particularly by husbands or boyfriends killing their wives or girlfriends. One reason the male guests on the show cited for being violent was that their self-image as head of the household was threatened by a woman who dared to voice her opinion or to disagree.

Unfortunately, domestic abuse is prevalent in this country and it doesn't just exist in disadvantaged neighborhoods. In one affluent community a shelter for battered women filled up quickly with victims who reported that their husbands were wealthy, well-liked captains of industry during the day, but drunk abusers at night. Many of the women had lived in fear and self-loathing for years, never able to summon up the courage to seek help until a place had opened nearby. Many also said that they had repeatedly taken the men back after kicking them out, hoping that time would change their behavior, although it never had.

Try to find the courage to seek help and information that will enable you to break the cycle of dependency and low self-esteem. If we tolerate abuse we are more likely to abuse ourselves through other self-defeating behaviors, so the first step to reclaiming our lives is to empower ourselves with knowledge, seek the proper help, and have the courage to protect ourselves from further violence.

I love myself enough to ensure that I am treated lovingly by others, too.

Silence is not a thing we make; it is something into which we enter.

—MOTHER MARIBEL

Whenever my son is acting up or is overstimulated, I give him a "time out" during which he sits quietly or goes to his room by himself. Although he's usually not happy about this, it doesn't take him long to calm down. It's amazing what a little enforced silence can do to change someone's temperament and get them thinking along different lines.

Because I'm too old to have someone forcibly give me a time out, I have to remember on occasion that my needs are no different from my son's. When I act bratty or I am sad about something, what I often need is to take some time in the middle of the day to be quiet and alone. I find that if I can slow down my thinking, remove distractions from my environment, and still my mind, life becomes more peaceful. I don't always emerge from my silent time with solutions or answers but I usually find that the mere act of caring enough about my well-being to take a time out is balm for my soul.

Give yourself enforced silence today if you haven't had any peace lately. Don't use the time to dwell on your problems; use it to change the course of your thinking, to do something you love, or to be grateful for anything that's going well for you. Just as small children must be removed from stressful situations to regain their composure, you'll find that taking time to reflect and be alone every now and then is important in reclaiming or maintaining your equilibrium.

I occasionally need time outs as much as small children do.

Without work all life goes rotten.

—ALBERT CAMUS

Just about everyone I know has lost a job at some point in his or her life. Some of these people have been able to bounce back pretty quickly and find jobs that are better suited to their skills in a relatively short period of time. But most of the people I know have spent long periods looking for work and have had their self-esteem and optimism plummet as a result.

Psychologists and other mental health experts say that in times of crisis we need to break up problems into manageable parts and take stock of the areas we *can* control. For example, if being laid off means financial problems threaten to undo us, we should seek out a financial planner to learn how to budget what we have. And if being unemployed increases our sense of isolation, we must make an effort to get together with those who can help boost our spirits.

If you're out of work today, try not to panic and sink into despair. Make a list of what needs to be done, break your solutions down into steps, and then begin your tasks. Also, don't add to your woes by blaming yourself if you've been caught in a corporate downsizing because your unemployment probably has nothing to do with you personally. Remember that as important as work is to feeling useful and creative, we must separate our worthiness as people from our ability to make money.

My self-esteem and happiness are independent of my employment situation.

A hobby a day keeps the doldrums away.
—Phyllis McGinley

Some of the most unhappy people I know are the ones who have no interests outside their work and families. Whatever creativity they possess has been subsumed into their daily routines and instead of using what free time they have on a hobby, they use it to clean a floor, do the laundry, or run an errand. Gradually, as this pattern repeats itself over the years, an activity that once brought great pleasure is forgotten in the daily rush and new ones are never fostered.

A therapist who wrote a book about this topic said that she was struck by the large number of women who came to her who had lost touch with their creative "wild woman." She encouraged them to stop cleaning and making beds so often and instead to do what made them happy, like painting, dancing, and writing. The women who allowed themselves to set free the "wild woman" on activities that expressed their inner selves reported feeling happier and more in control of their lives than women who didn't.

Are you "too busy" to have a hobby or be creative? Challenge yourself to leave a task undone—like ironing—and instead do something that you have neglected or always wanted to try. We may not realize how much the drudgery of our day is creating depression until we shake up our routines and find ways to let the "wild woman" come out to play on a regular basis.

I will find time for a pleasurable activity today even if it means going to bed with dishes in the sink.

Faith is what makes life bearable, with all its tragedies and ambiguities and sudden, startling joys.

—MADELEINE L'ENGLE

A dear friend of mine, Elisabeth, lost a baby when she was almost six months pregnant because its heart simply stopped beating due to a blood clot in the umbilical cord. Although she had wanted a baby for years and her age made the possibility of a pregnancy less likely, Elisabeth recovered her equilibrium rather quickly because of her faith that the accident—although painful and depressing—had been part of God's plan for her life.

When I saw her a week after her loss, Elisabeth admitted that she still had bad days but that good had already come from her tragedy: she and her husband felt more committed to each other than ever, her husband had snapped out of his midlife career crisis because the miscarriage had put his priorities in perspective, and her mother had expressed for the first time how much she had loved being Elisabeth's mother and how rewarding motherhood had been for her. "If I didn't believe the baby was sent to heal these parts of my life, the miscarriage would be harder to cope with," she admitted.

When we have faith that our tragedies and joys are part of an inscrutable plan for our lives, our crosses become easier to bear. Try to accept both your pain and your joy today as pieces of what are best for you. It may take some time to understand why certain setbacks occur, but having faith in God or a power greater than yourself can help you weather most storms.

My crosses will enrich and benefit me in ways I may not yet see.

Take away the miseries and you take away some folks' reason for living. Their conversation piece anyway.

—TONI CADE BAMBARA

I know a woman who is so wrapped up in her problems that there is no room in her life for anything or anyone else. Whenever I ask her how she is, I have to brace myself for a five-minute tirade on how much her foot hurts, how cruel her boss is, and how angry she is about "foreigners" taking over the United States. At one time I tried to offer sympathetic solutions to her litany of woes, but after several years I realized that this woman's problems have become her reason for living.

Seeing this tendency in my friend made me aware of how much time and energy I am capable of giving my troubles when I want attention and sympathy. It's one thing to go through legitimate spells of depression and to seek the solace and support of friends; it's quite another to complain and moan constantly about the state of our lives and never to take positive steps to address what's bothering us.

Are you letting your depression and problems run your life? Do you need them in order to feel alive and important? If so, consider how depression may have become your only way to enlist the concern and support of others. Instead of being known as someone whose response to "How are you?" is always negative, try today to focus on what is right with your life and then emphasize that as often as you can until it becomes a natural—and accurate —response.

I will not let misery become my reason for living.

As I see it, every day you do one of two things: build health or produce disease in yourself.

—ADELLE DAVIS

One day I watched a documentary about how the Chinese treat disease. They believe that the body is governed by *chi,* which roughly translated means energy. When the *chi* is balanced, the body and mind are healthy. There are many ways of balancing *chi* including t'ai chi ch'uan exercises, meditation, visualization, massage, acupuncture, and a judicious intake of herbs.

In the West, many of these practices aren't accepted by mainstream doctors who, instead, believe in medication and invasive medical procedures. But a growing number of people are turning to Eastern practices to supplement their traditional medical care because these foreign techniques have proved so effective in managing stress and mood swings. A friend of mine who suffered from morning sickness during pregnancy found that acupuncture was the only thing that helped her nausea and depression, and another friend gets regular massage therapy and practices t'ai chi, which she swears helps her beat the blues and stay focused during difficult times.

One way to build health and not disease is to try incorporating some Eastern healing techniques into your life. It makes sense that rhythmic exercise, meditation, and natural eating habits would be more beneficial than no exercise, constant stress, and processed foods, particularly if depression is a problem. So scrutinize your habits to see if you can find ways to incorporate Eastern wellness principles into your life, and you might be surprised by how much stronger and emotionally healthy a balanced body can be.

I will build health by balancing my energy today.

From the concert of life, no one gets a program.

—Anonymous

All of us at one time or another will be faced with events that threaten our happiness and self-esteem. We will probably be fired from good jobs, have relationship problems, lose parents, and do things that we regret. Try as we might we can do little to prevent many of these things from happening because no one is fortunate enough to be given a blueprint of their life ahead of time.

Sharon is a case in point. She developed throat cancer in her twenties, despite having no family history of cancer, and suffered from a deep depression. Basically she gave up on life, and it was only when faced with the possibility of having her voice box removed that she rallied, fighting back and living each day with as much vitality and enthusiasm as she could muster. Now, after several successful rounds of chemotherapy, she is grateful for every morning that she wakes up healthy and she doesn't take being alive in a week or a year for granted.

Because life is often unpredictable and filled with depressing occurrences, it's important to develop the resilience and flexibility that will give us strength to fight back when times are hard. Through developing our spiritual side, trusting that we can handle the burdens we're given, and taking advantage of whatever resources we need to cope, we'll discover that we are better able to catch whatever curveballs life throws us.

I will pray for the strength to accept the "program" of my life with grace.

A great step toward independence is a good-humoured stomach.

—SENECA

By most standards, Diane's recovery from alcoholism was successful. She didn't drink for more than two years and was an active member of a twelve-step support group. Diane, however, was far from healthy. Shortly after becoming sober, she was diagnosed as manic depressive with wide mood swings, bouts of insomnia, and chronic fatigue. "Sure, I wasn't drinking," Diane said, "but I was not comfortable emotionally, and I was falling apart physically."

Diane took matters into her own hands and educated herself about nutrition, which she believes saved her life. By following a nutritionally sound diet and taking the right nutritional supplements, she saw a dramatic, positive change. Some doctors believe that changing diet, especially while in recovery from an addiction, can spell the difference between success and failure in maintaining a drug-free or alcohol-free life. By balancing the body holistically, it is thought that persons can free themselves from the depression, insomnia, and listlessness that is common in early recovery.

Although changing your diet may not be the solution to your blues, it helps to eliminate substances that don't contribute to your health. Consider talking to a nutritionist or dietitian about your meals; a simple change may alleviate many of your symptoms. Although medication is often a key component of overcoming depression, a holistic approach may show you that how you eat has more of an effect on your moods than you once thought.

I will seek independence from depression by taking care of my stomach.

We can destroy ourselves by cynicism and disillusion, just as effectively as by bombs.

—KENNETH CLARK

Some of the unhappiest people I know are convinced that everyone's out to get them, no one can be trusted, and life is an adventure in looking out for oneself. They can't find time for volunteer work, they value money more than friends, and they cannot relinquish control of any aspect of their lives.

When we're tense, angry, and mistrustful it's difficult to experience lasting happiness. Chasing the almighty buck usually entails nights and weekends away from family and friends, and looking out only for our own welfare means we'll never know the joy of seeing the grateful face of someone we've helped. Similarly, glancing over our shoulder to make sure no one's going to "get" us keeps our minds filled with fearful, vengeful thoughts, not happy, positive ones.

Do you rate high on the cynicism scale? Is the glass always half-empty, not half-full? Do you think you might as well cheat on your taxes because everyone else does? If so, try to inject some trust, humor, and compassion into your life today and see how much freer you feel. If you can begin to see the world as a loving, harmonious place, you may be surprised to find that it can actually become more that way for you.

I will see the world in a positive, hopeful light today.

Those who are unhappy have no need for anything in this world but people capable of giving them their attention.
—SIMONE WEIL

I have two friends whom I have learned I cannot call when I'm depressed because they are incapable of giving me their full attention. One works on her computer while we talk and between the clicking of the keys in the background and her vague replies, I can tell she's not really listening. Another never fails to cook something or clean her kitchen when I call, and I'm hard-pressed to keep up my train of thought while I hear pots and pans clanging in the background.

When we're depressed we must find people to talk to who will sit quietly, make eye contact, and listen without distraction. This type of behavior says, "I care about you enough to listen to your feelings." Anything less than this courtesy is a nonverbal statement that our woes are of little concern to them.

Be careful about whom you seek comfort from today. Therapists will always give you undivided attention, which is partly why they're so helpful, but so can friends and family members who have good listening skills. You might even be surprised to find that just the simple act of someone taking the time to make us feel important and cared for is all that we need to chase the blues away.

I will seek the company of someone who can give me their complete attention.

Research tells us that fourteen out of any ten individuals like chocolate.

—Sandra Boynton

Although I've never been a chocolate lover, I have friends who cannot go a day without eating some form of it. These people usually have stashes of candy bars at work and their cupboards are full of cake and brownie mixes for late-night binges. My chocoholic friends may not know it, but indulging in their passion is an effective treatment for depression: Research shows that eating chocolate creates the same sense of well-being as does falling passionately in love.

Eating chocolate to beat the blues isn't the only way to use it. A psychologist at Duke University says that just the smell of chocolate can trigger mood-lifting endorphins because most people have a pleasant association with its scent. Apricot is another time-tested "happy" smell, and depending on our memories, other scents such as honeysuckle, jasmine, pine, and cinnamon can have similar effects.

If you need a mood elevator today, think about using chocolate to help you feel better. Since a moderate amount of candy or the scent of chocolate baking can be uplifting, it might be wise to visit a bakery, whip up some brownies, or indulge your sweet tooth. While these mild forms of therapy may not be the cure-all for what's ailing you, it can't hurt to try something that has brought so much happiness to so many.

I will use pleasant aromas to brighten my mood today.

For is it not possible that middle age can be looked upon as a period of second flowering, second growth, even a kind of second adolescence?

—ANNE MORROW LINDBERGH

One night I was watching a news show that focused on a large group of women who had been proposed for top posts in a new political administration. Although most of the commentary focused on the women's abilities, one of the female analysts broke into a smile and said, "The main thing I'd like to point out is that every one of these women is in or past menopause, which proves that women can have full, productive lives after their childbearing years are over."

Although her comment was slightly off the subject, it *is* heartening to see that middle age doesn't just bring the "empty nest" syndrome, sagging bodies, and atrophying of the brain. In fact, research has shown that after their children leave home many women actually blossom because they have more freedom to do activities that appeal to them. One friend told me that her forties and fifties were a glorious time of intellectual challenges, sexual experimentation, and freedom from schedules. "I'm happier in many ways now than I've ever been," she says.

Instead of looking at "the afternoon of your life" with dread, try to create the expectation that you'll only get wiser, more productive, and more energetic as you age. With the proper conditioning, nutrition, goals, and role models, you can turn a time that has traditionally been thought to bring nothing but depression and lethargy into the best and most fulfilling half of your life.

As I get older, I get better.

*All through the long winter I dream of my garden. On the first
warm day of spring I dig my fingers deep into the soft earth. I
can feel its energy, and my spirits soar.*

—HELEN HAYES

One of the pleasures I have discovered relatively late
in life is that of puttering around a garden and watching
plants I have nurtured grow. I had always pooh-poohed the
opinions of people who said that gardening is among the
most therapeutic of activities, but once I moved into a
house and inherited a lawn that needed flowers, shrubs,
and lots of water, I was converted.

But the benefits of gardening go beyond the pleasure
it brings. Several books have been published on gardening
therapy, and some prisons and psychiatric hospitals use it
as a tool for addicted and depressed patients. One inmate
said that planting a seed, tending the soil, and watching the
fruits of his labor bloom had given him hope that he, too,
could blossom as a new person if he took good care of
himself. Similarly, depressed patients say that the rhythmic
motions of digging, weeding, and watering help take their
minds off their troubles and give them the responsibility of
caring for something outside themselves.

Channel your energy into working with the soil today.
If you have a house, spend some time working around the
yard watering, pruning, or weeding and keep your mind
focused on the task at hand. And even if you live in a city
apartment, nurturing a pot of herbs or ferns can bring im-
mense satisfaction and act as a reminder that helping
something take root and flourish can be a healing and joyful experience.

My inner spirit flowers when I am in touch with the earth.

I sought the Lord, and He heard me, and delivered me from all my fears.

—PSALMS 34:4

A well-known baseball player in the city where I once lived suffered a very public, heart-rending tragedy. His six-year-old son was coming home from the park one afternoon when he darted in front of a car and was killed. While the local community mourned the little boy's death, the father courageously made decisions about donating his son's organs, spoke movingly at the memorial service, and then returned to the team two weeks later, strong and dignified despite what had happened.

I don't think many people could have weathered this type of tragedy as well as this man did, but he said that his faith in the Lord was what had carried him. "I know he's in a better place than I am," the man said, "and that I'll see him again one day when it's my time to go."

Sometimes when we're faced with problems that don't seem to respond to earthly ministrations, the only thing that helps is a belief in God. The strongest, most self-assured people I know are the ones who are deeply spiritual —not necessarily religious—and who trust that a power greater than themselves is orchestrating events in their lives for their ultimate good. If you are feeling bereft and despairing of solutions today, call upon the God of your understanding for wisdom, hope, and strength. The more you nourish this connection in both good and bad times, the stronger will be your inner peace when you need it.

God can give me strength when I feel the most vulnerable.

Everything that irritates us about others can lead us to an understanding of ourselves.

—CARL JUNG

One afternoon I returned from a gathering feeling down and out of sorts. As I searched my mind for the reasons, I focused on the behavior of the host, who can only be called contrary; he takes special delight in tearing people's egos down, jabbing their Achilles' heel, and deflating any pomposity he detects. I realized upon reflection that he had pinpointed areas in myself that bothered me but that I hadn't had the courage to face before.

Do you find yourself feeling angry, uncomfortable, or depressed after being with a certain person? Instead of dismissing them or putting them down, try to assess honestly what he or she has touched inside that might need to be examined and changed. The great saying that "we grow comfortable with people who agree with us, and grow with people who disagree with us," always holds true when someone affects us in this way.

Whenever I'm irritated, I'm close to identifying things about myself that need to be changed.

The main obligation is to amuse yourself.

—S. J. PERELMAN

As many of us get older we lose the ability to have fun and be spontaneous. Experts say that many of the people who succumb to addiction and stress either never learned as children how to play or have forgotten that skill. Part of the task, then, in recovering from an addiction or learning to cope with stress is to rediscover what playing is all about.

Play can be anything you enjoy free of coercion. If listening to the opera with your eyes closed is enjoyable, that's play. If playing tennis is fun and you're not obsessed with winning or looking good, that's play. And if you love your work, don't take it overly seriously and look forward to every day on the job, that can also be considered play.

Do you play enough to be a relaxed, happy person, or have you forgotten the joys of making up games and losing yourself in imaginary pursuits? Try to reintegrate play into your life today by taking time to do something enjoyable and that is free of pressures, deadlines, or self-imposed limits. Whether it's writing a short story, playing Frisbee with friends, doing the morning crossword puzzle, or painting with your children, finding the time and willingness to be childlike is important in keeping a perspective on life and allowing stress and frustrations to dissipate.

I will play today.

Dismounted from her dream, she could not find footing again on solid ground. Her realities repelled her.

—MARY O'HARA

Natalie is a middle-aged boutique owner who has always dreamed of being on Broadway, so despite her slim chances of making it, she pours time and money into singing and dancing lessons and gets depressed whenever she is turned away at casting calls. Because she's unable to accept the reality that she's probably never going to be a big star, Natalie's self-esteem has suffered tremendously.

Terry is another woman who has had trouble facing the fact that she is not a "company person." Because she resents taking orders from superiors, Terry has lost several jobs for "insubordination." After her last firing she decided to go into business for herself which, to her surprise, she liked and was good at. By acknowledging her difficult personality traits and trying to accommodate them, Terry accepted the painful reality that she wasn't cut out to hold a conventional job and that her future security would rest solely on her own efforts.

If we cling to unrealistic dreams for ourselves, we need to look at how our beliefs may be shortchanging us emotionally by robbing us of self-esteem. Giving up fantasies often creates depression, but learning how to work through them and create realistic expectations for ourselves will not just boost our self-confidence, it will lessen our chances of becoming depressed by "failure."

When I accept reality, the dreamworld loses its hold over me.

I hope you love birds, too. It is economical. It saves going to Heaven.

—EMILY DICKINSON

There are few things that bring me as much pleasure as the sound of birds singing in the spring. It is difficult to feel sad when I hear these musical expressions of nature heralding the return of longer days, green trees, and flowering shrubs. And during summers at the beach the cawing of the seagulls usually lulls me into a peaceful reverie.

There is a scientific reason why birds produce such good feelings in people. Pleasant, high-pitched sounds like bird songs have been shown to increase serotonin levels in the brain, which elevates your mood. Music therapists say that other repetitive sounds with seven or eight beats per second—such as a drum roll—have the same euphoric effect because the sound produces slower brain waves and a more relaxed mood.

Although there really are no substitutes for therapy and medication in some cases of depression, little mood lifters like listening to the birds or tapes of the waves crashing on the shore can increase the amount of serenity in your day. Make sure that you make the most of all of these types of natural solutions because not only are they free, but you can have access to them whenever you choose.

I will seek out the sounds of nature to soothe me.

We might well remember always that unless we control our thought, it will control us.

—ERNEST HOLMES

Before my second child was born I was seized with the certainty that her birth would make my life completely unmanageable. Rarely did I allow myself to visualize happy scenes; I thought instead about difficult deliveries, colicky babies, hassle-filled days, and sleepless nights. So as the end of my pregnancy approached I was sure that I was enjoying my last days of uninterrupted phone conversations and restful sleep.

Finally I confided my fears in someone who confessed to having felt the same way before the birth of her second child. "It wasn't anything like I imagined, though," she admitted, saying that her overwhelming love for her daughter had made all of the work lighter and that she had adjusted far better to the many changes than she thought she would. My friend suggested that I try to think about happy scenes of cuddling the baby instead of more negative ones. She also said it would be helpful to write positive affirmations about being a mother and to repeat them to myself often.

Within a few days of taking this advice I was calmer and happier about the upcoming change in my life. I realize now how much I allowed a little fear to completely dominate my thinking and actions, and I am more careful about giving time and energy to the unknown—something we all need to remember whenever our obsessions turn negative and start to control us.

Positive thinking helps create happy outcomes.

Don't make much ado about nothing.

—BALTASAR GRACIÁN

A manicurist told me one day that her clients often use her as a sounding-board for their problems. Because of the area in which she lives, many of her clients are wealthy and don't seem to have many serious problems. As a result of living fairly charmed lives, the manicurist said, sometimes the smallest problems send these women into an unreasonable tailspin of anger and depression.

One day, for example, a client arrived with redrimmed eyes and had obviously been crying. Assuming that something tragic had happened, the manicurist asked if someone had died in the family. It turned out that the woman's rambunctious two-year-old had taken an indelible pen and drawn on a new white leather sofa. As the woman related the story she broke into sobs, saying that she didn't know how to cope with having her favorite sofa so badly defaced.

Although this is an extreme example of making much ado about relatively nothing, many of us are guilty of overreacting to events that in the scheme of life weren't all that significant and that resulted in wasted hours or days of raging emotions. Ask yourself today if what you're upset about is truly awful or whether it's something trivial that in a month or a year will seem silly. If you can keep your problems in perspective and remember that much of what concerns us is often transitory, you'll have the strength required for a time when there *is* much ado about something.

I will not overreact to my problems.

Bad hair is hell.

—SHIRLEY LORD

As women we tend to place an enormous amount of importance on our appearance, and particularly on our hair. I know some very poised and successful women who have everything going for them, but if they feel their hair doesn't look "right," they slump into a depression.

One attractive friend of mine stayed in her home as a virtual prisoner for a month because a hairdresser mistakenly gave her a severe cut when all she wanted was a trim. For weeks she tied a scarf around her head, wore little makeup, and loudly fretted about how "ugly" and "deformed" she looked—something none of the rest of us saw. I had a similar reaction once when I boldly chopped off my long hair, only to wail to others afterward that I was "hideous" and "unfeminine." I learned from this experience how much of my self-esteem resided in having a safe, predictable appearance and how frightened I was of taking risks.

Examine today how much importance you attach to the superficial details of your appearance, particularly your hair. Are you locked into a certain look because you're afraid to change or because you rely on others to dictate what's best for you? One sign of self-confidence and inner joy is believing in internal, not external, beauty. Realizing that "bad hair" days don't equal bad days increases our chances of happiness.

I consist of more than what meets the eye.

Anyone who stops learning is old, whether at twenty or eighty.
Anyone who keeps learning stays young.

—HENRY FORD

Too often when women have low self-esteem they avoid setting goals that will increase their knowledge. Women frequently set "performance goals" that require positive feedback in areas they've already mastered. Men, on the other hand, tend to set "learning goals" that indicate a desire to learn a new skill or master a challenge. The difference is that men are more willing to risk making a mistake because they realize they're doing something new, whereas women feel like they're stupid if they don't do something perfectly.

This obsession with appearing flawless can trip us both professionally and personally. If we avoid learning a skill like using a computer because we don't want to look dumb, we can be passed over for career opportunities. And if we always turn down invitations to participate in a new activity for the same reason, we'll miss out on the feelings of mastery that come with new achievements. To always play it safe means that our self-esteem will probably remain low and our learning will stagnate.

A healthy, vibrant person is one who takes risks and who is always eager to learn something new. Make it a point to do something adventurous today that you won't necessarily shine at; you won't just gain a new skill, you'll also get a new outlook.

When I set learning goals I remain youthful and feel positive about myself.

The dead carry with them to the grave in their clutched hands only that which they have given away.
—DeWitt Wallace

One evening I was watching a report about how a local food bank was turning away whole families for lack of supplies. Because I grew up in a city where street beggars are common, I was somewhat hardened to pleas for assistance, thinking that everyone who asked for money really just wanted to buy alcohol. But this television report changed my mind. It focused on a family that had fallen on hard times; the parents had lost their jobs and were facing eviction. On top of that they were desperate for medical care to save their eighteen-month-old's life because he was struggling with a serious heart defect. Chastened, I gathered food and baby supplies and drove them to the food bank.

Although I wasn't particularly down on the day that I visited the food bank, I felt immeasurably better afterward and went looking for similar actions I could take to help people who were facing difficult times. The other unexpected benefit was that it minimized many of the difficulties I was facing at that time. I may have had problems, but at least I had healthy children, plenty of food, and a roof over my head.

Do something charitable today, no matter how small. Reach out to someone in need with your time or your money, and try to see the world through others' eyes. You'll always find that your life seems richer and happier than you may have thought, and that giving is often the best medicine for unhappiness.

The more generous I am, the richer a person I become.

For some of us depression is an occasional visitor who arrives quietly and vanishes without warning. For others, it's an invisible, aggressive intruder that seizes control of our bodies and our minds.

—ELLEN MCGRATH

When Sarah gets depressed her suffering is predictably tied to her menstrual cycle and to changes in the weather, so she knows from past experience that relief is only a matter of time. Jamie, however, suffers from bipolar disorder that runs in her family, so when depression strikes, it's often unrelated to an external event. Although these two women experience depression in different ways, it doesn't lessen the pain both feel when it occurs.

Because depression can manifest itself in different ways, it is often misdiagnosed by professionals. In fact, surveys have shown that doctors miss the diagnosis of depression in the vast majority of their female patients, attributing their symptoms to some other malady such as chronic fatigue syndrome or an eating disorder. Consequently, if we're misled by our doctors, we might discount the possibility of depression because we don't know enough about it, or we might treat an addiction under the assumption that it alone is responsible for our mood swings.

Be aware of your pattern of depression and see whether it is random or predictable. Check your family history for genetic links and clues that might help you understand yourself better. Be vocal about how you feel with professionals and remember that while physicians are important in our health care, knowing ourselves well is the best way to get the proper treatment.

I won't ignore symptoms of depression in myself.

The mother-daughter relationship is mano a mano.
—CANDICE BERGEN

Very few of my female friends have enjoyed smooth, trouble-free relationships with their mothers. At one time or another we have all feuded with our mothers over various issues including how we dress, who our friends are, what we believe in, and how we behave. More often than not we don't resolve our differences with our mothers until we reach adulthood and—quite frequently—we never come to a peaceful resolution without a lot of effort.

One friend of mine has a love-hate relationship with her mother that alternately delights and infuriates her. For long stretches of time she and her mother get along harmoniously, shopping together, talking often on the phone, and exchanging gossip. Then, inevitably, her mother says or does something to infuriate her daughter—insult her husband, criticize her children, or insist that she has no taste—and my friend cuts off all contact, vowing never to speak to her mother again. After a while they speak again and get close, and the whole cycle starts over.

We must remember that the nature of the mother-daughter relationship is a struggle: the mother tries to raise her daughter in her own image and the daughter fights to be independent. If we can accept this state of affairs, we can understand why our mothers can both enrage and enchant us, and we won't give them the power to make us depressed.

I will not allow my mother's behavior to influence my happiness.

Treating depression with all of its physical, mental, and emotional symptoms is treating wounded spirituality.

—LEO BOOTH

Quite often when people are depressed they have lost hope in their future and feel like their God has abandoned them. As a result, many psychiatric treatment centers address how spirituality influences our perceptions of ourselves and the world around us; ignoring this important issue leaves us vulnerable to future depression and self-destructive behavior when we're in another crisis and our emotional reserves are depleted.

Therapists often stress that being spiritual consists of being in touch with our creativity. It is this inner spark that brings us a sense of oneness with our Creator and allows us to feel passion. Artists often say they feel closest to God when they are creating, writers feel the same way when they are writing, and many of us have this sensation when we are doing something we love, like watching a sunset or cuddling our children. To know what awakens our sense of wonder and love puts us on the path to spirituality.

Your depression may be tied to feeling out of touch with your creativity and uniqueness, so think of ways today you can foster this. Some possibilities might include going to church, keeping a journal, walking on a beach at sunrise, or tending a garden. Once we can begin to express ourselves fully, our spirituality will be healed and our emotions will be steadier.

I will tend to my wounded spirituality today.

It is in games that many men discover their paradise.
—ROBERT LYND

Studies have shown that teenage girls who turn away from athletics and focus on dating and their appearance during the critical teenage years experience a dramatic drop in self-esteem. On the other hand, girls who work out, play in team sports and engage in athletic competition develop self-confidence, rarely develop alcohol or drug dependencies, and are three times more likely to graduate from high school.

If you did not engage in sports as a young girl, it's time to get your body moving. Any activity that moves your muscles and causes you to break into a sweat will make you feel stronger and more in control of your life. Joining a team, even the office softball team, will also make you feel like part of a group, which helps negate feelings of isolation. Even short sessions of calisthenics have a positive effect on a woman's mood and perception of herself.

It's never too late to become active. If you missed out as a teenager, make amends to yourself by finding an activity you like and doing it often. And if you have a daughter or friend in her teens, encourage her to be athletic. Exercise won't just make you feel happier and more energetic, it may provide excellent training to deal with the competition of life.

I will discover my emotional "paradise" in sports today.

One cannot be deeply responsive to the world without being saddened very often.

—ERICH FROMM

When I am very down, reading the newspaper and watching the news on television are torturous experiences. I find myself focusing on all of the grim and upsetting stories, such as car crashes, children dying of fatal diseases, families losing their homes, and innocent people being victimized by rapists, muggers, and con men. If I persist too long in watching the evening news, I usually find myself despairing that the world is unfair, everyone is doomed, and life is meaningless.

We must learn to be protective of ourselves when we are feeling fragile. One friend of mine simply avoids newspapers and television whenever she's depressed because it doesn't help her to be surrounded by such negative reports. Instead she sticks to listening to soothing musical pieces, reading favorite books, and playing with her children. At first I thought I'd lose touch with the world if I tried this tactic but I found that giving myself a few days off from current events puts things into better perspective.

Be gentle with yourself today if you're feeling particularly vulnerable; if you need to take a time-out from the news of the world, do it. The earth will continue to spin while you take care of yourself, and when you feel stronger you'll be better able to feel empathy for others without harming yourself.

I contribute to the stability and peace of the world when I am feeling that way myself.

Once you have heard the lark, know the swish of feet through hill-top grass and smelt the earth made ready for the seed, you are never again going to be fully happy about the cities and towns that man carries like a crippling weight upon his back.
—GWYN THOMAS

A recent study concluded that people who live in cities have higher rates of depression and mental illness than those who live in country settings. The researchers believed that part of the reason for this was that living in cities promotes feelings of apprehension and that city dwellers also witness more misery and violence than the country dweller.

There is something magical about being in a country setting that instantly uplifts the human spirit. At a low period in my life I often found that going for long drives in the Maryland countryside seemed to help me find perspective. And friends of mine who are gardening devotees swear that a few solitary hours of planting, mulching, and watering are a balm to their troubled soul.

Try to find opportunities to be outside in a garden setting today. Every city has a park, and most houses have yards where plants can thrive with the proper attention. Even better, try to escape to the country for a drive. Sometimes getting back in touch with the natural rhythms of life is just what we need to reground ourselves and find contentment again.

I will nurture myself with nature.

Cleaning your house while your kids are still growing is like shoveling the walk before it stops snowing.
—MARY KAY BLAKELY

One day I got a short letter from a friend who'd just had her third child. "Forget organization," she wrote. "Survival is the goal." She went on to say that she'd gone from being a compulsively organized person to someone who cared more about getting sleep than making beds.

When we have children or are juggling work and family life, it's nearly impossible to have an immaculate house unless we plan to devote ourselves solely to that effort. For several years I ran myself ragged trying to keep a clean house while working and being a mother, which only frustrated and depressed me. It seemed that no sooner would I finish mopping a floor than juice would splatter everywhere, and I'd react with unreasonable anger. Finally I came to terms with the fact that children can create chaos much faster than I can clean it up and that the only way to retain my sanity was to lower my expectations for order in my life.

Be realistic about what you expect from yourself if you are juggling a lot of balls. Forget about gourmet dinners, spotless floors, and wrinkle-free clothes—unless you're hiring someone to do them for you. Depression thrives among people who want perfection in their lives, so use today to eliminate at least one activity that can't be done perfectly and see if your satisfaction level doesn't rise very quickly.

I will keep my expectations pegged to reality today.

Ritual is the way we carry the presence of the sacred. Ritual is the spark that must not go out.

—CHRISTINA BALDWIN

Since the 1960s the number of people who feel depressed about themselves and their prospects for life has risen dramatically in America. Researchers trace some of this rise to the explosion in divorces and the breakup of nuclear families, which can bring about the end of comforting rituals that are important in molding happy, self-sufficent people. Without rituals like a shared family dinner or a familiar vacation spot, people can feel unanchored and unloved.

If we're depressed, we may not have grown up with consistent rituals or we may have forgotten to include them in our present lives. A friend of mine who usually spent every Christmas feeling blue because he didn't have the money to fly home to be with his family decided to trim a tree, decorate his house, and have friends over, which gave him a new sense of happiness and stability. Another decided to make herself hot chocolate with marshmallows whenever it snowed because it reminded her of the joy she'd shared with her mother when she was young.

Do you have rituals in your life that are comforting and predictable? Do you regularly buy flowers as a treat when you're depressed or do you take trips at a certain time every year to a familiar place? Be aware of the power of rituals today and strive to create some if you don't have any. Not only will these activities be soothing reminders of happy times, they'll create a sense of purpose in a life that may seem to have none.

I will include or create a ritual in my day.

Learning to live with what you're born with is the process, the involvement, the making of a life.

—DIANE WAKOSKI

One afternoon I watched a show on a condition that has been identified by mental-health experts as "imagined ugliness disorder." People who suffer from this problem perceive that they have a "flaw"—like a big nose—and they allow this belief to shape their attitudes and actions. For example, a man who thought his hair was excessively thin combed it constantly and refused to go to work on days he thought his bald spot was too prominent. He finally lost his job and his shaky self-esteem dropped further.

Although this is an extreme case, milder forms of this syndrome can still lead to misery. For example, some women become obsessed with their appearance and mistakenly think that other people are talking about their bad skin or wide hips. Such assumptions can lead sufferers to avoid social situations, become depressed and isolated, and undertake such risky procedures as plastic surgery.

If you are depressed today because you think you're "ugly," ask yourself if this perception comes from a comparison to the unrealistic and airbrushed perfection of models. And if your thoughts become obsessional, ask your doctor about medication that might be helpful in addressing misconceptions about your appearance. Whatever course, though, remember that accepting your appearance, and not thinking how you "should" look, is the only sure way to experience the happiness that comes from loving yourself unconditionally.

My appearance is a beautiful and unique expression of who I am.

You must do the thing you think you cannot do.
                                        —ELEANOR ROOSEVELT

Alison is the quintessential doormat. When her spend-thrift brother asks for money she loans it without question and never gets repaid. At work when she is told to take on additional shifts without additional pay, she meekly acquiesces. And when her husband informed her that his parents would be moving in with them, she inwardly fumed but said nothing. Not surprisingly, Alison is often depressed, suffers from stress-related headaches, and frequently cries when she is alone, wondering when she will feel happy or in control of her life again.

Alison is what psychologists call a Type E woman who is incapable of saying no to anyone. The Type E woman is usually afraid to offend others and would rather be put out than have someone else suffer. Women who wish to avoid falling into this trap must learn three essential skills: how to say no, how to delegate, and how to negotiate. For example, if we are asked to do something we cannot accomplish without negatively affecting ourselves in some way, we must either decline, say yes and ask others to carry some of the burden, or say yes but on terms that are more convenient for us.

If you cannot stand up for yourself and are depressed about a lack of inner strength, you must do what seems impossible: be clear about what your needs and limits are. Learning how to be assertive won't just be emotionally rewarding, it may also lead you down the path to a more exciting and rewarding life.

I will stand up for myself today.

A child is a curly, dimpled lunatic.

—RALPH WALDO EMERSON

When my son reached the age of two I learned what the "terrible twos" were all about. Suddenly my adorable, obedient child turned into an independent scamp who tried to thwart me at all turns. Some days were simply spent saying "No!" over and over again while cleaning up Cheerios, pulling toy cars out of our VCR, and imploring him not to tear his books. At the end of many of these days I was irritable and exhausted, and depressed about not having handled the day's crises in a responsible and loving way.

There is no harder job in the world than being a mother. Whether we choose to be at home with our children or to work outside the home, as mothers we're all faced with the difficulties of childhood such as independence seeking and misbehavior. As much as we adore our children we may react by snapping at them, behaving poorly, and saying things we later regret. This isn't uncommon, but it can be depressing if we hold ourselves up to some unrealistic standard and think we should always be reasonable and sweet.

If you're depressed about the demands of motherhood and you worry that you're not up to the job—relax. Childhood phases come and go, and maternal self-doubt and anxiety is normal. Talk to friends whose children are the same age or older and try to find comfort about issues that concern you. Once you can develop self-confidence in your abilities and tolerance for unruly children, you'll find that depression decreases while enthusiasm increases for this difficult job of being a mom.

I will be loving and patient with my children and myself today.

To fear is one thing. To let fear grab you by the tail and swing you around is another.

—KATHERINE PATERSON

Most of us are afraid of something: public speaking, being alone, driving in snow, outliving our children, or being fired. If we're emotionally healthy, we don't let our fears rule our lives and we take steps to address our phobias, such as enrolling in a public speaking class. But when we allow our fears to dominate us and dictate our actions, we run the risk of avoiding character-building lessons and becoming depressed about our cramped life-style.

One well-known therapist believes that people who are afraid that they will fail at something and allow their anxieties to rule them need to do "shame-attacking" exercises that prove to them that doing something fearful will not destroy them. His patients are asked to do something foolish, such as talking loudly to themselves on a crowded elevator or announcing the street stops on a bus. When they do this and attract puzzled stares or laughter, they learn that spontaneity isn't harmful and it frees them up to be more relaxed in other stressful settings.

If you're feeling frightened of something, the worst thing you can do is run from it because it will only continue to chase you and make you miserable. Face your fears and conquer them through "shame-attacking" exercises and other therapeutic techniques. You'll find that once you allow the "worst" result to occur, it will not only free you from your fears, it will also eliminate the depression that tells you life can never be different.

Facing my fears is never as awful as imagining them.

I have treated many hundreds of patients. . . . Among [those] in the second half of life—that is to say, over thirty-five—there has not been one whose problem in the last resort was not that of finding a religious outlook on life.
—CARL JUNG

One of the most profound things any of us will experience is when we look around at our lives and wonder, "Is this all there is?" This may be prompted by a tragedy, a letdown after attaining something we worked for, or the ending of a relationship. When this happens we need to be prepared for a period of depression and soul-searching while grappling with our beliefs and expectations and coming to terms with our own limitations.

One of the first steps toward developing a spiritual life is seeing it as part of our daily existence, not as something separate. A strong spirituality is often achieved through small daily acts of affirmation, and not necessarily through one major conversion. In eastern mystical traditions, where breath is considered the life-force of everything, daily "mindful breathing" exercises such as yoga are the building blocks of a strong spirituality. A more "western" approach is to practice compassion toward those who upset us and to volunteer time to worthy causes.

If you're feeling out of sync today, look at your spiritual life. Many books abound on how to find meaning in the small acts of life, and churches usually offer classes on nurturing the soul. By experimenting and having an open mind about spiritual options, you'll start to forge the inner strength that's needed when depression and other difficulties strike.

I will strengthen my spiritual outlook on life today.

Time pulses from the afternoon like blood from a serious wound.

—HILMA WOLITZER

When I'm feeling depressed I'm often unable to concentrate and my thoughts are scattered. When this happens days race by when I am unable to complete important tasks. I'll find myself making phone calls and forgetting who I'm calling, starting projects and leaving them unfinished, and frittering my time away on unnecessary drudge work. Until I learned how to better manage my time, my emotional swings were bleeding valuable hours and days out of my schedule.

If you're feeling depressed, make a to-do list every morning and put everything on it, even if it seems trivial, because you're liable to be forgetful now. Next, prioritize the list. Do you really have to buy birthday cards today when a project is due at work tomorrow? Group your tasks, too. While you're talking on the phone you can often weed out your purse, alphabetize your Rolodex, or fold laundry. If you can also figure out which tasks you're best at during which times of day, you'll be able to take advantage of your natural biological rhythms and be even more productive.

Make time your friend today. If you can make and follow a helpful, realistic set of daily goals, you won't stare in astonishment at the clock at the end of the day, wondering where the hours went. Depression is infamous for making days unproductive, but with some organization and determination you can fight back and take control of your time.

I will be disciplined about my schedule today.

It is around losses of love that the clouds of despair tend to converge, hover and darken . . . these are among the commonest causes of female depression.

—MAGGIE SCARF

At some point in our lives all of us will probably go through the end of a relationship and mourn its passing. Although men suffer when relationships break up, we women tend to place a higher value on our ability to maintain loving relationships and we blame ourselves disproportionately when they don't work out.

It's normal to be sad when we lose someone who has brought warmth and love into our lives, but if our sadness causes us to hurt ourselves more, our depression will only worsen. For example, a friend of mine was abruptly dumped by a man who quickly took up with someone else. Instead of recognizing that the relationship hadn't been good for her, my friend tortured herself by frequently driving by the man's house to see if he was with his new girlfriend. The longer she nursed her pain by dwelling on his life and not hers, the harder it was to move ahead and find someone who better suited her.

Try not to make the sadness of a lost love harder for yourself than it already is. Allow yourself a period of time for grieving and then dispassionately examine what you learned from the relationship that could be helpful to you in the future. Above all, try not to blame yourself for the breakup; romantic situations fail for a variety of reasons that have nothing to do with the scorned person, so when they do end, it's often for the best.

I will be whole and happy whether I am in a relationship or not.

To be rooted is perhaps the most important and least recognized need of the human soul.

—SIMONE WEIL

One day I was talking to an expert on postpartum depression about what factors contribute to the onset of depression after the birth of a child. One of the leading indicators, she said, is relocating shortly after the birth of a child. Going through the major hormonal and situational changes of a birth is difficult enough, she said, but losing your sense of belonging to a place can make the experience devastatingly negative.

Feeling unrooted at any time in our lives can be depressing. If we live in a city where we have few friends, no rapport with our grocer, and no sense of belonging, it will be difficult to feel as if we know our place in the world. It's also difficult to want to make new friends, join clubs, and reach out to others if we are planning to move or if we just don't like where we live. But the more we refuse to accept and enjoy our surroundings, the more likely we are to isolate ourselves and wallow in depression.

If you're feeling unrooted, try to lay enough of a foundation to provide a modicum of comfort wherever you are. Women who travel often take a favorite pillow or picture to help them feel "at home," so do something similar if you're new to a city. Whether it's attending a familiar twelve-step group or joining a walking club, becoming a regular fixture somewhere will not just provide you with new friends, it will give you the contentment that comes with feeling like you belong.

I will water the roots of where I am today.

When you stop drinking, you have to deal with this marvelous personality that started you drinking in the first place.
—JIMMY BRESLIN

When Mary stopped drinking and began to turn her life around, initially she was euphoric. As a sober woman she felt that she was seeing the world for the first time and she reveled in the newness of going to work without a hangover and losing ten excess pounds of bloat that she had carried around for years. But the "pink cloud" of sobriety didn't last forever; Mary suddenly found herself shy and insecure around men, depressed for no reason at all, and filled with rage at her father, who had sexually abused her at a young age.

The initial stages of recovery from an addiction such as alcoholism are often marked by euphoria at the progress we are making and by a feeling that nothing can go wrong. Inevitably, however, we are forced to face new challenges. If we've submerged ourselves in an addiction to avoid facing painful truths about ourselves or our lives, those issues will be waiting for us when we start to get well. And if we've been masking an underlying depression with addictive behavior, we might need to face the fact that we require intensive therapy or an antidepressant just to feel normal.

Remember today that early recovery from an addiction can be filled with emotional obstacles. As important as it is to celebrate progress, we have to acknowledge that depression isn't uncommon at this stage and that accepting and treating it is critical in avoiding a return to the addiction.

A life without mood-altering substances or behaviors means I sometimes feel pain acutely.

*If only God would give me some clear sign! Like making a
large deposit in my name at a Swiss bank.*
                                                    —WOODY ALLEN

One day I was very down about a variety of issues and
I felt unable to make any decisions about which direction
to go in to resolve them. So in complete desperation I re-
sorted to asking God to give me a sign as to how to restore
my tranquillity so that I could proceed with life again. A
few hours later I received a package in the mail containing
a review copy of a book on stress reduction. I promptly
read it and benefitted greatly from the author's suggestions.

I don't always receive such clear-cut signs when I ask
for help. Sometimes dreams warn me about people or situations, or I receive a timely phone call from a friend, or I
run into people who have been able to say just the right
thing at the right time. If I'm thinking clearly, I'll recognize
that my prayers were just answered, but usually it takes a
few hours or days to see that I've gotten the direction I
asked for.

If you're feeling stymied about something, try asking
God or your Higher Power for a sign. Then be alert to
anything unusual—or even routine—that seems to contain
an answer. Sometimes the best responses are the most sub-
tle, but if we're open we can always see them when they
come.

Answers to my prayers don't always come in obvious ways.

What is dangerous about tranquilizers is that whatever peace of mind they bring is packaged peace of mind. Where you buy a pill and buy peace with it, you get conditioned to cheap solutions instead of deep ones.

—MAX LERNER

When depressed, it's very tempting to seek a quick fix with a pill. When Ariel's depression led to insomnia, she begged her physician to give her tranquilizers so she could get some rest. He complied, and soon she was taking a powerful sedative that knocked her out so effectively that she had trouble rousing herself from bed every morning. Despite the fact that she remained lethargic and sad during the day, Ariel kept taking the medication because she enjoyed the sure-fire way to get to sleep every night and escape her misery.

When we turn to tranquilizers to help ease some of the side-effects of depression, we create additional problems for ourselves. Not only can sedatives lead to long-term addiction, they can sap us of any energy and initiative we *do* have. They can also worsen depression. One woman I know said that she felt worse while taking a sedative because her reliance on it underscored her feelings of powerlessness over her condition.

Tranquilizers and antidepressants are two very different things. Tranquilizers are sedatives while antidepressants work specifically on the chemicals that affect moods. Instead of using medication to ease sleeplessness and anxiety, try warm baths, biofeedback, vigorous exercise early in the day or a nutritious meal plan. When we persevere in finding solutions that aren't necessarily quick, we improve our chances of having long-term answers.

I will not succumb to "cheap solutions" to ease my pain.

Rule Number 1 is, don't sweat the small stuff. Rule Number 2 is, it's all small stuff. And if you can't fight and you can't flee, flow.

—ROBERT S. ELIOT

Living with stress has become second nature to some people. Deborah, the owner of her own company, is a perfect example. She gets to work before dawn, gulps endless cups of coffee throughout the day, smokes too much, and eats too little. She is often exhausted, depressed, and sick, and her employees are frustrated because she doesn't delegate well, erupts frequently in anger, and is insensitive to their needs for family time.

Stress often leads to depression, and if you aren't aware of how much stress you're under, you may not be able to fend off the blues before they hit. Psychologists advise us to take our "stress temperature" frequently by asking such questions as: Is my memory slipping? Am I having trouble sleeping? Has my appetite changed? Can I concentrate well? Am I often impatient? Do my moods swing? Am I irritable with people I care about? Answering yes to any of these questions can indicate a stress overload, which—if not caught in time—can result in depression and other illnesses.

Be conscious of how much stress you are living with today and try to remember the rules of how to cope with the "small stuff." By flowing with the stream of life instead of always fighting it, you can reduce stress significantly while enhancing your happiness and sanity.

Today I'll make sure my stress temperature is normal.

No man is the whole of himself. His friends are the rest of him.

—*Good Life Almanac*

Men and women differ in striking ways, including how they communicate. From the time they are little boys, males tend to share information such as sports scores with each other, while women share thoughts and feelings. Psychologists call this the difference between having "report talk" and "rapport talk."

But it's "rapport talk" that a person needs when they are blue. As women we have an easier time finding a sympathetic ear among our female friends. Personally I never have much luck with men—particularly my husband. Whenever I try to talk about something that is bothering me, he immediately lays out solutions in cut-and-dried, lawyerly ways. While he may have some very good ideas, I usually just want someone to empathize with me before they make me get to work, which is what my girlfriends are so good at.

Get yourself some good "girlfriend talk" today if you need support to deal with something that is depressing. Although it's a generalization to say that men can't be sympathetic and understanding, you'll probably receive more of what you need from your women friends. And during times when you're down, you'll undoubtedly find that "rapport talk" will, indeed, help you feel stronger and more hopeful.

My friendships can complete me when I feel fragmented.

It is not given to everyone to shine in adversity.
　　　　　　　　　　　　　　—JANE AIKEN HODGE

I always marvel at people who greet tragedy and sadness with dignity. For example, several years ago I read about a family whose trip to New York ended in a bloody brawl in which a son was killed for some pocket money. Instead of reacting hysterically and angrily, the parents established a scholarship fund honoring their son and asked others to pray for the souls of the murderers. "We're at peace with what has happened, and they need prayers more than we do," they said.

How we respond to setbacks is often a result of how we were raised. Therapists say that in dysfunctional families where the children weren't taught healthy coping skills, even the littlest setback can spiral someone into a deep depression. Through therapy or by observing others who handle challenges with grace, we can learn how to respond to problems without becoming self-destructive.

If your response to adversity has been to crumble while others have handled worse setbacks with dignity, don't get down on yourself. Coping skills are something we're taught and if our families didn't provide appropriate role-modeling, we can't fault ourselves for our reactions. We can, however, take the initiative as adults to learn to live a day at a time, get professional help, and strengthen our inner reserves so we always have something to draw upon.

I will learn how to shine in adversity.

Many persons have a wrong idea of what constitutes true happiness. It is not attained through self-gratification but through fidelity to a worthy purpose.

—HELEN KELLER

I heard a woman being interviewed on television one day who said that she had the very best life in the world. She said that she woke up every day delighted about her profession, that the people she consorted with were among the finest in the world, and that she felt privileged to do what she did. She wasn't referring to a glamorous position; this was a woman who used to be homeless but had turned her life around and now ran a soup kitchen and a shelter for the needy.

We don't necessarily have to dedicate ourselves as completely as this woman did, but it is important to devote energy each day toward a worthy cause. The activities that can achieve this goal are as simple as being selfless and loving to our families, running an errand for a friend, or organizing a neighborhood cleanup. It matters little what we do; the only thing that counts is that our activities be driven by a passion for something other than ourselves.

What portion of your day goes toward self-gratification and what portion goes toward furthering a cause with a worthy goal? Try to keep these parts of your life balanced because a life of too little service to others or the absence of a noble goal almost always results in feelings of emptiness, loneliness, and depression.

When I put energy toward a good cause, I energize and enrich myself.

It is only by risking our persons from one hour to another that we live at all. And often enough our faith beforehand in an uncertified result is the only thing that makes the result come true.

—WILLIAM JAMES

In her early thirties Vicky was suddenly hit with a clinical depression that was so deep she quit her job, sought inpatient treatment, and began a frustrating search for an antidepressant that would provide her with more benefits than side effects. Despite trying many combinations of medication Vicky couldn't find enough relief to return to her former state of contentment.

After several years of marginal functioning, Vicky chose to stop allowing her illness to rule her behavior. Instead of staying home and nursing her fears, she bravely decided to take such risks as volunteering and joining her church choir. "Depression had sapped all of my energy, but I mustered up enough to do something scary, and that snowballed into resolving to try a new antidepressant, which ultimately made the difference for me." Vicky now has more self-respect than ever and her depression is under control.

It's hard to take risks when we're down but the alternative is staying stuck in the "same old thing." If you can't do something that challenges your status quo, at least make a list of things to do if you had the nerve, like be assertive at work or run for a local political office. One day soon you might find the courage to follow through on your desires, and the result may well be an abatement of your depression.

Smart risks make me feel alive.

Fools mock at making amends for sin, but goodwill is found among the upright. Each heart knows its own bitterness, and no one else can share its joy.

—PROVERBS 14:9–10

In twelve-step programs such as Alcoholics Anonymous and Overeaters Anonymous, there is a step where members are encouraged to make amends for past offenses that have harmed others. There is also a step where it is suggested that they take a daily inventory of their actions and promptly make amends for anything they are ashamed of.

Every person I know who is recovering from an addiction and is thorough about making amends finds that these steps are helpful in restoring peace of mind. For those of us who are depressed, we may want to consider making amends to someone with whom we have had a disagreement. For example, Elaine had a big argument with her sister one afternoon that escalated into a screaming match reminiscent of their childhood fights. Instead of sulking for days, Elaine decided to call her sister and apologize for losing her temper. This action helped her feel in control of her emotions and not the other way around.

If you are depressed, it could be due to feeling bad about something you have said or done that has hurt another person. All of us have faults and make mistakes that need correction, and the sooner we can acknowledge this and take steps to improve our behavior, the better we'll feel about ourselves.

I will make at least one amend today.

If you've never been hated by your child, you've never been a parent.

—BETTE DAVIS

Some of my most depressing moments of motherhood have occurred when I've had to discipline my son and he's sulked afterward, refusing to look or smile at me for long stretches. Although he's still too young to understand that he's been reprimanded because he has put himself in danger, I try to explain it anyway, hoping he'll share a kiss or a smile with me. Until he does, I usually feel worse than he does.

Being a good mother often means not being a child's best buddy. When we discipline our children and set limits on their behavior, we not only ensure their safety but communicate that we care about them. These admirable goals can be obscured, however, when our children see us as bad guys who aren't giving them what they want and they let us know this.

Parenthood is one of the hardest—and occasionally most depressing—jobs in the world, and for the most part, we are thrown into it totally unprepared. If we can try to keep a sense of humor and some perspective about the constant trials of this important responsibility, and also remember that caving into our children's desires simply to make them happy is harmful to them.

I can accept being hated by my children when I know I'm acting out of love.

To hate and to fear is to be psychologically ill . . . it is, in fact, the consuming illness of our time.

—H. A. OVERSTREET

One day a therapist was talking to me about her theory on what drove people into depression and thus into her practice. She said she'd found that the root cause of the stress, anxiety, dysfunctional behavior, and addiction of her patients usually stemmed from hatred and fear, and that hatred was often a product of fear.

For example, she said, one of her patients was constantly sad and anxious because she felt unappreciated at her office. Whenever her memos went unanswered, salary reviews were put off, and phone calls went unreturned, she became depressed, fearing she was about to lose her job. Instead of taking the incidents as part of the normal course of doing business, every communication became an opportunity to see herself as deficient in some way and she'd work herself into a state of resentment toward her coworkers.

If you are depressed, examine whether your feelings are rooted in fear: fear of rejection, fear of abandonment, or even fear of losing your self-esteem. Understanding that fear usually leads to anger and depression can sometimes provide insight into why we behave the way we do while inspiring us to learn to manage our moods differently.

When I act from fear, I act from the dark side of myself.

Keeping off a large weight loss is a phenomenon about as common in American medicine as an impoverished dermatologist.

—CALVIN TRILLIN

A very close friend of mine has suffered from compulsive eating for many years. When she got married she starved herself down to a low weight but got heavier as the years passed. During her first pregnancy she gained over eighty pounds and after that she never got back on track. Now she despairs of ever being slim and attractive again and says that one of the low points of each day is having men turn away from her in disgust, seeing her as asexual and unattractive.

At any one time the vast majority of American women are depressed about their weight and trying to diet, regardless of whether they need to or not. Unfortunately most of these women want the weight they've gained over several years to come off quickly, so they resort to fasting or to unsafe, unsuccessful diets that leave their self-esteem lower than when they began.

If you truly need to lose weight, try to resolve that you will do it slowly and healthfully, and in a manner that increases the odds of keeping it off. Overeaters Anonymous is a free support group that can be helpful, and local hospitals often offer similar support groups. With proper nutrition, regular exercise and better coping mechanisms you can change not only your body but your emotions and self-image as well.

Moderate intake of healthy foods contributes to a sound body and mind.

A thousand good-byes come after death—the first six months of bereavement.

—ALAN GREGG

One of the most difficult transitions for a woman is the death of her father. Research shows that how a father treats his daughter is critical to her personality development and self-confidence. When our fathers die we tend to feel like we've lost the first man who ever loved us unconditionally and who always thought we were special no matter what we did.

A middle-aged friend of mine said that she was surprised by how difficult it was to deal with her father's passing. It didn't matter that his health had been failing for years or that their relationship had been difficult at times. "For the first time in my life," she said, "I truly felt alone, and I regretted how many things I'd never shared with him." Some of her coworkers didn't understand why she grew teary-eyed at times, or seemed distracted at work. "The fact that he was in his eighties didn't lessen the impact at all," she says.

Allowing ourselves to grieve after a loss is important, but especially so when the person is a family member. Mental health experts say that to process a death effectively, we need to say good-bye in a way that works for us, such as through a church service or a private ritual. Once we finish with our good-byes, which can take many months, it will be easier to hold on to the happy memories of shared experiences and to celebrate the person's life with joy, not sadness.

I will honor the spirit of those I've lost by remembering the happiness we shared.

There are no medals at the end of life for long-term sufferers.
—JO ANN LARSEN

At my son's day-care center there is one little girl who sobs for an hour every morning after her mother drops her off. I often hear the girl wailing, "I want my mommy!" as the woman leaves with a face etched in despair and frustration. Several times I've spoken with the mother about the guilt provoked by these scenes. She says that although she's a happily employed professional woman, she's begun to torture herself with thoughts that the girl will be maladjusted because of their difficulties separating every day.

This is a typical scenario for working moms who often shoulder loads of guilt, thinking that if only they didn't work, their lives and those of their children would be happier and more stable. For example, one woman who was on a business trip when her daughter fell out of a tree and was rushed to the emergency room said that although her daughter was fine and later remembered nothing of the day, the mother had carried around emotional scars for months, irrationally telling herself that if she'd been home, the fall wouldn't have happened.

If we're working mothers, we need to try to banish the "if only" thinking and the guilt from our lives. Instead of focusing on what our lives exclude, we need to remind ourselves that stay-at-home moms experience stress and unhappiness, too, and that providing a higher standard of living and being a good role model are just two of the many benefits we create when happily employed outside the home.

When I suffer from guilt, I lessen the quality of time I spend with those I love.

It wasn't raining when Noah built the ark.

—HOWARD J. RUFF

Karen comes from a family with a history of depression. Her grandfather was a manic-depressive, her mother had a history of mood swings that were managed with alcohol and later with pills, and her sister suffered from serious postpartum depression when both of her children were born. Knowing her family's record, Karen attended postpartum depression workshops during her first pregnancy to understand what might occur after childbirth. Educating herself about the causes of depression, the signs of it, and what resources were available helped Karen ease the fear of developing postpartum depression, as well as lessening her chances of experiencing it.

Sometimes when we're feeling invincible and happy, we don't want to deal with the darker side of life. But knowing where we can turn and what remedies are available to us when we go through a depression—which most women will experience at one time or another—is like putting money in the bank. And if we come from a family with a history of mood disorders, it's essential that we educate ourselves about it, just as we would if there was a family history of heart disease or cancer.

Do you know what resources are available if you need help for depression? What does your insurance policy cover in the way of therapy? Are there support groups in your area for addictions or grieving people? Instead of thinking that this is a morbid topic, remember that an ounce of prevention is worth a pound of cure, especially when you're dealing with mental health.

I will be proactive rather than reactive about my health today.

Hell is yourself [and the only redemption is] when a person puts himself aside to feel deeply for another person.
—TENNESSEE WILLIAMS

One day I saw the co-host of a popular television show talk about her recent miscarriage. As she discussed her painful experience, she added that she had recuperated while watching newscasts about the many people who had lost their homes, businesses, and other possessions in a devastating hurricane. "The only thing that helped my depression lift was to take all the clothes I had bought for the baby and send them to the people who had lost so much in the storm," she said.

That same day I watched coverage of the storm's cleanup and listened to a man talk about how he was coping with the loss of his home and all his possessions. Despite his grief over his own misfortunes, the man said that his spirits had been lifted by helping a neighbor quickly rebuild his house so that the neighbor's chronically ill son could have a safe, secure haven as soon as possible.

If you feel like you're in "hell" today as a result of dwelling on your own misfortunes, try to find someone else to assist. You might be surprised at how a change in focus can enlarge your perspective, raise your self-esteem, and banish feelings of helplessness and hopelessness.

I will put myself aside today.

Total absence of humor renders life impossible.

—COLETTE

I read an inspiring article one day about a woman whose symptoms of Alzheimer's began in her early fifties. After realizing that this disease would only get worse as she got older, she became very depressed. Every day she sat home with the shades drawn, crying about her uncertain future. And when she ventured out to run an errand, like buy groceries, she would often get lost on the way home, which only deepened her despair further.

What saved this woman was hooking up with a support group and learning to use humor to cope with her disability. Instead of living in a darkened house and being afraid to go out, she carried road maps in her purse and made jokes with friends about forgetting her own birthday because she didn't want to get older. Learning to laugh at a life-threatening diagnosis is also what helped well-known author and television personality Betty Rollin deal with losing a breast to cancer. In the book "First You Cry," Ms. Rollin describes how joking about wearing wigs, bathing suits, and bras lightened her load immeasurably.

Try to have some humor in the midst of your depression today. Whether it takes watching a funny movie or being with a friend who can make you laugh, tickling your funny bone when you least feel like it is one of the best ways to find hope in what may look like a hopeless world.

When I can laugh, I cannot be defeated.

If you want the present to be different from the past, study the past.

—BARUCH SPINOZA

I have a friend who has been miserable about carrying around the same extra fifty pounds for ten years. One day, after hearing her complain about the weight for the umpteenth time, I told her that her behavior was insane: "The definition of insanity is doing the same thing over and over, yet expecting different results. If you truly want to lose weight, you need to do something different!"

So often we're guilty of repeating self-defeating behaviors that depress us despite knowing that they haven't made us happy in the past. This includes all addictive behaviors, such as smoking, drinking, overeating, and overspending. For example, one friend of mine routinely runs up her credit cards on spending sprees and is depressed about her lack of self-control, but she always winds up doing it again when the balance is paid off.

Study your previous actions to determine if you're still doing something today that has depressed you in the past. If you can stop your insane behavior—whether it's being around someone who isn't good for you or quitting smoking—you'll find that some of the happiness that eludes you can be easily restored through changes in your own behavior.

I will learn from past mistakes, not repeat them.

Be kind; everyone you meet is fighting a hard battle.
—JOHN WATSON

A well-known politician's life was completely altered by the near-fatal accident of his young son. As the boy slowly convalesced the politician received hundreds of condolence cards from people he barely knew. He discovered that many of the people with whom he dealt on a daily basis had endured similar—and even worse—pains without his even being aware of it. The politician told a reporter that the experience had dissolved his former arrogance and taught him that everyone has their own battle to fight and that we can all use each other's sympathy and support.

Friends of mine who lost a son in a tragic accident feel the same way. When their son died they received cards and flowers from scores of other parents—some of whom they knew only slightly—who had also lost children. This outpouring of love gave them the strength they needed to carry on with their lives and cope with their loss.

If you are depressed today, bear in mind that many of the people you encounter may also be suffering and that you are not the only one who could benefit from kindness. The wisest course is to extend courtesy and thoughtfulness to everyone you meet because such generosity will be returned in your time of need.

I am not the only person who has problems.

If you want to do something with your life, never listen to anybody, no matter how expert they may appear. Go for it.
—MICHAEL CAINE

So often when faced with something new, we shrink from the challenge believing that we're not up to the task. And if we solicit the opinions of friends, we may become further discouraged because they'll throw cold water on our plans. "Don't do anything that risky," they'll caution, or "I wouldn't do that if I was you."

History is littered with stories of successful people who ignored the advice of their friends and relatives and tried something that they didn't necessarily have the tools or money for, but desperately wanted to do. A good friend of mine who wanted to stop practicing law in her early thirties was advised not to do so by all her friends and relatives. Her therapist encouraged her to pursue her dream, however, and now the woman owns a bed and breakfast inn. Although she had to save money for a year and drastically change her lifestyle, my friend is much happier doing what she loves, and she lives each day with passion.

If you are depressed because you want to make a change in your life but you aren't getting encouragement from family or friends, determine whether there are valid reasons for their lack of support. If not, you must begin to lay the groundwork for going after your dream. It's depressing to allow the opinions of others to color how we live our lives, but it is even more depressing if we never find the ability to believe in our potential and in ourselves.

When I believe in myself, all things are possible.

Whosoever knoweth the power of the dance dwelleth in God.
—MEVLANA JALALUDDIN RUMI

At weddings I'm fascinated by who dances and who stands uneasily on the sidelines, commenting on the dancers and their technique. Inevitably, I've found that the people who risk making fools of themselves in this simple, joyful act seem to be the ones with high self-esteem who seek pleasure in every moment, caring little what others think of them.

In the African culture a premium is placed on dancing with abandon so that the body will harmonize with the mind, which induces feelings of calm and happiness. American dance therapists are trained to help people find this rhythm and learn the freedom of expressing emotion. One chronically depressed friend of mine who had little luck with therapy, encounter groups, and medication said that it was dance therapy that finally brought her intense joy and a sense of control over her body.

Try to allow yourself the freedom to dance today, either by yourself or with someone else. You might feel silly, but after a while you'll find that dancing will even out your breathing and release pleasurable endorphins throughout your body. Once your soul finds expression through movement, you'll undoubtedly discover why dancing has been touted for centuries as a happiness booster.

I will joyfully move my body today.

If a man lives without inner struggle, if everything happens in him without opposition . . . he will remain such as he is.
—G. I. GURDJIEFF

One night while getting ready for bed, I realized that I was feeling very low but wasn't sure why. Upon reflection I realized that my depression seemed to stem from having spent the evening in the company of good friends with whom I had shared personal information about others. Although my friends are not likely to repeat such things, in hindsight I was angry about this compulsion to talk about other people's lives without their permission. The sick feeling about my gossipy behavior lasted throughout the night and forced me to make changes in my behavior the next morning.

Periods of sadness, guilt, anger, shame, and remorse aren't always all bad. These emotions are often what prod us to stop and examine what we're doing, and to ask ourselves if we're on the right track, consorting with the right people, or behaving wisely. Whenever I feel bad about something I've said or done, I am my own worst critic. However, without that little ache inside, I'd probably never take stock of what inside me needed upgrading or overhauling.

Boldly face your anguish and doubt today because it is what will transform you and keep you from stagnating. The nature of life is one of constant change, and fighting the emotions that allow this to happen will only prevent you from maturing and discovering fulfillment.

Depression and discomfort usually signal that something inside me needs changing.

Give me one friend, just one, who meets
The needs of all my varying moods.

—ESTHER M. CLARK

One of the most common hallmarks of depression is the tendency to isolate ourselves when we most need to reach out. I have often behaved this way because I didn't want to be a burden to someone else, or I didn't think that anyone could truly understand how I felt. Isolating myself has never been helpful, however; it has always left me angrier, more self-pitying, and less perceptive about my situation than if I had reached out.

Hard times can be a powerful reminder that self-sufficiency isn't always practical or helpful. While there are many things we can accomplish by ourselves, climbing out of a depression usually isn't one of them. I've discovered over the years that talking to one particular friend who has seen me in all of my moods, and who loves and accepts me anyway, is often my first step toward feeling better. She and I have such a long history together that she's able to remind me of similar dark times and my eventual return to happiness.

In times of crisis, having a large circle of friends is less important than having just one trusted ally to whom you can pour out your heart and receive love, acceptance, and confidentiality. Try to think of at least one friend or family member you can turn to today who can give you the support you need, and then remember to try to be there for that person when he or she needs the same kindness from you.

I will ask for support from a trusted and time-tested friend today.

No one is as capable of gratitude as one who has emerged from the kingdom of night.
—ELIE WIESEL

For many years I took many of life's blessings for granted. I lived with the illusion that life entitled one to such things as good health, a home, vacations, the love and support of two parents, and a general sense of well-being. As I matured into adulthood I learned more about the responsibilities and difficulties that come with being on your own, but it wasn't until my late twenties that I began to understand how blessed—and ungrateful—I had been.

Suddenly and without warning, many of the things I had considered my birthright were stripped from me. For the first time I couldn't pay the bills on time. New clothes and vacations became a distant memory. And my health began to falter, causing me to spend many hours in doctors' offices and in hospitals with stress-related problems.

But as often happens, life eventually improved, leaving me with a completely different outlook on life and a new sense of gratitude for even the smallest pleasures. Every morning that I awaken in good health is a blessing. Having food on the table and a roof over my head isn't taken lightly anymore. And paying my bills on time—even with nothing left over for "extras"—is something to be grateful for. Instead of being resentful of the years I spent suffering, I am now grateful for having been given the gift of gratitude that I could not have received in any other way.

My "kingdom of night" will bring me a dawn of gratitude and thankfulness.

The secret of life is balance, and the absence of balance is life's destruction.

—INAYAT KHAN

Many of the unhappiest women I know are those who have not achieved a balance in their lives. They are either consumed with work, overwhelmed with children, too focused on reaching a certain goal, or addicted to a certain substance or behavior. In each case one aspect of their life has assumed such enormous proportions that all other areas such as friendships, family life, hobbies, and basic caring for themselves have gone by the wayside.

Through a variety of painful situations I've learned that when I do too much of one thing—like working toward a professional goal—my friendships get neglected and I eventually pay the price. When I obsess about my children's lives, my own life suffers. And when I compulsively exercise, I lose valuable time with the people I love.

Make sure that today you devote enough time to the various aspects of your life that are important in keeping you healthy and functioning: spiritual growth, exercise, proper nutrition, friends, family, and play. As the Chinese believe, if you can keep the different polarities balanced—the yin and yang of life—you'll achieve the optimum in health and emotional well-being.

I will seek balance in my life today.

If you make money your god, it will plague you like the devil.
—HENRY FIELDING

I read a story one day about a man and his wife whose idea of success was amassing wealth and living life lavishly. For almost two decades they worked from twelve to fourteen hours a day, took expensive vacations, and bought things to proclaim their affluence, like expensive cars. Despite this supposedly charmed life, however, the couple felt vaguely empty as they entered middle age.

The turning point came when they visited a historic park on a family vacation. The couple was struck by the pride the artisans took in making crafts from a certain period in history. Suddenly they realized that making money meant nothing if they took no pride in their work, so they both quit their jobs, found work that directly contributed to their community, and scaled back their lifestyle. They earn a fraction of what they once did but they love their work, have more time for family events, and are happier now that making money is not their chief goal.

Sometimes depression stems from worshipping the wrong things in life. Examine your priorities today and ask yourself if this is the case with you. You may not need to take the drastic measures this couple did to find inner peace, but a small shift in how you spend time or what you are striving to achieve may be the answer to your blues.

Great satisfaction often comes from humble pursuits.

If happiness truly consisted in physical ease and freedom from care, then the happiest individual would not be either a man or a woman; it would be, I think, an American cow.

—WILLIAM PHELPS

A lot of us mistakenly think that our moods will lift and our problems will be solved when our lives are devoid of stress and the various concerns of daily life. When we believe this, however, we severely underestimate the importance of stimulation and conflict and the satisfaction that comes from solving problems.

I once read a study that said the happiest people were working women with children and the unhappiest were single men. My experiences have confirmed this because my happiest days have been those spent engaged both in my work and with my family. Although it's very difficult to do both well, striving to be the best I can in these areas has been a very effective way to help ward off depression.

If you're feeling low, aim to increase the activity in your life, not decrease it. Try to value the stress and uncertainty because that is what will keep you questioning, alive, and vibrant. A placid life may be a nice dream, but in reality it's a recipe for unhappiness.

The busier I am, the less likely I am to be depressed.

*Give sorrow words; the grief that does not speak
Whispers the o'er-fraught heart and bids it break.*
—WILLIAM SHAKESPEARE

When Charlotte's sister and her children were brutally murdered by the sister's estranged husband, Charlotte felt as though her world had caved in. After taking a few days off to attend to the details of the funeral, she returned to work because it made her feel "useful." For several weeks afterward, her coworkers expressed their sympathy, but when they stopped, Charlotte became depressed because no one seemed interested in comforting her anymore.

Something similar happened to Bill when he lost his wife to breast cancer. For a time his colleagues asked how he was feeling, but when they stopped and he was still grieving, he decided to speak up and ask for support. Bill found that bringing up his wife's death first made others more comfortable with the topic, which gave him the opportunity to give voice to his sorrow. Charlotte never took the step of telling people that she still needed their support, and she wound up struggling for months with a depression that was eventually treated with medication.

Give your sorrow words today, by either speaking them or writing them. Bring up something that's troubling you even if you think those around you aren't interested. You might be surprised to find that people would like to be supportive but don't know how to express themselves, and that all it takes to get some emotional relief is to open your mouth and ask for what you need.

I will speak of my pain today.

Love yourself first and everything falls into line. You really have to love yourself to get anything done in this world.
—LUCILLE BALL

So often I hear bright, accomplished friends of mine denigrating themselves because they don't feel they measure up in certain areas. Some of the most common complaints are "I'm not smart enough," "I'm not outgoing enough," and "I'm too old." In a world that is tough enough to get by in, these are people who are beating themselves up before anyone else has a chance!

Psychologists say that women are more likely than men to harbor low self-esteem, even if they've been raised in supportive, loving families. Part of this is due to the overwhelming pressure society places on us to be and look a certain way, and part of this is because we are more likely than men to experience harassment and abuse, and then blame ourselves for its occurrence.

What are the messages you send yourself? If you've been laid off, do you immediately assume that you weren't "good" enough, or do you stop to think that the company needed streamlining? Do you think you are unattractive because you're not a size six, or is it possible you have a larger frame? We must learn to love ourselves and send ourselves approving, supportive messages because once we can do that, we'll discover that happiness with ourselves and our lives is easier to attain.

I love myself just as I am.

Life is an adventure in forgiveness.

—NORMAN COUSINS

For six years Lucy was plagued with nightmares, fits of depression, and raging anger because her husband of seventeen years had slept with Lucy's closest friend—her sister. When Lucy found out about the indiscretion she was incredulous. The only way she could cope with her pain was to shut her sister completely out of her life, refusing even to see her sister's two children when they were born.

After six years of carrying her grudge and experiencing extreme mood swings, Lucy decided to forgive her sister in an effort to find peace. "I was only hurting myself," she said. "Every time I saw a picture of her or heard her name mentioned, I felt the rage all over again." Lucy contacted her sister, explained her feelings, and said she wanted to bury the hatchet. Not only did her actions bring her peace, Lucy said she felt whole and happy for the first time in years.

Are you suffering because you won't forgive someone for something they've said or done? Think about how much you're hurting yourself and imagine how much freer you'd feel if you weren't carrying so much resentment. Forgiving someone is one of the hardest and boldest, but most healing, actions we can take if we're in pain.

I will go on an adventure of forgiveness today.

Let us always meet each other with a smile, for the smile is the beginning of love.

—MOTHER TERESA

When I was young I remember being told that the act of frowning used thirteen muscles and that smiling used only two, so to conserve energy it would be prudent to smile. Although that made a big impression on me, it wasn't until I was older that research convinced me of the importance of smiling: Even if you aren't happy but you move your mouth to form a smile, you will be happy shortly because the contracted muscles will change the bloodflow and release "feel good" endorphins in your brain.

This suggestion really works for me. When I try to hide a down mood by pretending to be happy, it usually isn't long before my mood matches my phony face—which at that point becomes one of genuine pleasure. Like the slogan Fake It until You Make It, which is used in twelve-step recovery programs, you need only make believe for a short period until the body is in synch and you've achieved a better mood.

Try to put on a happy face today no matter how you're feeling. It may not heal any underlying strife or treat a chemical imbalance that requires medication, but if an exercise this simple can improve your mood and help you see the world in a happier light, then you are one step closer to emotional health.

I will smile today even if I don't feel like it.

We are most deeply asleep at the switch when we fancy we control any switches at all.

—Annie Dillard

Sometimes when unforeseen events like death or natural disasters happen, the people who might appear to be best-prepared to cope actually handle it the worst. A study of widows and widowers showed that the greater a person's intelligence, self-confidence, and income, the more depressed he or she was likely to be after a partner's death. The researcher theorized that people who feel a sense of self-mastery about their lives are probably more shaken by upsetting events than those who don't.

For example, I once read an article about a financial titan whose life consisted for many years of attaining status, wealth, and citations in the society column. When his only son was killed in a car crash he was quoted as saying that for the first time he discovered that money didn't insulate him from tragedy. Within a year he had begun dismantling his empire and spending more time and money on helping causes that would further his spiritual life and benefit those less fortunate than himself.

Try not to make the mistake of believing that outside trappings protect us from depression or devastating events. Instead, accepting that we don't control all the switches in life and believing in a power greater than ourselves can give us the strength to handle tragedy when it occurs.

I cannot control events, but I can control my reactions to them.

There is no perfect solution to depression, nor should there be. As odd as this may sound . . . we should be glad of that. It keeps us human.

—LESLEY HAZLETON

Glenda is a seventy-four-year-old grandmother who has suffered from depression all her life. Although her mood swings were difficult to cope with, she prided herself on the fact that she never missed a day of work. Upon retirement, though, Glenda's depression became so overwhelming that she stopped eating and sleeping. Only after her physician intervened did she agree to try one of the most controversial cures for depression—electroconvulsive therapy (ECT)—which successfully relieved her of the symptoms.

There are no perfect cures for depression. Some have side effects, and what works for one person may not work for another. However, many doctors say that ECT is so stigmatized because of its negative portrayal in movies and books that many of the depressed people who could be helped by it never consider its potential benefits. Only in recent years have people begun to express appreciation for ECT and its long-lasting effects on depression; a well-known talk-show host is one such person who says that ECT saved his life and sanity.

Try to be open-minded about ways to relieve your depression. Ask your physician about all of your alternatives and research them carefully. ECT has some side effects, such as mild memory loss, but even that could be better than allowing depression to take over your life. Depression is a very treatable illness, but only when you persevere in finding the solution that works for you.

I am open to new ways of combating depression.

So long as women are slaves, men will be knaves.
—ELIZABETH CADY STANTON

One day I saw a woman and her husband on a talk show discussing how the husband ran every aspect of his wife's life. He was so overprotective and suspicious of her that she was forbidden to have a car, a phone, or any friends. The woman was clearly depressed and angered by the situation, but she managed to keep a smile on her face while she admitted that she never did anything to speak up against her husband or fight for her rights.

The couple could learn a few things from a friend of mine who used to be in a similar situation. Although very assertive at work, my friend let her husband walk all over her at home. He frequently enjoyed a "boys night out" but forbade her from doing something similar with her friends because he wanted her home with their son. After years of mounting anger and depression about the inequity, my friend confronted her husband, explained her need for more time to herself, and took a monthly subscription to the ballet. This one step—although difficult—opened the door for them to address other issues that had become divisive.

As long as we let the men in our lives be "knaves" in their treatment of us, we'll be "slaves" to them. Is there an inequity in your relationship with a man that is depressing you but that you've kept silent about? Start to see yourself and act like someone who deserves love, equality, and dignity and before long this will be exactly what you'll get.

I will not be anyone's slave.

The goal is to live a full, productive life even with all that ambiguity. No matter what happens, whether the cancer never flares up again or whether you die, the important thing is that the days that you have had you will have lived.

—GILDA RADNER

Cancer, particularly breast cancer, has never been at higher rates for women than it is now. By the time we reach middle age, all of us will either know someone who has contracted cancer or we will have experienced it ourselves. While it's impossible not to suffer after learning of a cancer diagnosis and fear the worst, survivors say that there are some positive things to be gained from this experience.

Shock, denial, anger, and bargaining are steps that anyone given a diagnosis of cancer is bound to experience. On the other side of these steps, however, is hopefully acceptance and a decision to rejoin life. Many cancer survivors say that their diagnosis not only taught them to live for the day, but also gave them the courage to leave bad relationships and stop accepting abusive treatment from others. Instead of wasting time doing things that didn't challenge them, these survivors decided what they really wanted to do and then pursued it with a vengeance.

If you had cancer, how would you spend today? Even if you are fortunate enough not to have a life-threatening disease, you can take the positive lessons survivors have learned and decide what you want to do, how you want to live, and who you want to emulate and then set about making today the beginning of the rest of a precious and meaningful life.

I will act today as if I may not get another chance tomorrow.

People are like stained glass windows. They sparkle and shine
when the sun is out, but when the darkness sets in, their true
beauty is revealed only if there is a light from within.
—ELISABETH KÜEBLER-ROSS

One day I was watching a former prisoner of war describe how he'd survived seven and a half years of torture
and solitary confinement without breaking down or giving
up hope that he'd eventually be free. At first, he said, he'd
been distraught at the thought of dying in a foreign country
and never seeing his family again. Then he'd gradually felt
a deeper, fighting spirit emerge and a belief that God
would be with him, no matter what. "Once I was in touch
with those emotions," he said, "I knew I'd make it."

Darkness in our lives is an opportunity to discover how
much inner light and strength we have. Some of us may
have a lot because we were raised with so much love that
our self-esteem is unshakable. Others, however, may find
that hard times shake us severely, revealing that our foun-
dations are rocky and that we have to work incredibly hard
to shore up our confidence and optimism.

Whichever scenario describes you, strive to sparkle today no matter how much darkness is around you. Read
inspirational books, pray, meditate, or talk to a spiritual
leader in your community, but do something that will nourish your inner spirit. Remember that you can always shine
when the sun is out, but that true courage and strength
involves sparkling from within even when the storms are
raging.

I will allow my inner light to shine brightly today.

The guilt that you carry because of your inability to provide an ideal home environment regardless of the circumstances will not do you a bit of good. It will not do your children a bit of good, either.

—JANET WOITITZ

Surveys have shown that over 50 percent of American mothers work outside of the home and that most of these mothers returned to a full-time job when their children were infants. Because of this vast change in female working patterns, many women of my generation, who had mothers who stayed home, have themselves become working mothers. This dichotomy has led many of us to wonder if what we're doing is best for us and for our children.

Sometimes this guilt can result from listening to women who chose to raise their children differently. Johanna has had several babysitters quit on short notice, causing her to lose valuable days at work. Instead of offering to help, Johanna's mother never misses a chance to tell her daughter that the parade of sitters is harming her grandchildren and that Johanna should quit her job because "it's not important, anyway." Although Johanna's career brings her pleasure, and she feels her children are well-adjusted, she always has spells of depression and self-doubt when her mother weighs in with her opinions.

If *we* can be happy and confident about our decisions, our families will reap the fruits of our positive emotions. Carrying around unnecessary loads of guilt won't just harm *you*, it will have an adverse effect on those you love. Try today to nip guilty feelings in the bud and use the time you have with your family to show them your happiest side.

The greatest contribution I can make to a happy home is self-confidence in my decisions.

We humans are full of unpredictable emotions that logic cannot solve.

—CAPTAIN JAMES T. KIRK, *STAR TREK*

Several years ago Elise broke up with a man she'd been inseparable from for over five years. Although they'd spent many holidays and special times together, the man decided that he didn't want to marry Elise when she unexpectedly got pregnant. Devastated, Elise ended the pregnancy and the relationship. But, even today, she's still tormented by feelings of love for this man, and she often wonders about the child she aborted and whether or not she did the right thing.

Whenever we are wronged by someone, our friends are often quick to tell us how much better off we are without that person in our lives and how lucky we are to have learned the truth about them. But if we've shared intimacies with someone, to just cut off our feelings for them is nearly impossible. Depression, regrets, and thoughts of revenge are all common emotions when an intimate relationship ends, particularly if it wasn't our choice.

Emotions are, indeed, unpredictable, so trying to be rational about pain and grieving is often impossible. Be gentle with yourself today and try not to feel pressured to behave in a certain way because others think you should be further along in your recovery. Learning how to cope with depression is a process we all must go through, and what works for us may not always be the most logical or understandable approach for others.

I will allow my emotions to be irrational if it helps me heal.

He who cannot rest, cannot work.

—HARRY EMERSON FOSDICK

Several years ago I felt overwhelmed by various obligations, and almost immediately my sleep patterns became completely disrupted. No matter how tired I was when I went to bed, my eyes would snap open at 1:45 A.M. and I wouldn't be able to get back to sleep. For the rest of the day I'd drag myself around, tired, dispirited, and unable to get any work done. The next night, the pattern would repeat itself followed by another dreary, unproductive day.

Although I didn't know it at the time, I'd entered into one of the classic phases of clinical depression—a change in sleep patterns. Initially I dealt with the fatigue by drinking lots of coffee, which only gave me headaches, more mood swings, and a crash when the caffeine wore off. Other people turn to sleeping pills or a nightcap to make them sleepy, but these solutions only provide more problems in the long run.

If you are depressed and your sleeping patterns have changed markedly, seek professional help to alleviate the suffering. Through a combination of therapy, stress-reduction techniques, and the proper medication, you'll again get the proper amount of rest necessary to work, enjoy life, and feel normal.

When I get enough rest, everything in my life is more manageable.

The one serious conviction that a man should have is that nothing is to be taken too seriously.

—SAMUEL BUTLER

One day I read a story about a celebrated country music singer who sank into a deep depression after losing her mother, going through menopause, and experiencing career burnout. The singer hung up her microphone and retreated to the country where she underwent psychotherapy, spent time in her garden, and reflected on what she wanted in life.

After three years the woman realized that she had attached too much importance to things that in the long run were insignificant. For example, she'd wanted to be a recording star so much that in the process she neglected her friends and other interests. And because she valued her independence so much, she'd never gotten married and known the joys of motherhood. In hindsight she saw that her depression was partly a result of recognizing how much time she'd already squandered—which menopause had underscored.

Are you taking something so seriously that it is crowding out other things? Obsessing about a goal or attaching too much importance to something that is ultimately transitory can cause emotions to become unbalanced. Strive to wear life like a loose-fitting cloak each day and you'll undoubtedly find that life will never wear *you* out.

I will strive for balance and moderation in my life.

Fond as we are of our loved ones, there comes at times during their absence an unexplained peace.

—ANNE SHAW

When I was in high school a friend's mother came to address the student body about how she coped with the challenges of being a busy career woman and the mother of six children. One of her remarks struck me at the time as very strange and selfish; she said that occasionally when she was overstressed, she checked into a nearby hotel and sat in a bubble bath with the phone off the hook. A night or two of that, she assured us future mothers and professional women, was all she needed to regain her sanity.

Two decades later I understand what she was talking about. During a tough phase when my infant daughter was still waking up several times each night and my three-year-old son was demanding extra attention, I couldn't wait for a business trip to take me out of town. After a day's work in a distant city I would repair to my hotel room, get in bed with the television's remote control and a good book, and catch up on my sleep. Within a day or two I always regained my energy, felt more centered, and was eager to get back into the family fray again.

No matter how much you love your family and friends, remember today that getting away from them occasionally is like a balm to the soul. Try to plan a retreat—either a walk in a park, a trip to another city, or an overnight stay in a hotel—where you can become restored and renewed. Although this may feel selfish at first, remember that caring for yourself is also a gift to those in your life who will benefit from a happier you.

An occasional absence is good for my soul.

It is frightening how dependent on drugs we are all becoming and how easy it is for doctors to prescribe them as the universal panacea for our ills.

—CHARLES, PRINCE OF WALES

One of the biggest mistakes doctors make is to prescribe pills automatically to women when they complain of anxiety, sleeplessness, and depression. In fact, women take two-thirds of all of the anti-anxiety and antidepressant drugs in this country. Unfortunately, medication is too often the first remedy tried because it's easy to take a pill and see immediate effects; what's harder is finding out what is truly wrong and how it can be resolved without a prescription.

In our "quick fix" society we are conditioned to believe that pills can do everything from relieving a headache to helping us lose weight. The sad truth is that medication is only a fraction of the solution to many of these problems; diet, exercise, therapy, holistic remedies, and adequate rest can supply much of what we need to cope with depression and stress.

Drugs are not the panacea to all ills and we need to understand alternative solutions before taking any medication that might be addictive or have undesirable side effects. Antidepressants and other drugs can restore energy, clarity, and focus to lives that feel out of control, but it's important that we understand them and be properly diagnosed and monitored so that they don't worsen what we're already struggling with.

There is no "quick fix" for my problems.

More things are wrought by prayer
Than this world dreams of.

—ALFRED TENNYSON

For most of my life I was a very jaded person who didn't believe in God or the power of prayer. If I was in a situation where I needed help and someone said something thoughtful like, "I'll say a prayer for you," I'd always think cynically, "Yeah, a lot of good that will do me." But in recent years my attitude toward prayer and what miracles it can bring about has changed dramatically as a result of some wonderful experiences.

A number of scientific studies have borne out the power of prayer. For example, when people in one wing of a hospital were unknowingly prayed for by a prayer group, while those in a separate wing were not, the ones who had been prayed for recovered more quickly and showed a lower death rate than those who were not prayed for. Even plants that have been randomly prayed for have also repeatedly been shown to flourish and grow faster than those that were not.

Try prayer today if you never have. It's free, it's private, and it can be as quick as just saying, "Help!" If you don't feel comfortable praying, try asking someone to pray with you or for you. You might be surprised and comforted to find that calling upon an unseen force brings you greater relief and more results than if you tried to solve your problems single-handedly.

I will entrust myself to the power of prayer today.

Follow your bliss.

—Joseph Campbell

So many people I know are miserable because they spend their days doing things they don't like. They go to jobs they don't enjoy, fill their life with people they don't like, and pursue activities that aren't beneficial or pleasurable. It's not surprising that at the end of the day they are down because they have a nagging feeling that something better is out there, but they don't know how to get it.

Mary once fit this profile. Several years ago she was unmarried, unchallenged in her job, and stuck in a rut of going home to her cats and watching television. At the suggestion of her therapist she wrote a "wish list" of things she wanted to do and then methodically went about trying to make them happen. Instead of griping about her job, she wrote a résumé and looked for a position in a different field. She also joined a ballroom dancing club and worked on smiling more. Within six months she had a new circle of friends, found a more fulfilling job, and even started dating. By identifying her "bliss" and then going after it, Mary transformed herself from a depressed, self-pitying woman to a self-confident and happy one.

What is on your bliss list? Is it working to better the world, writing a novel, or traveling? Whatever your answer, there are always ways to bring more of what you love into your life even if it's just in small ways. You'll find that knowing what brings you joy and taking steps to experience it more often won't just result in more satisfaction, it will reduce your likelihood of succumbing to depression.

I will do at least one thing today that makes me blissful.

*Things may come to those who wait, but only the things left by
those who hustle.*

—ABRAHAM LINCOLN

Patricia is a friend who was abruptly laid off from a
well-paying job when her company faced a restructuring.
Because she had never imagined being unemployed, she
didn't know what steps to take to find another position.
Compounding this problem was her embarrassment about
being out of work, which she didn't want to communicate
to others. So instead of reaching out and networking to find
a job, Patricia stayed home alone and dwelled on her predicament, hoping that something would come along and
find her.

Patricia's way of dealing with this crisis is not uncommon. Studies show that when women are dealt a blow they
tend to retreat inward, repeatedly rehash their hurts, and
take little or no action to resolve their problem, whereas
men usually take immediate action. Thankfully, biology is
not destiny; women who have been trained to take immediate steps to address problems not only lessen their chances
of getting depressed, but also improve the probability of
getting what they want.

Sometimes when we're down, getting out and hustling
is the last thing we think we're capable of. But that's exactly
what we must do if we are to overcome our depression. Set
a goal of calling someone every day and networking if
you've lost your job and ask them to suggest helpful people
to call, too. Whether it's a job or something else you're
seeking today, remember that staying home and sulking
only guarantees that you'll never be the early bird catching
the worm.

When I take action I am always empowered.

You have a wonderful child. Then, when he's thirteen, gremlins carry him away and leave in his place a stranger who gives you not a moment's peace.

—JILL EIKENBERRY

I had coffee one day with a friend of mine who had undergone a huge change of attitude toward her son since our last meeting. When we first met she had regaled me with stories about how fabulous, smart, and handsome he was. Although she had a fulfilling job and a good marriage, it seemed as though her son was the center of her life and that the sun rose and set on him. Several years later, however, that all changed.

"What's wrong?" I asked as she sighed with impatience when I mentioned her son's name. "I can't wait for him to leave for college!" she snapped, detailing his transgressions. When I expressed amusement that he had gone from being the world's greatest child to the typical teenager, she rolled her eyes and said that in about ten or fifteen years I wouldn't be laughing because I'd be going through the same thing.

Whether we have a teenager at home or not, we need to remember that many friends and family members will go through stages that are painful and upsetting to us. No one stays the same over many years, nor should we expect them to. Be tolerant and forgiving of the foibles in others, just as, hopefully, they would be for us. And remember that if it is a teen you are dealing with, the struggle for independence during these years does eventually end and is usually replaced with a more mature, sensitive young adult.

I will try to meet change in others with flexibility, humor, and tolerance.

We have all known the long loneliness and we have learned that the only solution is love and that love comes with community.

—DOROTHY DAY

When Juliet's first child was born, she decided to combine motherhood with a flexible career from her home. Her employer agreed to the arrangement, allowing her to do work by phone, fax and computer. To her surprise, Juliet found that this "dream job" didn't suit her; in fact, she felt depressed much of the time. Although she enjoyed being near her newborn, she missed the camaraderie of the office, the talk around the water cooler and the positive feelings she got from getting dressed nicely each morning and being complimented on her appearance.

If you are a gregarious person, the isolation of working alone can be depressing. There are other difficulties, too. One woman who returned to the office after trying to work from her home said she'd still needed to hire fulltime babysitters in order to get quality work done. Even then, whenever she'd heard her child crying, it had been hard for her to stay at her desk and concentrate.

If you've found that working at home hasn't brought the benefits you thought it would, consider that you may not have the right personality for this type of arrangement. Being with other adults during the day is a powerful stimulant for happiness, so if you need this type of company, you'll do yourself and your family more good by being in an environment that brings you joy as well as job satisfaction.

Being in a community is sometimes better for me than being alone.

The human soul has need of security and also of risk. . . .
The boredom produced by a complete absence of risk is also a
sickness of the soul.

—SIMONE WEIL

Researchers have discovered some surprising ways that successfully help people jolly themselves out of apathy or boredom. One of them is risk taking, such as buying a lottery ticket or bungee jumping. For some reason, doing something that has unknown consequences can help a person feel alive again.

Everyone has a form of risk taking that acts as a mood lifter. For some people it's betting on horse races and for others it is pushing themselves to their physical limits, such as skiing down a dangerous slope or entering a triathlon. For yet others it is dramatically altering their hairstyle, striking out on their own professionally, or placing an ad in the personals section of a local newspaper or magazine.

If you are depressed, you might need to take a measured risk that will make you feel vibrant and alive again. Think of something new and different that won't have adverse consequences if it fails. For example, having an affair is not an acceptable risk; asking someone interesting to join you for coffee is. Our souls will indeed become sick and our minds stagnant if our lives consist of predictable, routine actions, so challenge yourself to bring excitement through risk into your life and you may be surprised to find that happiness—not just exhilaration—is a pleasurable benefit.

I will take a life-affirming risk today.

Humor is emotional chaos remembered in tranquillity.
—JAMES THURBER

My friend Jill wins the award for having the Wedding from Hell. The morning of the big day the diamond fell out of her ring and the ring bearer refused to wear his outfit because it was "sissy." When Jill got to the church she discovered that her mother had had words with her mother-in-law, the organist was sick and the bouquets were the wrong color. At the altar Jill fainted from hunger and the ceremony was completed as she sat in a chair. And then, to add insult to injury, her honeymoon was cut short because of a bat-infested cabin.

To hear my friend relate all of the mishaps now you wouldn't know that she cried for weeks after the wedding, convinced that her marriage was jinxed. She also had to mediate arguments between the mothers-in-law and struggle to find something enjoyable to recall about "the biggest day of her life." But ten years later she can laugh about the uproar and even find positive things about the whole experience.

Try to be light-hearted today about the events in your life where Murphy's Law reigns supreme and you are surrounded by emotional chaos. It's an attractive quality to be able to laugh at yourself and your misfortunes instead of being depressed, and the sooner you can bring humor to bear on a bad situation, the sooner you'll find it bearable.

I'll laugh at my chaos today.

There is a certain melancholy in having to tell oneself that one has said good-bye . . . to the age and the circumstances that enable one to observe young children closely and passionately.
—COLETTE

When I brought my second child home from the hospital, I went through a melancholy phase when all I did was think of the future. I often got teary imagining how she was going to grow up, become a rebellious teenager, and leave me without a backward glance. Instead of appreciating her at that very moment, I could only think about how she wouldn't be around in twenty-some years so I'd better have another baby soon to replace her.

Thankfully this phase passed, but I still go through periods with both of my children when I am so enraptured with them that I wonder how I'll survive when they no longer come to me to hold them or tell them bedtime stories. Every mother I know has grappled with depression over watching their children pass through the innocence of childhood. Although normal, it's an emotion we all must overcome if we are to allow our children to become self-sufficient, healthy, and independent people.

If you're sad because your children are growing up too fast, remember that childhood isn't the only wonderful time; adolescence and adulthood can bring marvelous and treasured moments, as well. The more we can look forward with anticipation, the less likely we'll be to look forever backward at what once was.

Every stage of my children's lives is special in its own way.

A woman is always buying something.

—OVID

I have a friend whose response to every setback in life has been to go shopping—with a vengeance. I always know when she's depressed because her house begins to bulge with deliveries from mail-order catalogues, television shopping networks, and department stores. To assuage her guilt about buying things she can't afford and doesn't need, I and others are the constant recipients of such useless items as stuffed animals, decorative knickknacks, and cheap jewelry. Shopping never brings my friend any lasting happiness; her spending sprees are always followed by remorse, lies to her husband, and terror that her credit line will be eliminated.

If we compulsively shop for ourselves or others as a response to depression, we're probably unconsciously suffering from the misconception that our self-esteem will rise with the next new pile of cosmetics or the next generous gift to a friend. Shopping cannot fix our emotional problems, however. Running up our credit charges, buying things we don't need, and spending beyond our means only indicates that we're not facing deeper feelings of inadequacy and sadness.

Be aware of your spending habits today, particularly if you are using shopping to avoid facing depression. Several helpful groups exist for people whose spending is compulsive and self-destructive, so consider seeking the support of your peers. Moderation in our activities is a key to establishing contentment and happiness, but learning this important skill only comes with vigilance, practice, and commitment.

I will shop only for what I need today, not what I want.

The most beautiful thing we can experience is the mysterious.
—ALBERT EINSTEIN

Often crises and life-changing upheavals bring with them unusual spiritual occurrences. This has frequently been documented in cases of near-death experiences when people are clinically declared dead but are then miraculously revived. When they "return" to their bodies they usually speak of having met angels or of seeing a light that radiates pure love. Almost always these men and women are so changed by this occurrence that they seek out ways to share their experience of peace and harmony with others.

Other friends of mine in distress have witnessed "mysterious" events in more earthly surroundings. One friend who suddenly lost her job was soothed in a series of dreams by images of finding a better job shortly. Another friend whose husband left her discovered that daily sessions of meditation gave her sensations of peacefulness that she couldn't get anywhere else and that helped her get through a difficult time.

Today, be aware of the fact that depression and hard times can open the door to unusual feelings of spirituality and peace that we may not have had before. The God of our understanding sometimes has an easier time reaching us when we're most vulnerable, so use this period to be aware of the many ways in which we can be comforted when we need it most.

I can always find the peace I need, but not always in ways that I understand.

What a wonderful life I've had! I only wish I'd realized it sooner.

—COLETTE

When we're depressed the normal tendency is to "awfulize" everything and to see our lives as bleak and forbidding. I've gone through enough down periods to recognize that when I get depressed I'm apt to cast my entire life in a state of terribleness. No matter what anyone says to me, I'll insist that I've never been a good person, I've never produced any worthwhile work, I've never truly been happy, and I've wasted a lot of time making stupid mistakes.

Because I've gone through this cycle before, I know now that it's a mental state that will pass. Before too long I'll be back to normal and I'll marvel at the terrible things I've said and thought about myself. Before I understood my pattern and the dynamics of depression, though, I'd lose weeks and months to this self-defeating behavior; now it's closer to days or hours, for which I'm grateful.

If you're in the midst of "awfulizing" your life, remember that depression breeds inaccurate thinking. Everything looks worse and less hopeful when you're down, so wait until you're in a better frame of mind before making big decisions or taking important steps. Above all, try to remember that the days you're stuck in a mental rut are irretrievable and that the sooner you can regain clarity on your life, the more of it you'll have left to enjoy.

There is always something to give thanks for in my life.

When friends stop being frank and useful to each other, the world loses some of its radiance.

—ANATOLE BROYARD

At one time I was depressed because a trivial issue had come between me and one of my closest friends. I was sure I was right so I refused to offer the olive branch, and she didn't seem to want to breach the chasm. So weeks went by without either one of us making a gesture as I became increasingly sad about the loss of our frequent talks and her companionship. Finally I swallowed my pride and called, saying that I missed her and that I wanted to resolve what had come between us. She agreed and we had one of the best and frankest talks we'd ever had.

Friendship is one of the things that women count on most for support and comfort in difficult times. When a friendship founders on the rocks of jealousy, anger, or misunderstanding, it can be extremely painful, particularly if you were very close to the person. Although it's very humbling, one side must take the initiative to mend the friendship; it's very easy for both people to harden into positions of anger and defensiveness, which only increases the pain of losing the friendship.

If you're depressed about a rift that has come between you and a friend today, ask yourself whether the good times you've had outweigh the problems. Then, if you decide that the person is someone you want in your life, reach out to them and be frank about your hurt feelings. A good friendship is worth its weight in gold because of what it can provide emotionally, so don't let one slip away over an issue that is less important than the relationship itself.

I will work at my friendships today.

The total deprivation of [sex] produces irritability.
—ELIZABETH BLACKWELL

A friend of mine whose husband is in the military often endures periods of separation from him of six weeks or longer. One of the worst parts of the separations, she says, is her lack of sexual fulfillment. Although a monogamous woman at heart, she finds it impossible not to flirt and fantasize while her husband is away. To overcome her subsequent guilt, she exercises endlessly, becoming so exhausted by the end of the day that she doesn't have time to feel sexual.

All of us will, at one time or another, probably go through spells of no sex. We or our partners may lose interest temporarily, we may go on extended business trips, or we may take medication that kills our sex drive. Also, given the high divorce rate and the fact that the average woman can expect to be widowed for fifteen years of her life, it is probable that we will be left at sometime without a steady partner.

Whichever situation best describes the reason for your sexual desert, take heart that there are solutions. If we've lost passion for our partner, couples therapy can help teach new ways to relate sexually. Medication can also be altered to reignite the libido if that is a problem. And there is a new trend of women turning to other women for sexual satisfaction in middle age. Don't overlook masturbation as a healthy tool for remaining sexually alive, either. Finding a way to keep sexual pleasure in your life isn't just good for your body, it's great for the mind.

Satisfying sex is one road to happiness.

Many of us spent our first twenty years learning the ways of the wounded; the next twenty were spent healing those wounds. . . . I am convinced that the second half of a woman's life is a profound opportunity for transformation.
                                                —CATHLEEN ROUNTREE

As we get older we face a variety of emotional obstacles such as passing through our childbearing years, losing our youthful figure, and watching loved ones die. Partly as a result of these types of changes, women are more likely to suffer from depression than men, with the risk peaking around middle age.

Hillary Rodham Clinton said that of all the things written about her during her husband's presidential campaign, the one that bothered her the most was seeing herself described as "middle-aged." This reluctance to being forty-something embodies society's emphasis on youth, which may cause us to devalue ourselves. But with the right attitude, we can accept middle age as a wellspring of opportunities, a release from restrictions, and a chance to realize who we are.

Aging is a natural process, and preparing for it and accepting it is an important part of being able to take advantage of what it offers. Midlife can be a culmination of using what we've learned, or it can be a bleak time when we feel like we're falling apart. Ultimately it's up to us to choose which path we'll take and how gracefully we'll age.

My real age is my state of mind.

A worldly loss often turns into spiritual gain.

—INAYAT KHAN

One day I read about a wealthy California architect who lost his company, his possessions, and his marriage all within one year. He was consumed with anger and depression about the adversity in his life until he decided to seek a deeper faith in God that might help him cope with his losses. A church pilgrimage to the Holy Land filled him with awe and wonder, and when he returned to America to rebuild his life, he found that many of the material trappings that had seemed so important to him before had diminished in importance. A spiritual life gave him more satisfaction.

Although this is a dramatic story, it's true that whenever we lose something we often replace it with something stronger and more significant. For example, people who've been robbed often discover that their most valuable possession is their life, and they develop a renewed appreciation for the small things of life. Similarly, many divorced women say that their initial feelings of sadness and fear about being alone are eventually erased by the satisfaction they receive from learning they can be self-sufficient.

Try not to be depressed about a worldly loss today. While you might feel empty and traumatized for a while, by being patient and introspective, you'll undoubtedly find that you've created a space into which something more valuable and spiritual can enter.

I will not be frightened by the voids in my life.

*The repressed memory is like a noisy intruder being thrown
out of the concert hall. You can throw him out, but he will
bang on the door and continue to disturb the concert. The
analyst opens the door and says, "If you promise to behave
yourself, you can come back in."*

—THEODOR REIK

Sometimes people can be depressed without even
knowing why. Kay couldn't figure out why she despised her
infant son and why she felt suicidal. Cynthia had bouts with
depression throughout her life but didn't have any one specific reason she could point to. Later both discovered
through therapy that repressed memories of sexual abuse
were the seeds of their self-destructive behavior and periodic depression.

Repressed memories often start to surface as the adult
feels secure in her life or her children reach the age at
which her abuse occurred. Once the memories surface,
they come in bits and pieces—such as discomfort at a certain smell—and they can never be pushed into the unconscious again. At this point it's imperative that a therapist be
consulted because processing the memories in a safe environment can help the sufferer deal with complex issues and
help her understand the reasons for her depression.

If your mind has a "noisy intruder" you can't cope
with and that is contributing to or causing depression, talk
to a therapist about the possibility of repressed abuse. Putting yourself into professional hands can help you unlock
the reasons for mood swings while also providing a secure
haven in which to start healing.

*My memories can heal me when I process them in a healthy
way.*

Oh sleep! It is a gentle thing, beloved from pole to pole.
—SAMUEL TAYLOR COLERIDGE

A recent study of women showed that most were sleep-deprived and that married women routinely averaged an hour less sleep than their husbands. "These women," one researcher said, "talked about sleep the way starving people talk about food!"

There are lots of reasons why women deprive themselves of sleep. In the working world, staying later at the office than our male colleagues can "prove" our worth. If our parents need care, we're more likely than our male siblings to be the ones juggling their concerns with our own. And if we're mothers, we sleep far less soundly than our husbands because we often are more in tune with our children's needs than they are.

If you're not getting enough sleep, go on a campaign to change your actions so that you will. Skip a television show, simplify your morning routine, and try to take restful catnaps if your schedule allows. Since fatigue is a key instigator of irritability, depression and tension, the more ways you can guarantee getting some "gentle" sleep, the less likely you'll be to experience sadness and mood swings during the day.

I will get enough sleep to function in top form today.

Smell is a potent wizard that transports us across thousands of miles and all the years we have lived.

—HELEN KELLER

One day I read an article called "34 Surefire Ways to Beat the Blues." Most of the ways listed were familiar to me but one was particularly effective because it instantly transported me to a place of happiness. The suggestion was to bake something that smelled wonderful, the idea being that most people have happy memories associated with delicious smells such as warm bread or mulled cider. My response was to think back to summers at the seashore when I bicycled to a doughnut shop in the morning to pick up breakfast for my family before a day at the beach. Just the thought of how heavenly that store smelled and how happy I was as I anticipated another lazy day altered my mood for the next few hours.

Of all our senses smell is the most directly linked to memory because it is located in the brain's limbic system, where scent perceptions are recorded and emotions are stored. Even more importantly, smells don't require verbal decoding for the memories to be retrieved so they are especially accessible to us.

Think back to a happy time in your life and what smells you associate with it. Does the scent of chocolate-chip cookies remind you of visiting your grandmother, or does salty air take you back to a visit to the seashore? Discover the smells that bring you joy and recreate them in your environment, because having this important tool at your disposal can bring instant relief whenever you need it.

I will create an aromatic environment that brings me happiness.

Noble deeds and hot baths are the best cures for depression.
—DODIE SMITH

When you are feeling blue there is no shortage of things you can do to try to make yourself better. However, some techniques are more successful than others in helping us shake depression, regain hopefulness, and find renewed joy in life. All of us respond differently to proposed solutions and it's important to learn what works best and to stick to it.

Reminding yourself of what you have to be grateful for and giving yourself a treat, like a hot bath, are two of the most effective ways to relieve depression. Getting together with others can also be helpful, but only if you don't endlessly rehash your troubles. Exercise is another mood booster, and is particularly effective if you're normally sedentary. Sensual pleasures like making love, getting a massage, and listening to favorite music also repeatedly turn up as proven ways to beat the blues.

Just as there are many forms of depression, there is a diversity of solutions. Try a number of techniques and carefully observe your reactions to them. For example, if reading romance novels is a guaranteed stress reducer, try to always have one available, and if music is your cure, make sure you surround yourself with it. Learning what is most soothing to the soul is a powerful tool in heading off depression before it takes root or in restoring your equilibrium when you need it most.

I will do something today that has alleviated my depression in the past.

I never think of the future. It comes soon enough.
—ALBERT EINSTEIN

When I am down I tend to focus on how the future is never going to be bright again, and I create awful scenarios that I'm sure will befall me. For example, if I hear about a tragedy, I imagine myself struggling with the same problem, or if I read that the unemployment rate is climbing, I become convinced that I'm next in line for layoffs. Whenever these gloomy ruminations begin I lose hours of precious time not appreciating what I have and thinking about things that probably will never occur.

Happily I've found that I'm unable to predict the future—especially when I'm depressed. But it's still hard to completely erase the hopeless feelings that engulf me when I'm down and tell me life will never get better. A good antidote to imagining a negative future, I've found, is to repeat over and over to myself that I must live in day-tight compartments and not worry about tomorrow. When I can do this I bring more attention and focus to what I have before me and I don't weaken my mind and body with unhappy thoughts.

Don't worry about tomorrow today. Depression tends to worsen when we allow our mind to dwell on "what ifs," so try to interrupt this train of thought today with positive affirmations or purposeful activity. If you can successfully train yourself to start seeing what's hopeful in life instead of the potential negatives, then the future is guaranteed to be brighter than you may once have thought.

I will dwell only on what I can accomplish today.

Prayer is indeed good, but while calling on the gods, a man should himself lend a hand.

—HIPPOCRATES

I know a man who has a statue of the Virgin Mary on the dashboard of his car. One day while I was riding with him I asked him about his faith. It turned out that he was devoutly religious and went to Mass every morning before work. He said that he turned all of his problems over to God and the various saints in his faith whenever he needed help. He believed that this was the most effective way to deal with anything that disturbed him or threatened his well-being.

While part of me thinks that this man's devotion is admirable, the other part thinks it's a cop-out. There's no question that having a strong spiritual compass is helpful when hard times hit, but I also believe that you need to help yourself, too. For example, this man wasn't known for dealing with any of his professional or personal problems in a healthy way. Whenever conflict emerged in his department at work, he retreated into his office. And when his children were in trouble, he drank a lot. He may have turned his cares over to God in the mornings, but during the days it seemed he lacked the energy to help himself.

Remember today that faith in the God of your understanding is invaluable, but that prayer is best when combined with a little elbow grease and aggressiveness. Don't expect miracles to happen unless you're doing your best to make them happen.

A helping hand always starts at the end of my arm.

*In California everyone goes to a therapist, is a therapist, or is a
therapist going to a therapist.*

—Truman Capote

In some parts of the country it's chic to have a therapist and to discuss what he or she is working on with us to
solve. Many people even find it a badge of honor to seek
out professional help and announce how much better we
feel afterward. Others, however, may find it difficult to pick
up the phone and make contact with a professional because
we're afraid it will make us appear helpless, weak, and in-
decisive.

I grew up on the East Coast and spent most of my life
in progressive cities where getting therapy was considered a
smart choice if you were faced with emotional problems.
This doesn't hold true everywhere, though; friends of mine
in the Midwest say that the "pioneer spirit" of solving your
own problems makes it especially difficult to seek help
there. And friends from the south say that women are still
primarily valued for their appearance, and that getting
therapy is often considered frivolous and unfeminine.

If you need professional help but are afraid to call a
therapist because it's not considered acceptable in the culture in which you were raised, try to challenge the stereotypes by asking yourself if they are helpful or hurtful to
you. Although it's very difficult to break a mold that you
feel pressure to conform to, it's only by fighting passivity
and others' expectations for us that we find our individual-
ity and create our own happiness.

I will act in my own best interests today.

Too many people, too many demands, too much to do; competent, busy, hurrying people—It just isn't living at all.
                                              —ANNE MORROW LINDBERGH

Like many other women with small children, I have arranged a work schedule that is flexible and allows me to work from my home with a computer, copier, fax machine, and phone. There are many pluses to this arrangement, but there are also several minuses that can leave me feeling depressed, powerless, and angry when I'm not careful about how I spend my time.

Because my office is at home there is no clear demarcation between my home hours and my office hours, and if I'm not careful I slip into my "work mode" or my "mom mode" at inappropriate times. For example, if I get a writing idea I want to turn on the computer, even if it's dinnertime. Or if I get an important business call and I'm reading a book to my children, I'll want to take it in order to appear professional despite the fact that it's my designated family time. My solution has been to create clear boundaries of when I can fulfill which roles and then to adhere to them, no matter what. Although exceptions *do* crop up, it has made me happier and more organized to have an established policy.

Learning how to set limits on our time and being able to say no is important because, until we're careful about how we spend our time and who we spend it with, we're setting ourselves up for the "women who do too much" syndrome of depression and exhaustion.

I will be the master of my time.

Spirituality is simply superaliveness.

—FRITJOF CAPRA

During one very lonely period in my life I felt strongly that God didn't exist and that religion was just a crutch for people who had problems. In early adulthood, however, as I grappled with some self-destructive behavior through support groups, I began to see things differently. I was advised to find a power greater than myself that would help restore me "to sanity" and that would help me remember that I didn't pull all the strings in my life. My journey down that road helped my life become richer, more meaningful, and happier.

People who shun God because they find religion stifling and hypocritical need to remember that having a sense of spirituality is different from being religious. When I began to explore my own spirituality, I felt like I had awakened from a long period of drowsiness. Instead of wondering if life had focus, I found a purpose and my days became more alive. My creative juices flowed again, I felt my emotions more acutely, and I was able to reexperience the pure joy I remembered from childhood.

If you don't feel superalive, you may have lost touch with your spirituality. There are many ways to foster this: trying your hand at poetry, exploring your physical limits, meditating regularly, and going to church are just a few. Whatever you have to do to connect or reconnect with your spirituality is vital because without it, you'll always have a shadow over your happiness and an emptiness inside.

When I am in touch with my spirituality, I am filled with vitality.

Don't kid yourself. Those women [on Jane Fonda's exercise tape] have never had babies. Their children were all born by professional stunt women.

—DAVE BARRY

With both of my pregnancies I worked hard to stay in shape. I stretched religiously, walked a few miles every day, and watched what I ate so that I wouldn't have a lot of excess weight to lose afterward. I started and ended at the same weight with both pregnancies, and had the same size babies both times. The first time I returned to my prepregnancy weight within weeks; the second time I carried 15 extra, uncomfortable pounds for many months—eventually becoming extremely depressed about how I looked and my inability to get back to my previous weight.

It was only after discussions with friends who'd also had two children that I regained my perspective and my depression lifted. They helped me remember that the most important thing was that I had another healthy child. In addition, my body was three years older than it was during my first pregnancy and that snapping back into shape was probably going to take at least twice as long.

Be nurturing and patient with yourself if you're depressed about how your body is reacting to childbirth. With time, exercise, prudent eating, and rest, you'll once again feel energetic and more like your old self. Keep in mind, too, that no one's body is identical to yours and that your journey of recovery is going to be unique and special, just as your child is.

I love my body and the miracles it can perform.

August is a wicked month.

—EDNA O'BRIEN

Every August without fail, I experience a sense of melancholy. Along with the hot and muggy weather, my energy disappears and my ambition fizzles. I know I'm not alone in this as most people I know schedule August vacations and mentally prepare themselves for not getting much done. In fact, I'm told that this phenomenon is so common in Europe that entire countries simply grind to a halt in August while people go off to recharge themselves.

For some people, summer depression is related to the heaviness of the air and a relatively rare condition called summer seasonal affective disorder (SSAD). When this condition strikes, sufferers find that the abundance of heat and light makes them feel depressed, even manic. A change in climate, medication, and therapy can all benefit people with this condition. Those of us who don't have SSAD, however, may simply have depressing childhood memories of our summer vacations ending in August, or we might just prefer cooler months.

If August has always been a problem time for you, try to schedule activities this year to make it different. For example, if your work productivity has always dipped in previous years, try to make sure you take a break to recharge and relax. And, above all, remember that although the dog days of summer usually seem endless, some advance planning can make the weeks fly by.

I will plan ahead to ensure that August is not "wicked" for me.

It hardly seems to matter how many years have passed, how many betrayals there may have been, how much misery in the family: We remain connected, even against our wills.

—ANTHONY BRANDT

Hannah is a successful middle-aged woman who runs her own business, has a great marriage, and whose children are a credit to her. Despite her professional and personal successes, Hannah feels like an utter failure because she is estranged from her parents with whom she has a longstanding disagreement over money.

Hannah is not unlike many women who consider their accomplishments insignificant unless they also have warm family relationships. This, however, is not always possible. Hannah has sought joint counseling with her parents, but they have always resisted this and any other overtures at peace Hannah has made. Despite the fact that she has done everything humanly possible to work out a solution, Hannah still considers herself a "bad daughter" and to assuage her depression she frequently binges on huge amounts of food.

When faced with fractured family ties, we sometimes just have to let go and concentrate on finding happiness in other areas of our lives—particularly if we can't make headway in fostering harmony. Try to apply the powerful emotions that are stirred up through family feuds to create a healthy space for yourself that includes people who feel like the "family" you want around you. Remember, too, that while you may always feel tied to family members who depress you, you have the power to ensure that those ties don't strangle you.

I won't allow unhappy family ties to cause me to hang myself.

The capacity to sacrifice, like any skill, always needs some fine tuning. It is one thing to sacrifice briefly one's sleep to comfort a child with a bad dream; it is quite another for a mother to sacrifice her whole career for a child.

—CAROL PEARSON

One afternoon at a brunch, I discussed with some friends what types of sacrifices we were making for our children. It turned out that despite our similar backgrounds and the similar ages of our children, we had all made different decisions about how to best combine motherhood with a professional life. But despite our different approaches, all of us suffered periodically from depression, concerned about whether or not we were doing the right thing.

This is a hard time to be a mother. With so many career options available, many of us feel guilty if we pass up opportunities that previous generations could only dream of. Yet most of us also have a desire to be with our children during their tender years. There are many ways women can combine these goals with parttime jobs and working from home. But if we choose to completely jettison a career because we think it's best for our children, we must make sure it's something we'll be happy about. One woman who gave up a prestigious position chafes when she hears about the success of her former colleagues and is often resentful that her family's standard of living has been dramatically lowered without her income.

While it's difficult to be a completely happy working mother, studies have unanimously shown that a career produces optimum well-being among mothers. So before you sacrifice your career for the "good" of your family, make sure it's a decision that you will be happy about in the long run.

I can make certain sacrifices without becoming a martyr.

The fullness of life is in the hazards of life.
—EDITH HAMILTON

One of the reasons most frequently cited for depression is a feeling of missing out on life and not living up to one's potential. When I feel this way, the cause is usually a desire to do something new combined with a fear to take the risk.

A well-known motivational expert says that one of the best ways to fight low self-esteem and depression is to take such chancy but self-affirming actions as expressing your opinion more often, standing up to someone who belittles you, or taking concrete steps to advance your career. Doing something that scares you is confidence building, while running away from it only underscores the belief that you "can't," or that you'll never find your purpose in life. Rewarding yourself, with flowers for example, after taking these risks is an important way to reinforce the value of putting yourself on the line.

Life isn't risk-free, and self-doubt is an inevitable part of doing something new. Accept that you may feel uncomfortable when trying to break out of a depression, but resolve that you will follow through and learn something no matter how it turns out. The more you can risk, live, and learn, the more self-confidence you'll amass and the greater the positive changes in your life will be.

I will experience the fullness of life today by facing one of its hazards.

The wheel that squeaks the loudest
Is the one that gets the grease.

—JOSH BILLINGS

I remember coming home from one of my first jobs drained and unhappy at night. The main source of my discontent was my inability to articulate my needs—whether for help, a longer deadline, or a raise—and so I suffered and stewed in silence. I had always thought that when people needed or deserved something at work they automatically received it; I found to my chagrin, however, that until I learned to be assertive, I was going to stay mired in the same place.

Women tend to be more unobtrusive and polite than men because we usually learn when we're little—consciously and subconsciously—that being ladylike means never making waves. But when we are unable to communicate our wants and needs in our personal or professional lives, then we are hurting ourselves. Feeling frightened about speaking up just ensures that we'll always be at the mercy of others, often suffering from depression, repressed anger, physical ailments, and other stress-related ills.

Being a squeaky wheel doesn't mean being unpleasant. Saying in a firm, friendly voice that we are due a raise, we need more help from our husbands with chores, or that we don't appreciate being the object of sexual or verbal harassment can empower us without causing alienation. Assertiveness-training courses proliferate for those who don't know how to be straightforward, but the first step is always to identify what you're afraid of and then to muster up the determination to behave differently.

Silence doesn't always serve me well.

Every blade of grass has its Angel that bends over it and whispers, "Grow, grow."

—THE TALMUD

Once I read about a single mother whose life was one of juggling a demanding job, childcare hassles, and housework. One night after spending the day trying to cope with work deadlines and a sick child, she went to bed exhausted, wondering if she'd ever not feel tired and frazzled again. Several hours later her daughter woke up crying because she had wet the bed. Dragging herself into the girl's bedroom, the mother felt a presence beside her as she changed the sheets. Reflecting on the strange experience the next morning, the mother concluded that it had been an angel giving her strength and support, enabling her to press on despite her fatigue.

Many people I know feel that they have a guardian angel who appears in odd ways when they most need comfort. One woman swore that a man who gazed sympathetically at her each morning at the bus stop was an angel aware that she was caring for a dying father. Another friend thinks that a man who appeared to change her flat tire on a deserted stretch of road and then melted back into the night was her personal angel.

Be alert today to receiving unexpected help or comfort when you are down and exhausted. Whether you are aware of it or not, there is usually a caring person who will appear when you are most in need.

There is always an angel bending over me.

*If one advances confidently in the direction of his dreams,
and endeavors to live the life which he has imagined, he will
meet with a success unexpected in the common hours.*
                                                    —HENRY DAVID THOREAU

I read in the newspaper one morning about a very
successful mystery writer who had endured years of failure
and rejection before he found his niche. For a long time his
novels and short stories were turned down by various pub-
lishers. This discouraged the author because deep down he
knew that all he wanted to do was write. Finally a friend
suggested he try his hand at mystery writing instead, which
proved to be great advice. The author's books are now read
and enjoyed by millions.

Depression can cause us to give up on our dreams,
especially when we're not sure if we're on the right track.
But like this author who withstood many rejections before
he found a way to reach his goal, we sometimes have to
direct our efforts a bit differently. Perhaps this means giving ourselves more time to reach a goal or learning a skill
that will help us, but it's important that we not completely
give up on ourselves because of a temporary setback.

Reading biographies of people who have succeeded
against the odds is a good way to reignite a passion for life
when it's flagging, as is recalling what inspired you at one
time to go after a certain goal. But whatever you do, try to
hold fast to your dreams because without dreams, as a poet
once said, "life is a broken-winged bird that cannot fly."

*No matter how severe my obstacles, I will not abandon my
dreams.*

We're all of us sentenced to solitary confinement inside our own skins, for life.

—TENNESSEE WILLIAMS

A best-seller by a Jungian therapist uses myths and archetypes to demonstrate the ways in which women lose their personal power. One of the stories is about a group of women who are transformed into sleek seals that cavort in the ocean at night and then return to human form in the daylight. One of the women has her "seal skin" stolen while she is in female form and the result is that she is unable to transform into the playful, loving seal she was at night. For years she wanders sadly because she has "lost her skin." Only when it is returned to her does she again have happiness in her life.

The moral of this tale is that all of us have a "skin" in which we are comfortable and happy and that when we temporarily lose that cloak we experience depression. There are many reasons why this happens: stress, troubling relationships, and unfortunate occurrences are some of them. To reclaim the "skin" that gives us life we must do what brings us joy and serenity. For some women this might mean making regular time for exercise, meditating, going to a museum, or seeing a therapist to learn what brings us pleasure and feelings of confidence.

Are you comfortable in your skin today? If not, give some thought to what evokes playfulness, creativity, and feelings of self-love, and then take steps regularly to incorporate those people or activities into your life.

I will wear the skin that brings me joy today.

Medication without explanation is obscene.
                                    —TONI CADE BAMBARA

Several years ago an antidepressant hit the market that was heralded as one of the greatest breakthroughs in the treatment of depression. Because the pill had fewer side effects than other antidepressants, many flocked to it, convinced that it would solve all of their problems. Doctors, too, were often impressed by this medication's good press and they doled it out like candy to some people who didn't really need it.

The vast majority of therapists and doctors who dispense medication are reputable and know a great deal about what they prescribe, but there are some who don't take the time to discuss in detail a medication's side effects. For example, some antidepressants relieve mood swings but cause dry mouth, constipation, lowered sexual drive, and weight gain. Others induce lethargy or sleeplessness. Many side effects wear off over time but you must be an educated consumer before making the decision to take a particular drug.

Don't leap for a medication because a friend is doing well on it or you've read about its wonderful effects. Know your body and your options and be prepared to switch medications if the first one doesn't work. The proper antidepressant can make the difference between feeling alive or listless, but you must be cautious when dealing with them and remember to be an active partner with your doctor in monitoring your reactions and progress.

I will be responsible about any medication I take for my emotional health.

Sometimes the greatest adversities turn out to be the greatest blessings.

—CHARLES COLSON

In the early 1970s, Charles Colson was convicted for his role in the Watergate scandal and, as a result, was sent to prison. While there he experienced a conversion to Christianity, and when he was released he turned his new beliefs into a crusade to help others behind bars. In 1993, Colson was awarded the Templeton Prize for Progress in Religion as recognition for his work. "I see now how God has used my life," Colson remarked at the time.

When we're groping in the dark for answers, it's easy to think that we'll never find our way back to the light. But Charles Colson is a good example of someone who was publicly disgraced and who fought depression and hopelessness before finding work that not only redeemed him and his sense of self-worth, but benefited many others as well. Other figures implicated in Watergate found similar ways to overcome their shame and pain; Jeb Magruder became a minister, and the disgraced Richard Nixon retreated for over a decade before reemerging as a respected analyst of world politics.

No matter how depressed you are today, take comfort in the fact that many others who at one time felt the same way learned from their mistakes and managed to rebuild their lives. Tragedies often turn into personal blessings, and although we may be unable to fathom the reasons for our pain now, the future will undoubtedly show us how enriching our experiences were.

My greatest adversity could be my greatest blessing.

Kindness is contagious. . . . One truly affectionate soul in a family will exert a sweetening and harmonizing influence upon all its members.

—HENRY VAN DYKE

Research indicates that moods are "contagious" and that humans tend to mimic the actions and expressions of those they are with. So if you spend time with a depressed person who has a downcast manner, you will probably find yourself doing the same thing, regardless of how you really feel. And being with happy people tends to energize us, even if we're in a bad mood to start with.

Be aware today of the people you choose to be around. If you're the depressed one, it makes sense to try to find people who can help lift your mood. And if you're with another person who's down and you become angry and drained, excuse yourself and give them the space necessary to work out their problems. Carefully selecting who you spend time with and observing their effect on your mood could be one of the easiest ways you can learn to change how you feel.

I will "catch" a good mood from an optimistic, cheerful person today.

One friend in a lifetime is much; two are many; three are hardly possible.

—HENRY ADAMS

When I went through a serious depression I really found out who my friends were. Previously I had thought that I had a huge circle of friends who would lend support in a crisis. What I found, however, was that only a tiny handful of people really cared about how I felt, supported my efforts at change, and visited me despite my protests about being too down to see anyone. By the time I pulled out of my slump, those I chose to call true friends had been whittled down enormously and I had learned some very valuable lessons about how I too could be a better friend.

Sometimes it takes adversity to uncover what is really valuable in life, particularly with regard to friends. If you're suffering from depression, a true friend will go out of her way to help you find solutions, will listen without judgment, and will remind you of how unique and lovely you are. Such friends are rare and to have one or two in a lifetime is to be truly blessed.

If you feel down today because you mistakenly thought you had a large circle of friends to call upon, don't be. Quality is far more important than quantity in this case, and learning who those special people are is one of the valuable insights we can glean from dark times.

I am thankful for my true friends.

A man's sorrow runs uphill; true it is difficult for him to bear,
but it is also difficult for him to keep.

—DJUNA BARNES

There are few things more devastating to a woman
than the death of a child, but the emotional pain caused by
miscarriage isn't always given the same consideration. Miscarriages occur frequently—but it still takes a long time to
recover from the loss. Not only does the mother have to
cope with the passing of her joyous expectation but she
must deal with the mood swings brought on by hormone
changes.

Some women whose miscarriages occur late in the
pregnancy often find it takes a significant amount of time
to readjust their emotions and process their loss. One
friend's fetus died because of genetic complications in her
second trimester, and part of her recovery included talking
with friends who'd had miscarriages and avoiding baby
showers. Another woman who lost her baby during the
sixth month had a private service at her church so that she
could have some emotional closure to the sad event. Yet
another woman had her doctor take pictures of her still-
born child so that when she felt strong enough she'd have
an image of the baby to keep.

If you've experienced the tragedy of miscarriage, recognize that you will need time to recover physically and
emotionally from your loss. Don't expect to jump back into
activities that engaged you before the pregnancy, and give
yourself ample time to adjust emotionally. With time,
friendship, and some rituals to help mark your grief, you'll
eventually emerge from this period intact.

I cannot carry my grief "uphill" forever.

Life is like a game of cards. The hand that is dealt you represents determinism; the way you play it is free will.

—JAWAHARLAL NEHRU

One day I visited a friend in the hospital who had just been diagnosed with cancer. I had expected to find a morose, self-pitying person; instead, my friend was upbeat and determined to make the best of what was ahead of her. "This is the hand I've been dealt, for better or worse," she said. "I'm just going to play it the best I can."

Unfortunate things, over which we have no control, happen to all of us at times. Perhaps we have been born into a family with a history of medical problems, or we've founded a business that went bankrupt because of an ailing economy. Or maybe we've suffered through the problems of infertility or the loss of a loved one. These are all depressing situations that require a period of adjustment and mourning. However, at some point we need to square our shoulders and accept what has befallen us. If we waste time wishing life were different, we'll only prolong the sadness. But if we can pick ourselves up and try to make the best of the situation, we'll always come out ahead.

Instead of being discouraged about the hand you were dealt, try to put energy into finding solutions to what troubles you. Support groups exist for many problems, resources abound for the disadvantaged, and friends are often willing to help when asked. While some unfortunate events are inevitable, how we exert our free will determines the final outcome to our problems.

I will accept the things I cannot change in my life.

To the person in the bell jar, blank and stopped as a dead baby, the world itself is the bad dream.

—SYLVIA PLATH

A large number of people who suffer from depression experience hallucinations and delusions at some point during their illness. One woman to whom this happened says, "It feels so weird to tiptoe around the brink of reality and to *know* that you perceive it differently from other people." She says that when her depression was at its nadir she felt everyone was conspiring against her and that they all wanted to see her hurt or dead.

When depression results in delusions and a feeling of unreality, as it often can with manic or severe postpartum depression, we must put ourselves into the care of a professional. These types of mood disorders will not respond to mild solutions or self-help groups alone; depression depletes the body of many chemicals that we need to regulate our thoughts and behavior, so combining medication and therapy is often the only way to feel sane and happy again.

If you are tormented with thoughts of hurting yourself or others, or your thoughts have become unrealistic and inappropriate, seek medical care immediately. Allowing destructive misperceptions to continue unchecked without consulting a professional to help sort out reality from unreality can only result in you harming yourself and possibly others, when you could be addressing a very treatable problem.

When the world feels like an unending bad dream, I will seek help.

No day is so bad it can't be fixed with a nap.
—CARRIE SNOW

When I was growing up I often heard stories about how famous inventors and other geniuses often took the time for an afternoon nap. Supposedly Albert Einstein "discovered" some of his more important theories during his naps and he often swore by their restorative powers. In countries that are less rushed than America, the afternoon siesta is almost considered a sacred event because stores close and everyone takes a leisurely break, and then later return to their tasks refreshed and more energetic.

Biologically we're programmed to rest in the hours after lunch when energy and alertness levels dip. But in this country where we're always rushing, the nap or restful break is often forgotten and even thought of as selfish. But it's the rare person who doesn't come away from a catnap or a meditation session in better humor and with a better perspective on her problems. In fact, meditation experts aver that two 10-minute sessions can boost brain power and energy, as well as help fight depression and anxiety.

Most of us don't have the luxury of napping, but we usually *can* take the time to find a quiet place and close our eyes for a few minutes. So give yourself a short break today and allow your mind to leave behind its worries and sadness. Although you may not be able to solve your problems by doing this, if you schedule relaxation into your day, you'll reduce the chances of allowing anxiety and fatigue to lead to depression.

I will give my mind and body rejuvenating breaks today.

[H]uman beings are not born once and for all on the day their mothers give birth to them, but . . . life obliges them over and over again to give birth to themselves.
—GABRIEL GARCIA MARQUEZ

One day I said to my therapist in exasperation, "I'm sick of working on myself! When does this get easier?" Unfortunately, for those of us who engage in self-scrutiny and seek improvement in our lives, our task may never be done. Because just as we finish coping with a thorny issue, we're likely to find something else that needs attention.

A close friend of mine expressed the same sentiment to me one day. She lamented that if she wasn't working on her relationship with her mother, she was dealing with being a better parent, trying to be more assertive at work, or addressing her compulsive eating. "I just want to yell, 'Enough!' and take a break," she said, "but I never seem to have time to catch my breath before something else comes up."

If we're committed to being the best we can possibly be, life is going to present us countless opportunities in which we can give birth to ourselves over and over again. While this may be painful and depressing at times, ultimately it is in our best interests to change and evolve. Try to look at all of the issues facing you as opportunities for growth and improvement, not as events to be endured, and you'll find it easier to be grateful for this important birthing process that healthy people engage in regularly.

Being "reborn" is a painful process but is followed by the euphoria of beginning anew.

Retirement revives the sorrow of parting, the feeling of abandonment, solitude and uselessness that is caused by the loss of some beloved person.

—SIMONE DE BEAUVOIR

Although many people look forward to retirement—a time when they will sleep late, pursue hobbies, travel, and have more time for friends and family—leaving a job can be a trigger for depression. Experts say that depression often comes to older people who have had a lifelong predisposition to it, but who don't experience a full-blown episode until their lives change dramatically, Retirement, a serious illness, or the death of a spouse can trigger depression.

People over sixty are more likely to suffer depression than any other age group, including teenagers. However, they are the least likely to seek help or recognize the signs of clinical depression, partly because the elderly still consider depression a sign of weakness. If periods of sadness persist after an event like retirement, it's essential that the person suffering overcome this stigma and get help. For older people, the first step is a physical examination to rule out illness that may be affecting brain chemicals. Once that is done, the elderly benefit from the same treatment as younger adults: antidepressants, exercise, and group support.

If you or someone you know is experiencing depression related to an event like retirement, don't write the sad feelings off as something that will disappear with time. The elderly need support and treatment for depression more than most, so be aware of the events that can trigger the blues and be sure to take action when it's called for.

I will remember that the sorrow of parting can be followed by joyous beginnings.

The man that lays his hand on woman,
Save in the way of kindness, is a wretch
Whom 'twere gross flattery to name a coward.

—JOHN TOBIN

Anne is a thirty-nine-year-old mother of three who has an abusive relationship with her boyfriend. When he drinks he usually loses his temper and becomes irrational, punching and screaming at Anne until one of the children intervenes, at which point he turns on them. Although Anne has demanded her boyfriend move out a number of times, she has also taken him back repeatedly, broken down by his abject apologies and promises to change. Inevitably, however, the abuse reoccurs and Anne gets depressed about her inability to break away from someone so cruel.

A lot of women put up with abusive relationships for a variety of reasons. Some have known abuse all their lives and thus come to accept it as inevitable. Some feel like they will not have enough money to support themselves without the abuser's financial help. Some are comfortable with the chaos that accompanies violence and is sometimes followed by passionate sex. And all suffer from low self-esteem that tells them they don't deserve better.

If you are depressed because you're enmeshed in an abusive situation, take steps to get out. There are many shelters that offer assistance and counseling, and therapy can empower women to learn that any type of abuse is undeserved and inappropriate. Once you can recognize that you deserve love and respect from others, it will be easier to learn how to give that to yourself, as well.

Any man who touches me without gentleness does not deserve my presence or love.

Suicide is a permanent solution to a temporary problem.
—PHIL DONAHUE

A few years ago, in my hometown, two top government officials committed suicide within six months of each other. In both cases the men had been depressed for a long time and their behavior had concerned those around them. The tragedy, however, was that neither one was aggressive about getting professional help because they feared their actions would look "weak" and "shameful." Consequently they avoided taking medication that could have stabilized their moods and helped them see that their problems were just temporary events that could be solved.

Most people who commit suicide suffer from some form of depression, with alcohol and a chronic medical illness often exacerbating the situation. Experts say that a major disappointment in one's life—like a divorce, losing a job, or being implicated in a scandal—can act as a trigger sending them into a spiral of hopelessness. Perfectionists especially lose sight of potential solutions because of rigid thinking.

If you are considering suicide, you must seek professional help. It usually takes a confluence of factors—a family history of depression, a major event, or a problem with alcohol—to bring about a suicide, but any one of these could be the straw that breaks the camel's back. Don't delay in getting the support you need regardless of how you think it will look to others because, while suicide may seem preferable now, it is an extreme response to a solvable problem.

Depression is never permanent.

*Do not let Sunday be taken from you. . . . If your soul has
no Sunday, it has become an orphan.*
                                          —ALBERT SCHWEITZER

Carl Jung once said that every person over the age of
thirty who was in crisis was having a spiritual crisis. What
he meant by this is that once you reach a certain maturity
you begin to wonder about your place in the world and
about humanity in general. What was I sent here to accomplish? How can I be a better person? Why is there so much
suffering in the world?

To weather the storms that we undergo and to develop
a perspective on the vicissitudes of life require some sort of
spiritual grounding: a strong sense of right and wrong, a
belief in a power greater than ourselves, and the fulfillment
that comes from active efforts to help those in need.

The spirituality we need when we're depressed doesn't
necessarily come from weekly church attendance, but for
many people a quiet hour on Sunday devoted to introspec-
tion and worship is restorative. If organized religion isn't
for you, try to create "Sunday" moments throughout the
week to read spiritual literature, give of your time, meditate, and pray. There isn't a "right" way to foster spirituality, but if you make no effort at having a rich and
empowering inner life, you will indeed have an "orphan"
for a soul.

I will have some "Sunday" in my day today.

Worries go down better with soup than without.
—JEWISH PROVERB

One of the biggest temptations when we're depressed is to eat. Unfortunately we don't always want to eat things that are nourishing and healthful; we tend to veer toward things that don't benefit us, such as chips, sweets, and sodas because either they provide a temporary lift or they soothe us. But when we're depressed, it's more important than ever to pay attention to what we eat and make sure that we take in foods that strengthen, not weaken, us.

Research has shown that the old wives' tale about eating chicken soup when we're ill may have some merit to it. Chicken broth has some infection-fighting properties that are helpful in times of stress when our bodies need nourishing input. Other foods that provide steady surges of energy include low-fat proteins, grains, fruits, and vegetables. If we reach for coffee, pastries, and french fries, we'll not only feel depleted and tired, we'll also pack on a few extra pounds.

Be prudent today about what you eat while depressed or under stress. What goes into your body plays a big part in how you feel and react to situations, and how well you sleep at night. If you treat your body like the important vessel it is, it won't turn on you when you most need it to perform.

I will take in foods that are good for me today.

If depression is creeping up and must be faced, learn something about the nature of the beast: You may escape without a mauling.

—R. W. SHEPHERD

Linda looked forward to the birth of her first child with great anticipation and joy. After an uncomplicated delivery of a beautiful little boy, however, Linda was hit with a crippling depression that lasted over a year. She inexplicably wanted to hurt herself and her child, and she suffered from such bad mood swings that she was afraid to be alone with her baby. Although her depression gradually lifted, Linda feels she was emotionally absent during her son's first few years.

When Linda got pregnant again, she crossed her fingers and hoped that her depression had been a one-time thing. Unfortunately, her sadness and mood swings returned when her daughter was born and only through her husband's intervention did she finally seek help and get the treatment she needed.

Learning as much as we can about depression—particularly if we are vulnerable to it or notice it manifesting in our lives—is a smart act of self-preservation. Understanding the nature of this beast and not being afraid to confront it significantly reduces our chances of being beaten by it and increases the likelihood of finding solutions that will return us to a level of normal functioning.

I will fearlessly face the "beast" of depression.

Just remember enough never to be vulnerable again: total for-getting could be as self-destructive as complete remembering.
—HELEN MACINNES

There is a growing area in psychology called "past life therapy" that specializes in helping people with addictions, phobias, depression, and other ailments find out if the problem is related to a past-life event. Many have report-edly found that relaxing, exploring memories of a previous existence, and then reliving its unrelieved traumas can be a powerful tool for healing themselves.

I once met an older woman with chronic liver prob-lems who didn't respond to medical treatment. One day she prayed tearfully for an answer to her pain when she suddenly saw in her mind a picture of a medieval Crusader lying dead on a battlefield with a spear through his abdo-men. She realized that she had once been that man, and as a result, she never experienced a recurrence of liver trou-bles again. Another woman said that an unhealthy addic-tion to a man who was abusive to her had been cured when she discovered through past-life therapy that she'd been involved with him in numerous past lives. This realization helped her see that while there might always be a pull toward this man, she didn't necessarily have to act on it.

Therapists say that even those who do not believe in the concept of reincarnation can still be helped with past-life therapy. If we can allow ourselves to be open to uncon-ventional treatment and use our imagination to assist in finding solutions to our problems, we increase the chances of attaining peace and happiness.

I will not impose narrow limits on what can heal me.

Anger is a signal, and one worth listening to.
                                    —HARRIET G. LERNER

Depression does not always express itself with weepy, self-pitying behavior. One of the ways depression masks itself is in anger—toward people, institutions, and ourselves. Sometimes this anger stems from childhood victimization, sometimes it is because of professional discrimination, and sometimes it is the result of feeling old in a youth-oriented society. Whatever its roots, anger needs to be confronted and addressed before depression can be conquered.

One of the most popular ways counselors help depressed people cope with their feelings of rage is through art therapy. For example, women who have been sexually abused are encouraged to draw pictures of how they view themselves and their attackers. Pictures of the victimizers are often burned, stomped on, or cut up so that there is a symbolic destruction of the source of the pain. Several female friends have found this therapy so illuminating and healing that drawing has become a wonderful outlet for their energy.

Is your depression taking the form of anger, either toward others or toward yourself? Try to visualize the source of your anger and draw it in the colors and shapes it takes in your mind. Don't worry about creating the perfect picture; the goal of art therapy is to vent your emotions safely and in a way that allows you to see your pain in a new way. By using such therapeutic methods to express emotion without fear of retaliation, you are one step closer to lifting the cloud of depression from your life.

I will draw my feelings today.

I'm not going to "should" on myself today.

—ANONYMOUS

One day a friend was lamenting that she was a bad mother because she had her two daughters in preschool for a few hours twice a week. She felt that instead of sending them to school she "should" be watching them herself rather than working at a business she loved and was good at. I pointed out that most mothers in her position sent their children to full-time day-care and that she was doing a Herculean job in accomplishing as much as she was. That didn't seem to matter to her; my friend was obsessed with what she thought she "should" be doing and nothing would change her mind.

I had a bad case of the shoulds myself several years ago. I wanted to nurse my son for a long time but a hectic traveling situation forced me to wean him earlier than I wanted to. Although I had little choice in the matter, I beat myself up regularly, comparing myself to my nonworking friends who were nursing for a year or longer and who often made comments like, "Breastfed babies are smarter than bottle-fed babies." It was only after the passage of several years and seeing that I had a bright, happy, and well-adjusted son that I started to let up on myself.

Be kind to yourself today and don't have unrealistic expectations about what you think you "should" be doing. Just doing the best you can and refusing to nurse regrets is the smartest and healthiest thing you can do for yourself.

I will eliminate the word should *from my vocabulary today.*

[Your body is] the harp of your soul.

                                          —KAHLIL GIBRAN

A depressed woman usually carries herself in a certain way: Her eyes are downcast, her shoulders are slumped, her walk is not purposeful, and her body communicates a feeling of fatigue. Friends and acquaintances don't even have to ask how she is feeling because her entire demeanor gives away the negative answer.

Sometimes learning how to carry ourselves with more authority and confidence is helpful in beating depression and stress. A California personal trainer says that when she teaches clients how to walk properly, they often feel better physically as well as emotionally. She instructs them to stand in front of a mirror and imagine the big toe anchored to the ground so that weight is slightly forward. Then move up the legs, bend the knee, and tighten the buttocks. Next, pull in the stomach toward the spine, lengthen the torso by lifting the rib cage, and press the shoulders down and back. Finally, imagine a rod running through your spine and a string holding your head high.

Assertive, confident people hold themselves upright in a way that conveys optimism and a can-do attitude, so if we can learn to carry ourselves this way and to imagine ourselves as winners, we may be able to empower ourselves to change not just our bodies, but also the way we approach life.

I will walk with pride today.

In families there are frequently matters of which no one speaks, nor even alludes.

—Joyce Carol Oates

One of the most important things we must do during a depression is to investigate our genetic heritage to determine if we suffer from a biologically inherited disease. Unfortunately this isn't as easy as it might seem. Depression wasn't always identified as such by previous generations—partly because of the stigma—and when a family member was treated for depression, it was often hushed up.

A therapist who specializes in treating depressed women advises her clients to research their history with tact and resourcefulness. Some of the questions to ask relatives include finding out if a person was known as being "self-absorbed," having a "nervous condition," suffering from frequent "accidents," or being addicted to drugs or alcohol. If there is a history of suicides or mood swings, those need to be noted, as well. A genetic counselor can also be useful in locating death certificates and identifying patterns in a family.

Take a hard look at your family today and analyze whether you may have inherited a tendency toward depression. Studies show that some types of depression do get passed along genetically, and being armed with that knowledge can not only help find an effective course of treatment, but it can assist in laying a plan of action to help future generations, as well.

I will be a sleuth about my emotional heritage today.

I write to find out what I'm thinking, what I'm looking at, what I see and what it means. What I want and what I fear.
—JOAN DIDION

When Abraham Lincoln lost a major battle during the Civil War, he sat down and wrote a scathing letter to the general whose blundering had cost the Union many lives and much land. Although the letter was well worded and accurate in its details, he deliberately never sent it. A recent former First Lady admitted that she used this same technique whenever she was angry with one of her husband's adversaries; she composed angry missives but then burned them, feeling better that she had vented her spleen without doing any lasting damage.

Writing is well known as a way to process our feelings without hurting anyone else. Researchers say that spilling our emotions onto paper in letter form can not only purge ourselves of hate, but it has been shown to improve people's emotional and physical health. Some people also like having a computer dialogue with their sadness and frustration; they pose questions to their inner feelings in small letters and then allow their emotions to respond in capital letters.

Don't keep your feelings bottled up inside today. If you're angry or depressed, write about it. If a specific person is upsetting you, compose a letter but don't send it. Also, try to store your daily thoughts in a journal or a safe computer file. While this exercise may seem time-consuming and silly at first, over time you'll discover that it is one of the cheapest and best forms of therapy around.

I will write to find out what I'm thinking today.

Being popular is important. Otherwise people might not like you.

—MIMI POND

All of us at one time or another go through a stage in life when we wrestle with whether we're popular or not. In high school, popularity is usually based on having the right looks, clothes, or boyfriend. As we get older, though, popularity is often dependent on other things that don't have anything to do with external trappings, and if we learn the necessary skills, we can enjoy the happiness that comes with being sought after and well liked by friends and family members.

In the classic book "How to Win Friends and Influence People," the authors outlined some excellent time-tested principles for making more friends and becoming more outgoing and self-confident. One is to be interested in other people; if you're always droning on about yourself and your problems, no one will want to be around you. Also, compliment others; no one likes false flattery, but a genuine thoughtful remark is always appreciated. Also, smile! The person who is always smiling will attract others like bees to honey.

It's never too late for us to brush up on our personality skills. If we can get along better with our fellow man, we'll undoubtedly feel less depressed and more confident about ourselves. Above all, learning to be a good friend means that when we're down and in need of support, we'll have friendships that can sustain us and provide the solace necessary to get back on our feet again.

I'll always have friends when I'm a good friend to others.

The sight or sound of perfect things causes a certain torment.
                                    —ADRIENNE MONNIER

One day I was listening to a panel of models talking about their lives and how "misunderstood" they were. "Women hate me," one model moaned, commenting on how hard it was to enter a party and not have women glaring at her in envy. Another chimed in that it was impossible for her to have women friends unless they were very secure or very accomplished in some area of their lives, and therefore not threatened by their attractive, attention-getting friends.

It's a rare female who isn't jealous of a beautiful woman because her seeming perfection highlights our own insecurities about our looks and body. In fact, seeing anything "perfect" can cause us to feel terrible about certain areas of our lives if we use perfection as a yardstick by which to measure our happiness. So if a friend makes a huge salary and can afford certain luxuries, we may deem her life "perfect" and become depressed because ours doesn't measure up. Or we might see someone else's gorgeous house, beautiful clothes, or wonderful husband and be down that our own lives pale in comparison.

Try not to let the "perfection" in someone else's life get you down today. Not only is comparison odious and unproductive, but it also doesn't take into account that what looks great on the outside isn't always happy on the inside. Remember also today that even if you and your life aren't flawless, you too have special qualities and traits that others admire.

I will remember that all that glitters is not gold.

I am worn to a raveling.

—BEATRIX POTTER

Family experts say that with the increase in two-income households and the decrease in the amount of time parents spend with their children, a new phenomenon has been observed that is often mistaken for depression: parent burnout. Up to 50 percent of all parents suffer from burnout—regardless of income level or the number of children—and it is an inevitable condition if Mom and Dad have too much to do, too little time, and too little support.

Some of the signs that parenthood is taking too steep a toll include focusing on your children to the exclusion of yourself, frequently being sick, disliking or abusing your children, drinking alcohol or taking drugs to control your temper, and dreading weekends. To counter these tendencies, experts advise learning to accept the negative feelings about your children, taking time to pray or reflect, not expecting all weeknights to be "quality time," and taking regular, short trips with your family. They stress that ignoring burnout or pretending that it doesn't exist only leads to depression and chronic self-destructive behavior.

Burnout is not just a problem for parents; it is a problem for any woman who does too much and has lost enthusiasm for her life. Try the suggestions above to counter this condition and remember that if the excessive stress causes you to reevaluate and change your life, it has served a useful purpose.

I will address burnout in any area of my life today.

. . . [W]e could never learn to be brave and patient if there were only joy in the world.

—HELEN KELLER

Whenever we look at all of the horrendous things going on in the world, it's hard not to wonder how a loving God could allow them to happen. It's easy to come to the conclusion that there is no Supreme Being and that the world is out of control. If we observe closely, however, we can usually find positive things that result from tragedies—even if they're not headlined in the news. For example, I've noticed that food shortages usually result in offers of help from those who have food resources, abused children often receive offers of adoption, and random cruelty can result in remarkable compassion from Good Samaritans.

Whenever the sadness of the world feels overwhelming, try to notice the good that can come from it—and even challenge yourself to be one of those who gives love or assistance to those in need. Not only will you feel less enervated whenever you hear about tragedy, but you'll lift your spirits by giving unselfishly of yourself.

I will see the positive side of suffering today.

All women become like their mothers. That is their tragedy. No man does. That's his.

—OSCAR WILDE

One of the quickest ways to start an argument in a marriage is for the man to say to his wife, "You're just like your mother!" or for the woman to say to her husband, "You're just like your father!" These are emotionally laden phrases that shouldn't be thrown around lightly because of their capacity to evoke strong feelings on both sides.

It's true that as we get older and have children, many of us will begin to mimic our mothers' actions and attitudes —unconsciously or not. Some of these may be positive behaviors; for example, we may be generous volunteers in the community, attentive and caring parents, or capable businesswomen. We may also, however, take on traits that depress us, such as nitpicking, competing with our children, or ceasing to take care of our bodies. It's when we begin to adopt the parts of our mothers that are detrimental to our happiness that we need to sit up, take notice, and do something constructive to change ourselves.

Be mindful of both the positive and negative qualities you have inherited from your mother and make a conscious decision to work on the ones that are self-destructive. While mothers give life and a framework with which to see the world, happiness resides in being able to separate from your mother and use her as a role model to help create a persona that will serve you well.

I appreciate the good traits I learned from my mother.

Certain signs precede certain events.

—CICERO

Quite often when devastating things happen to us we say that we never saw it coming or that we were totally taken by surprise. Sometimes this is true, but I've learned through experience that more often than not we are given plenty of warning about such an event.

One friend of mine whose engagement was broken spent two years recovering from the pain of rejection. She wishes now that she'd paid more attention to her fiancé's mood swings and the cold phrases in his letters because in hindsight they were clear indications that he no longer loved her. Another friend of mine has dreams of destruction before people close to her die, so whenever they start she knows to prepare herself for a shock.

Are you depressed about something today that you could have prepared yourself better to handle? Were there any clues you ignored that may have indicated that a relationship was about to end, a job would be terminated, or you would be disappointed in some other way? Were there signs you were becoming depressed that you chose not to notice? One way we can protect ourselves from suffering emotional devastation is if we have a "heads up" attitude about what we're experiencing and we're observant of the people and situations in our lives. Learning what signs precede upsetting events can give us time to prepare ourselves and help ensure that our emotional health remains intact.

When I pay attention to the subtleties in life, I am given clearer vision.

One can never consent to creep when one feels an impulse to soar.

—HELEN KELLER

Heidi at one time aspired to be a professional opera singer. But marriage and children intervened and her desires were put on the back burner for "the good" of the family. Heidi often became distracted and moody whenever she read about well-known singers, and she increasingly resented her family and the choices she'd made to accommodate them.

At a therapist's urging Heidi decided to try out for a local theater production, and when she was accepted a light went on in her life. Once her passion for singing was stoked —albeit on a smaller scale than she'd once imagined— Heidi found new reserves of love and energy for herself, and instead of being jealous of other accomplished singers, she came to appreciate their talents more readily and is less likely to become depressed by their success.

Are you down because you're creeping through life when you really want to soar? All of us have something that brings us bliss and makes us feel special, and once we can find ways to unleash that passion and become fulfilled, we'll always have a source of happiness right at hand.

I will find a way to soar today.

We cannot direct the wind, but we can adjust the sails.
—ANONYMOUS

One of the well-known definitions of serenity is being able to accept the things we cannot change. Although this may sound easy, it's not. All too often we see something that is unchanging and inflexible—like an overbearing boss, an alcoholic parent, or a colleague that hates us—and we assume that if we just tried harder, the immovable object would move to our satisfaction and we could achieve peace of mind.

Grace has the omnipresent in-law problem that is so common to women. Although she has been a thoughtful and respectful daughter-in-law for many years, her husband's family continues to resent her religious affiliation. After ingratiating herself but finding them unreceptive to her overtures, Grace has changed her tactics. Instead of becoming depressed by their rejection, she has decided to "adjust her sails" and accept the fact that she'll probably never be friends with her in-laws. Now their visits don't depress her because Grace has no expectations and thus cannot feel disappointed by their behavior.

Is there a situation that is depressing you because you feel that no matter how hard you try, nothing's ever going to change? If so, analyze whether you might be better off "adjusting" your sails instead of trying to direct the wind. Once you have the wisdom to know where to put your energies and where to call a truce, the less likely you will be to create situations that lead to depression.

I will adjust my sails when it's to my benefit.

A request not to worry . . . is perhaps the least soothing message capable of human utterance.

—MIGNON G. EBERHART

Six months after my daughter was born I was stricken with anxiety attacks that were so debilitating that I stopped sleeping through the night. As I dragged myself through the days on little or no sleep, I became increasingly depressed about what was happening to me. Others who had never had a moment's trouble sleeping urged me not to worry so much or to just "take it easy" for a few days. But anxiety attacks cannot be managed by "not worrying" or simply going to bed; often there are complex medical and psychological factors that need to be examined.

Fortunately, through a combination of appropriate medication, brief hospitalization, and a reorganization of some of the stressors in my life, I returned to health within a few weeks. But I'll never forget how frightened I was when something I took for granted—a good night's sleep—was taken from me so quickly and without warning. When this type of thing happens, feelings of powerlessness and depression can spiral out of control, and unless quick treatment is sought, panic attacks can become lifelong, chronic illnesses.

If you are suffering from anxiety attacks that are depressing you, seek appropriate medical and psychological care immediately and forget well-meaning admonitions "not to worry." Until you understand the ways that these occurrences can be controlled and prevented, they will rule your life and deplete your capacity for happiness, spontaneity, and optimism.

I will not allow anxiety to cripple and depress me.

*Surround of rainbows / Listen / The rain comes upon us /
Restore us.*

—MERIDEL LE SUEUR

There is a woman in California who has become one
of the most carefully watched people because whenever she
experiences a migraine headache there is sure to be an
earthquake happening somewhere in the state. Although
this may sound strange, quite a few people are extremely
sensitive in this way and for them the weather forecast is an
accurate barometer of how they will feel emotionally that
day.

Research has shown that the air preceding a big light-
ning storm is loaded with positive ions, which cause surgi-
cal complications, slower reaction time, industrial and road
accidents, and mood swings. Dry winds, also known as "ill
winds," which afflict various parts of the world, are loaded
with positive ions that cause greater amounts of depression, irritability, and headaches. On the other hand, negative ions—which are released by sunlight shining through
clean air and by heavy rainshowers or waterfalls—produce
lower blood pressure, greater productivity, and feelings of
exhilaration.

Does the weather seem to govern your moods? Keep a
journal of how storms, cold and warm fronts, or air pollu-
tion alerts (high in positive ions) affect your well-being.
And whether you think the weather affects you or not,
keep in mind that any water—the seashore, a fountain, or a
shower—is rich in negative ions that induce sensations of
satisfaction and happiness.

*I will try to arrange my environment so that it positively en-
hances my mood.*

I was raised to believe that you need to have a man to identify who you are. I don't feel that way anymore. I'm glad I have a man, because I love him and I would feel lonely without him in my life. But he doesn't validate me to myself.

—SALLY FIELD

One day I was watching a show about "kept women" who lived their entire lives to please the men who took care of their every need. Although each of the women interviewed seemed intelligent and capable, they all spoke of feeling worthless without the attention and companionship of men.

Too often we women make the mistake of thinking that if we aren't dating someone or aren't married, we have failed in defining who we are. However, buying into this traditional notion of femininity can be very damaging; studies have shown that if a woman marries and has children because she believes this is the only way she'll ever be validated, the greater her chances of suffering from depression are.

If you're defining your worth based on whether or not you're in a relationship with a man, you're selling yourself short. We women are fascinating, complex, and important people in our own right, but the only way to know this is by pursuing activities that interest, empower, and absorb us. Try to make sure that today and every day contains periods in which you validate yourself by doing what you want to do, and not what anyone else *thinks* you should do, because living according to others' expectations is a sure recipe for misery.

I am a complete and worthwhile person regardless of whether I have a significant other.

Joy makes you open and light. Joy counteracts the pull of gravity. Joy can be real loud and a little primitive.
—VERENA KAST

One day the author of the above quote was working as a grief counselor when she noticed the healing and strengthening power of joy. "My client was grieving about the loss of her husband when she suddenly recalled some happy memories and burst into a smile. I saw then that joy was very much an emotion of remembering," she said, "and that flashes of joy could blaze through even the deepest blues."

Some of us may feel that joy should be confined to holiday seasons, and that displaying it at other times is inappropriate, and even a bit risky. But some psychologists believe that expressing joy helps people to feel hopeful, which in turn helps to combat depression. And the more joy we can call forth into our lives, the stronger will be our emotional foundation.

To get back in touch with your inner joy, do a "joy biography." Think about your childhood and identify moments of exhilaration. Ask yourself what has given you joy and who you were with at that time. Recall and recreate a movement you loved as a child, such as spinning around as fast as possible or skipping stones in a lake. If you can train yourself to reclaim joy from your childhood vault, you'll more easily recognize the joy that surrounds you today.

I will reconnect with some childhood joy today.

Loneliness seems to have become the great American disease.
—JOHN CORRY

In this modern world it's very easy to become isolated and lonely in the course of our days. It's normal to work out with headphones on, to drive to work alone, to eat lunch with a book, and to return to an empty apartment where television is our main companion. The more we are isolated from the needs and concerns of others, the more we are free to focus on ourselves and to feel as if the world is an uncaring and cold place.

Loneliness feeds on itself and the more we sink into it, the harder it is to fight our way out. One solution is to pick an isolated time and deliberately reach out. That might mean jogging with someone instead of with a radio, or of carpooling instead of driving alone. One very lonely person I know decided to combat her isolation by vacationing with groups of people rather than by herself. The friends she has made this way have made a real difference in her attitude toward life.

Being alone is not a natural condition because humans are social creatures. Fight your depression and loneliness today by being a friend or companion to someone else or by making a phone call or visiting someone who needs a lift. Inevitably you'll find that the more you reach out to others in ways you'd like to be included, the less likely you'll be to catch "the great American disease."

I will make an effort to include people in my daily life.

We are able to laugh when we achieve detachment, if only for a moment.

—MAY SARTON

Sometimes when we are depressed it's because of a situation over which we have no control. This is frequently the case when a loved one is engaging in self-destructive behavior, such as drug-taking or alcoholism, and nothing we've said or done has been effective in helping them treat their addiction.

Jeanne became very depressed after a planned intervention on her alcoholic father was unsuccessful. After listening to a roomful of family, friends, and work colleagues express how his drinking had adversely affected them, Jeanne's father thanked the group for coming and said he didn't think he was alcoholic; he just liked to "have a good time" occasionally. "My heart felt like it was breaking when he stood up and walked out," Jeanne says, adding that the most effective antidote to her sadness has been attending support groups where she can gain strength from others who have been through a similar situation.

When we're overwhelmed with depression because of a loved one's self-destructive actions, it's probably time to detach ourselves from the situation and work on taking care of ourself instead. Trying to fix someone who doesn't want to be fixed can only drain and dispirit us, and even drive the person farther away from us. If we can pull back and learn healthy ways to cope with someone else's negative behavior, there's a chance that our actions may have a more positive effect than any of our well-meaning attempts to help.

Detachment can ease my depression.

I long to accomplish a great and noble task, but it is my chief duty to accomplish small tasks as if they were great and noble.
—HELEN KELLER

A lot of my friends entered a personal slump around the age of thirty. Many began to feel as if they were in the wrong profession or in the wrong relationship and that life was passing them by so quickly that they'd never achieve the goals they'd set for themselves. Around this time they also came to grips with the painful realization that they might have to scale back some of their youthful expectations and settle for less professional success than they had originally hoped for.

All of us will probably go through a period when we realize that we probably won't win the Nobel Prize—or even the local school board election—because our talents lie elsewhere. The challenge is to accept that fame and fortune may not necessarily come to us but that our lives can still be meaningful and rewarding. Therapists say that people who go about their daily activities—both the mundane and the important ones—with reverence and complete attention are far happier than people who are always wishing that they were doing something else.

If you believe that happiness will only come from doing work that brings acclaim and attention, try to redirect your focus. Being a good neighbor, mentoring a colleague at work, or staying home to raise your children may not always feel like the most noteworthy tasks in the world, but by assigning importance to your performance, you can create much joy for yourself.

Every task of my day is great and noble.

I like living. I have sometimes been wildly, despairingly, acutely miserable, racked with sorrow, but through it all I still know quite certainly that just to be alive is a grand thing.
—AGATHA CHRISTIE

There is always something happening to Janet that keeps her blood pumping and her emotions at a feverish pitch. Either she's feuding with a friend, tending an injury, mediating a quarrel between her parents, or coping with a career crisis. Although she says these events depress her, I suspect that this type of chaos makes Janet feel most alive and vital. It also ensures that she'll always have some attention-getting drama in her life.

Experiencing depression can be a double-edged sword. While it can render us "acutely miserable," it can also be the only way we feel engaged in life. My friend Linda recognizes this tendency in herself and has to strive to find enjoyment in the peaceful lulls of her life. "Whenever things were going well for me, I'd go to a bar and pick up some loser, guaranteeing that my emotions would go on a roller-coaster for a few weeks," she says. Now Linda finds safer ways to create passion and drama in her life, mostly through her artwork.

Take stock of your patterns today. Is there always some type of drama going on in your life? Is it possible that you are creating chaos in order to feel alive? If so, acknowledge this tendency and think of other ways you can experience excitement. While periodic bouts with the blues *can* leave us grateful to be alive, it's unhealthy for us to invite them into our lives.

I will not create my own blues.

Beware of allowing a tactless word, a rebuttal, a rejection to obliterate the whole sky.

—ANAIS NIN

There are times in my life when my attitude is such that no matter how well things are going, I allow the tiniest criticism or negative event to ruin my day. For example, if I give a speech and ninety-nine people tell me it's great but one person tells me it wasn't, I obsess about the dissatisfied one person and make myself completely miserable.

It takes strong self-esteem and a good perspective on life to allow negative comments to roll off our backs. I've learned this skill by constantly reminding myself that criticism often contains a kernel of truth that can help me. And one friend of mine inwardly repeats, "I'm not a gold coin so not everyone is going to love me," whenever she encounters people or situations that are negative or off-putting.

Try not to allow someone else's tactlessness or rude behavior ruin your day. Concentrate on the sunshine in your life and affirm it often so that any clouds that roll in won't obscure your happiness and block your clear vision.

I won't let anyone else's behavior affect my happiness.

The great secret of doctors, known only to their wives, but still hidden from the public, is that most things get better by themselves; most things, in fact, are better in the morning.
—LEWIS THOMAS

In the well-known book "Gone with the Wind," the heroine, Scarlett O'Hara, is a famous procrastinator. No matter what the dilemma her response is always, "I'll worry about it tomorrow." To her way of thinking, the following morning always brings a fresh mind, a different perspective, and new solutions to her problems.

We go through few things that aren't more manageable after a night's sleep. I saw this evidenced on television one day while watching the reactions of a town's residents who had lost their homes and businesses to a hurricane. The first day they had all been in shock, crying about how they'd lost everything and despairing of ever getting back on their feet. The following day they were still depressed but had mustered the energy to start fighting back. Instead of focusing on their losses they were wielding chainsaws to clear fallen trees, pooling their resources, and vowing they'd survive.

If there's something you can put off until tomorrow that's bothering you today, do it. Troubles that look overwhelming today could be manageable tomorrow, and chances are you'll have more energy and creativity after a good night's sleep. But don't confuse putting something off with refusing to deal with it at all; a little procrastination may save your sanity, but denying a problem exists only ensures that it will return some other time.

When I sleep on my problems, they often improve.

Hunting God is a great adventure.

—MARIE DE FLORIS

I once read a story about a now-famous authority on love and spirituality who said that a nervous breakdown in her twenties was one of the best things that had ever happened to her because she had been forced to discover a faith to sustain her. Through reading books, seeking out the opinions of others, and following her instincts, she developed beliefs that have now helped millions in similar straits.

Troubled times are often the catalyst for us to turn inward and redefine our belief in God. One friend of mine rediscovered his childhood love of God after alcoholism made a shambles of his life and he turned back to the Catholic church for comfort. Another friend has spent years examining and researching her faith in an effort to understand why so many women in her family have developed breast cancer. Her intense self-scrutiny has led her to many joyous awakenings and has given her a renewed sense of peace and zeal for life.

Try to use your depression as a marvelous opportunity to explore your place in the universe and discover what your feelings about God are. "Hunting God" can provide a worthwhile goal when life seems purposeless, and what you discover can not only provide the strength to withstand difficult times, it can imbue you with a better sense of perspective on your life.

When I hunt God I find something greater than myself.

The most powerful ties are the ones to the people who gave us birth . . . it hardly seems to matter how many years have passed, how many betrayals there may have been, how much misery in the family: We remain connected, even against our wills.

—ANTHONY BRANDT

Gloria is part of a large Italian family that gathers periodically to celebrate birthdays, anniversaries, and holidays. The family is very dysfunctional—the father physically abused his children and the mother was emotionally absent and pill-addicted—so every gathering is fraught with conflict and unresolved issues. As upsetting as every visit is, Gloria continues to travel across the country on a regular basis because she feels she wouldn't be a "good" daughter if she didn't.

Breaking the emotional ties with dysfunctional parents is tough, but if our parents have caused us misery and we don't acknowledge or process it in therapy, we'll strive to get their approval and then becoming depressed when we don't receive the nurturing we seek. One prominent therapist says that until we can view our parents with detachment, acceptance, and unconditional love, we will never have satisfaction or happiness as adults.

Be aware of the dynamics between you and your parents today. If visiting them and interacting with them causes you to experience depression, seek out a therapist who will help you cope with your emotions. Parental ties are potent, so deal with them before you recreate an unhealthy version with your own family.

I will be conscious of the emotions—both good and bad—that my parents evoke in me.

The road to Hell is paved with good intentions.

—SAMUEL JOHNSON

Years ago, during the height of my eating disorder, I was almost always depressed because I could never follow through on my good intentions. For example, if I woke up and vowed to follow a careful diet, I usually cheated. And when I promised myself I would try to get help, I wouldn't. This chronic inability to be good on my word with myself and others bothered me and contributed to my low self-esteem.

We'll never feel good about ourselves if we always intend to do something but don't do it. One area where this often happens is at our jobs, where we want to advance in our careers, but become bashful when it comes to promoting ourselves. Or we may frequently tell people we'll call them or invite them over, but we don't. The more we promise and don't deliver on large and small items, the harder it is for us to have feelings of self-worth and happiness.

Talkers are a dime a dozen; achievers are rarer. Do something today that you've been intending to do but have never found the time or courage to do. If you can cross just one thing off your to-do list and take action to address something that's been bothering you, you'll earn not only the respect of others, but also self-respect and some assurance that you won't wind up in the "Hell" of good intentions.

Today I will walk the walk, not just talk the talk.

I consulted the moon
like a crystal ball.

—DIANE ACKERMAN

One January morning I was vacationing at my parents' beach house when a brutal nor'easter whipped up the coastline and sent waters slicing through the town, destroying houses, the boardwalk, and countless motels, restaurants, and stores. The major culprit in making the storm so devastating was a total lunar eclipse. Because of the moon's effect on the tides, what might have been just a bad storm turned into one of the worst devastations I'd seen in my thirty years of visiting this seaside town.

Although the moon's effect on water is well known, it's less well known that the moon has a documented effect on humans, too. It's been said that full moons bring about more homicides and crimes of passion than partial moons, and women are more likely to go into labor on full moons. Some women even find their menstrual cycles are synchronized according to the moon's phases and that their emotions are at a frenzied peak around eclipses, full moons, and other major lunar events.

You don't have to be an astrology devotee to understand that the moon governs the gravitational pull of the tides and the fluids in our bodies. Try to chart your moods and see if the moon's phases are connected with changes in your emotions. If they are, you have another powerful tool to help you understand those periods of disorientation and sadness.

I will consult the moon today.

Turn your face to the sun and the shadows fall behind you.
—MAORI PROVERB

Millions of women begin to suffer each fall from a depression that has been shown to be linked to a lack of sunlight. Called seasonal affective disorder (SAD), it produces lethargy, irritability, carbohydrate cravings, and rapid mood swings. For those who suffer from SAD, often the only effective remedy is the onset of spring. Almost magically, they report feeling happier, more energetic, and less addicted to sugary foods as the days get longer.

Although there is a wealth of data indicating that too much sun can result in serious physical problems, a dose of sunshine is still one of the best things we can do for ourselves. Not only can it lift our moods—even if we don't have SAD—but it can give us a respite from our cares, provide us with a bit of color in our cheeks, and help us to assimilate important vitamins. Combining sun with a bit of exercise can also lead to an improved mood, providing us with a sense of purpose as well as more energy.

If you have the blues every year starting in the fall, it might be wise to find out if you suffer from SAD. Treatment could be as simple as light therapy or a trip to a sunny climate during the cold dark months. And if you are plagued with binging during this period, support groups and medication in some cases can also be very effective. Treatable conditions like SAD are only problems when we fail to educate ourselves about the many solutions available and we allow our situation to fester.

Sunshine can be an effective antidote to my inner darkness.

The life which is unexamined is not worth living.

—PLATO

I have two friends who were once in despair over their financial situations. Both had spent lavishly on themselves by overextending their credit cards and never being able to say no to a sale or "bargain." By the time they realized what they had done, both were tens of thousands of dollars in debt and had lost the respect of family and friends. They sank into depression and panicked over what they could do to fix their problems.

The first person chose to declare personal bankruptcy, thus absolving herself of all debts—and her depression. The second person took the harder road and sat down with a financial counselor who advised her on how to work out a manageable budget, pay her creditors over time, and change her spending habits. This friend gradually worked herself out of the hole, and by doing so not only developed self-esteem, but saw that she'd used buying things as a way of dealing with mood swings and sadness. By learning how to cope with debt, this woman also learned how to cope with life.

Whenever we are depressed about an uncomfortable situation, like indebtedness, it behooves us to examine whether our motivations and behaviors are self-destructive. Pain is a marvelous catalyst for change, so take advantage of the situation you're in today to create the kind of life that *is* worth living.

Honest self-appraisal is a beneficial side effect of my pain.

You cannot have a proud and chivalrous spirit if your conduct is mean and paltry; for whatever a man's actions are, such must be his spirit.

—DEMOSTHENES

Sometimes we may be down and not even know why. We could be happily married or in a fulfilling relationship, gainfully employed and healthy, yet still feel empty and sad. When this is the case it might be wise to examine what kind of people we are and how we conduct ourselves and our affairs.

I find that when I go to bed at night unsettled and sad without knowing why, it's because I've done something of which I'm ashamed. Some examples of behavior that can bring this type of "hangover guilt" include gossiping, taking frustrations out on a child or store clerk, or telling a lie. Through a self-help group in which I participate I've learned that making daily amends for these types of transgressions is imperative if I want to halt the behavior before it overwhelms me and creates major problems in my life.

Take a look at your recent actions and reactions. Are you proud of everything you've said and done? Are you taking advantage of someone because it's easy and convenient? Have you taken credit for something that you had nothing to do with, slandered someone needlessly, or deliberately ignored someone out of spite? Even though these may sound like trivial and unimportant incidents, you'll never have the gift of peace and inner joy until you acknowledge and work on aspects of yourself that may not be immediately obvious, but that nevertheless could be causing you pain.

My spirit is a reflection of my behavior.

A vigorous five-mile walk will do more good for an unhappy but otherwise healthy adult than all the medicine and psychology in the world.

—PAUL DUDLEY WHITE

One of the best things I ever bought to help fight my depression was a treadmill. No matter what the weather is like outside, I have a guaranteed way of getting my heart rate up, moving my body, and breaking a good sweat. I know from experience that a day without movement is a day I'm more prone to the blues, so I'm careful to budget some time into every day to walk, run, swim, or stretch, and the results are so positive that it's been easy to make daily exercise a part of my life.

Dr. Keith Johnsgard, author of "The Exercise Prescription for Depression," writes that everyone can learn exactly how much exercise they need each day in order to fight depression effectively. Exercise, he contends, mimics the effects of antidepressant drugs by activating the neurotransmitters in the brain that release pleasure-inducing endorphins. Running, he and other experts add, is so efficient in this task that it ought to be viewed as a "wonder drug," similar to penicillin and morphine.

Try some exercise today to combat mood swings and depression. Although you might start reluctantly, once exercise becomes a habit it can be psychologically addictive as well as physically beneficial. If you can learn how to unlock your body's own healing abilities, you'll find that you can prescribe the right dosage of well-being whenever the blues strike.

I will raise my heart rate today for at least twenty minutes.

Failure is an event, not a person.

—ZIG ZIGLAR

I am always intrigued by how different people deal with failure and its accompanying stresses. A lot of people, myself included, have at times equated failure with what type of people we are. For example, a well-known football player retired after a successful career and decided to open a chain of restaurants bearing his name. The chain failed, the athlete lost a lot of money, and his humiliation led him to attempt suicide. He was quoted in the paper as saying that he didn't feel he could face anyone again because he was "nothing but a failure" and no one would ever respect him again.

Unlike this athlete, there are people who see failure as a stepping-stone to something better. I've read profiles of business leaders who have risen to the top of their chosen professions, but who on their way up have committed horrendous blunders. They refuse to personalize these failures, however, saying that their mistakes made them smarter and savvier professionals in the long run.

We can learn valuable lessons from these successful people about how to cope with failure. We will all fail at things from time to time but we don't have to turn such events into catastrophes, or personalize them as character flaws. Failures are simply signs that we are creative risk takers who are willing to try new things, and we must remember that unless we fail at relationships, jobs, and daily events from time to time, we aren't learning anything or moving forward.

When I fail, I gain in wisdom.

There is no aristocracy of grief. Grief is a great leveler.
—ANNE MORROW LINDBERGH

One morning I was listening to the news on the radio when the announcer read an item about how the king of a Scandinavian country had entered a treatment center for depression. I was angered that the announcer and his cohost then joked about how depressed they'd be if they were a king, implying that this man's suffering was frivolous or undeserved because of his great wealth and social standing.

It is misguided to believe that only certain types of people suffer from depression or that being at a certain social or economic level creates unlimited joy in a person's life. This type of stigma keeps many suffering people from getting proper help. Depression is a medical condition that respects no social or economic boundaries and strikes 25 percent of all women at some point in their lives. The tragedy is that most of these women won't get help because they don't take depression seriously or they feel guilty about needing professional help.

Don't judge your depression today. There doesn't have to be a "good" reason for your feelings; if they exist, they need attention. Depression is an illness that almost always responds favorably to treatment within a few months, so instead of wondering why you have become depressed, use your energy and time to ensure that you get the best help you can find.

External conditions can't protect me from internal pain.

The farther behind I leave the past, the closer I am to forging my own character.

—ISABELLE EBERHARDT

My friend Emily was dumped by her fiancé shortly before her wedding, and although she has since married, she's still paralyzed with thoughts of revenge, and the mere sight of a man who resembles her ex-fiancé or who went to the same college can send her into a day-long depression. Another friend, Marie, once botched a big project at work and has second-guessed herself ever since, unsure of her position among her colleagues.

Although these are two very different situations, both women have been unable to let go of the past and have suffered as a result. Experts say that the best way to get over these types of events is to give ourselves permission to have "emotional memories" that reignite our feelings of rejection and depression. If we try to repress them they'll always be waiting to emerge and devastate us anew. It's not unusual for this healing process to be lengthy and painful, with every two steps forward being countered by a sideways or backward step.

Is there an upsetting situation in your past that you can't forget and that intrudes on your thoughts frequently? Do you tell your friends that you've moved on from it when you secretly spend a lot of time feeling depressed about it? If so, try to let go by revisiting your pain occasionally. Once you are able to open the door on past heartache and fully accept what has happened to you, the emotions around it will gradually subside and lose their power to make you depressed.

I can foster future happiness by fully accepting a negative past.

[Moderation is] the inseparable companion to wisdom.
                                    —CHARLES CALEB COLTON

Sometimes it's hard to believe, but too much of a "good" thing can result in depression. Betsy discovered this when she took up running. First, she ran short distances every other day. Gradually she increased her mileage because she enjoyed the "high" she got from the activity as well as the effect it had on her waistline. It wasn't long before Betsy was hopelessly addicted to daily runs, upping her mileage to seventy miles a week. Instead of being exhilarated by her regimen, however, she felt depressed and tired most days, unable to derive pleasure from life.

As Betsy's situation demonstrates, something that helps us feel energized and happy can be detrimental when we take it to an extreme. It wasn't until Betsy developed shin splints and had to cut back on her running that she realized how much better she felt when she ran less frequently. Not only did her body become stronger and more resilient, but she had more time for other pleasures.

Remember today that things we do because they are good for us will hurt us if we do them excessively. So if we are overdosing on vitamins, exercise, herbs or even volunteer work, keep in mind that balance is the key to happiness. Too much of anything—even something "positive"—can leave us feeling tired, irritable, and depressed.

I will strive for balance in all my affairs.

Life itself still remains a very effective therapist.
—KAREN HORNEY

A well-known talk-show host often tells her audiences that when she was in her mid-twenties she was involved in a relationship that brought her more pain than happiness. When the man finally ended the romance, the woman went into a suicidal depression and wrote good-bye notes to her friends, saying that she couldn't go on without him. Luckily, she didn't act on her threats and her job took her to another city where she immersed herself in work. More than a decade later the woman says that what healed her depression was getting on with life and moving forward.

Depression can be an immobilizing condition but if we can summon up the energy to carry out day-to-day activities, we might be surprised to find how much better we feel. It's very empowering to live through a devastating occurrence but still adhere to as much of our daily routine as possible. In fact, I've often heard people say that just showing up at work saved them when they were trying to overcome a loss and their only other option was to sit home and cry.

We can receive a tremendous amount of healing through therapy and medication, but sometimes just getting on with life when we're depressed can be effective, too. Even if you don't want to, make an effort to go through the motions of a normal day. Picking up dry cleaning, feeding your pet, and going to work may feel insurmountable, but using life as therapy may be a very effective way to fight the blues.

I will get on with my life today.

Never fear shadows. They simply mean there's a light shining somewhere nearby.

—Ruth E. Renkel

All of us, no matter how wonderful, pure, and loving, have a "dark side," also called our "shadow." When I first became aware of my shadow, I shied away from it and didn't want to accept that my personality contained facets that are not socially acceptable. But gradually I learned that my less lovable side was as much a part of me as my better one, and that until I could accept this, I would continue to be in situations and with people that reminded me of my shadow.

If you aren't acquainted with your shadow you can identify it by thinking about the people and behaviors that upset or depress you. For example, do you resent someone because she always tries to grab the limelight? Are you morally outraged by adultery or people who abuse their children? If so, these could be tendencies that you, too, possess but that you have learned to repress either because your parents or the world around you deem them unacceptable. To avoid acknowledging that you have a dark side is to be unable to love yourself completely.

The poet Robert Bly says that once we "eat our shadow" we release energy, open our ability to change, fairly judge others, and become more tolerant. Take some quiet time to write down behaviors that shock or enrage you and then contemplate circumstances under which you might act them out. Once you can accept that you have a shadow that may not necessarily ever come to light, you'll free yourself to become completely whole.

I accept both the dark and light sides of myself.

I always thought it mattered, to know what is the worst possible thing that can happen to you, to know how you can avoid it, to not be drawn by the magic of the unspeakable.

—AMY TAN

One of the best pieces of advice I was ever given on how to cope with an upsetting situation was to spin a problem I was facing out to its worst possible conclusion and then to come to peace with the chances of it actually happening. Once I could do that, I was assured, I'd have a more tranquil outlook and would be better able to cope with whatever ultimately happened.

A friend of mine who wanted to ask for a raise but was depressed because she couldn't get up the nerve to do it found this advice helpful. She imagined the worst possible conclusion—that her boss would refuse her request—and then worked on how she'd gracefully deal with that possibility. Once she felt she could handle being turned down, she put together a list of reasons why she deserved a promotion and then presented her request. Surprisingly her boss was receptive and agreeable. By living through the worst possible scenario beforehand, she empowered herself to behave assertively and positively.

If you are depressed because you're afraid of addressing something that's upsetting, settle down in a quiet place today and imagine the worst possible thing happening as a result of your taking action. Then work on mentally accepting that conclusion and see yourself coping with all of its ramifications. Quite often this type of preparation and a lot of determination are the recipe for achieving goals and having the emotional stability to go after them.

Although the "worst" may never happen, accepting its possibility helps to prepare me for the "best."

Hating people is like burning down your own house to get rid of a rat.

—HARRY EMERSON FOSDICK

One day I read a heart-breaking story about how two sets of parents responded to the same unfortunate deaths of their sons in war. Both young men had been killed by "friendly fire" when their plane was accidentally shot down by a fellow soldier. Because of the grief and sincerity displayed by the officer who made the tragic mistake, one set of parents chose to forgive and move on with their lives. The other family, however, could not put the tragedy behind them and spent every day declaring their hatred for the man to anyone who would listen.

Losing a child is one of the worst things that can happen to anyone, particularly when the death is senseless. But miring yourself in hatred only makes grief deeper and healing that much further away. Hatred causes the body to weaken, allows depression to set in, and the immune defenses to drop. In the long run, carrying a grudge and actively nursing it could cause more problems than confronting the loss head-on.

Learning to love and forgive is very tough. Therapists advise that we try to see a situation from someone else's viewpoint and that we try to pray—even if it's grudgingly—for the welfare of the person we dislike. Although we may feel that we're the ones who deserve the compassion, practicing these techniques will bring us the greatest amount of healing.

Hatred never accomplishes a worthy goal.

Sometimes one has simply to endure a period of depression for what it may hold of illumination if one can live through it, attentive to what it exposes or demands.

—MAY SARTON

I know some masochists who enjoy periods of suffering and depression because they believe that it is unnatural to have nothing but joy in their lives, and they argue that they always learn something valuable from their sorrowful times. Although this attitude is admirable, most people hate the feeling of an oncoming depression and eagerly anticipate the days when they can wake again without a heavy heart and a doubting mind.

Years of experience have taught me how to anticipate an oncoming depression. First, I begin to fixate on suffering in the world, worry incessantly about the future, and, friends tell me, talk in a sad voice. Then something happens to take me very low and I enter a period of intense grief when I feel things very deeply. Although I always receive some type of illumination or wisdom from these times, I've never come to the point where I welcome or enjoy these episodes.

Try to be aware of the signs that precede mood swings and be mindful that once the depression hits, we are close to achieving or understanding something important. Although we may never embrace these down times like some people do, at least with preparation we can learn how to expect them, live through them, and then come away with some valuable illumination that helps us to live a more balanced, compassionate, and joyful life.

I will be attentive to what depression can teach me about myself.

The price one pays for pursuing any profession or calling is an intimate knowledge of its ugly side.

—JAMES BALDWIN

I have a friend whose résumé is filled with brief stints at many companies in a variety of fields. Her problem is that she enters each new career with enthusiasm and optimism, but is eventually disillusioned by some part of the job. She once worked at a television studio because she wanted to be a reporter but she quit because she didn't like the unpredictable and long hours. Similarly, she tried to sell real estate because she wanted flexibility but she eventually gave that up, too, because most buyers wanted to see houses at night and on weekends—the same times she wanted to be home. Not surprisingly my friend is depressed about her inability to settle down, and she fears for her financial future.

At some point most of us are forced to face the "ugly" side of our job. For example, a social worker told me that as much as she loves helping others, she hates feeling drained at the end of the day. And a full-time mother said that while she treasures being with her daughters, she hadn't counted on being so bored and restless at times. Whenever we have these feelings, we need to recognize that there are no "perfect" jobs and that we often have to make trade-offs to reach the goals that we've set.

If you are depressed about your job or career, ask yourself whether your expectations are realistic. There are undoubtedly downsides to every career, so instead of pinning happiness on finding the "ideal" situation, it might be better to work on adapting better to what you already have.

I will focus on the positives of my job today.

It is hard to fight an enemy who has outposts in your head.
—SALLY KEMPTON

I have often been told that I am my own worst enemy, and I know it's true. When I'm down, I'm my own worst critic. I beat everyone to the punch by telling them how bad a job I've done on something, how poorly I look, or how stupid something I've said is. Although intellectually I know that I ought to be building myself up, it's hard for me sometimes to shut off the negative voices in my head.

This is something that women do far more often than men. When men are injured or hurt, they frequently become physically active (kicking a chair) or angry ("How dare he do that to me!"). Women, on the other hand, are quick to blame themselves for problems and to ruminate on how sad or lonely they are. When we do this, we only marshal our own forces against ourselves when we should be finding ways to feel and think positively about ourselves.

Although it's hard to go against ingrained habits like self-criticism, we *must* if we are ever to know contentment. Monitor your self-talk today and try to avoid thinking negatively. Instead of telling yourself that you're dumb or destined to fail, congratulate yourself for trying something new or for taking a risk. Find something about yourself to praise and say it to yourself in front of a mirror. The more you can reprogram yourself to be your own best friend, the less likely you'll be to give your enemy "outposts in your head."

I will not be my own enemy today.

It is in his pleasure that a man really lives; it is from his leisure that he constructs the true fabric of self.

—AGNES REPPLIER

One day I read an article about what researchers have discovered about a person's ability to feel happiness. The worst thing to do when depressed, they said, was to ruminate about one's problems. Sharing one's sadness with another person was shown to cut one's suffering in half. The best prescription however, for beating the blues, they offered, was "a noisy game of tennis!"

It's simplistic to assume that all forms of depression will respond to an activity like tennis, but having leisure time and using it with gusto can only help us if we're feeling sad. Not only does exercise improve our well-being and our health, but it takes our mind off whatever is troubling us. Friends of mine swear that a round of golf without a golf cart is the fastest and cheapest way they've discovered to feel better when they're down.

It's imperative to find leisure time every week, and preferably every day, in which some activity prevents any thoughts about our troubles. Whether you take a brisk walk, play some noisy tennis, or swim a few laps, if you make leisure time a high priority, you'll always have a guaranteed block of time when you won't be depressed.

When I move my body, I soothe my mind.

You are to have as strict a guard upon yourself amongst your children, as if you were amongst your enemies.
—GEORGE SAVILE

When we are down on ourselves one natural tendency is to vent the rage and frustration on others. Unfortunately we may end up being angry with or abusive to people who are least able to understand such moods—our children—and although we may not intend to harm them, physical or emotional abuse can severely scar them for many years.

I've seen a very powerful ad on television for Parents Anonymous that features a man speaking forcefully into a mirror, saying, "You do not hit when you are angry, especially people who are smaller than you are. Do you understand that?" Even calling our children names in the heat of anger, or saying things like, "I never wanted to have you," "You're worthless," and "I don't love you," can be as devastating as a physical blow.

Be aware today of the people you are affecting with your emotional swings. If you think you're hurting your children, it's time to get help and break that cycle of depression and anger. Seek out a therapist, counselor or self-help group like Parents Anonymous and put some distance between yourself and those who might be most vulnerable to you. And as much as you are hurting, try to keep in mind that like a pebble that falls into a puddle and creates a ripple effect, our behavior always creates waves that touch others.

I won't victimize my children with my depression.

He lived a life of going-to-do
And died with nothing done.

—J. ALBERY

One day a friend of mine, Beth, called in a fit of pique. For weeks she had been trying to make headway with her feelings of anger toward her parents; during this time I had sympathized with her, gently given her ideas that I thought might help, and provided names of professionals who could assist her. But all she did was continue to complain without ever taking action.

This particular day I lost my patience and told her that I had nothing more to offer in the way of ideas or support. I said I felt powerless as I watched her continue to hurt herself and I added that until she could take some action to help herself she'd be wallowing in the same problems for years. Thankfully my outburst had an impact, and that day she made an appointment to see a therapist who has now successfully guided her to resolution on many of her problems.

Depression can often cause procrastination about solving problems, but until you address a problem, you'll be stuck in the same rut forever. Try to pick one action today that will help you, whether it's revising your résumé, making a decision about something, or committing to an activity. Breaking the cycle of "going to do" and actually taking a positive step can break the gridlock of depression and result in higher self-esteem and contentment.

Today I will do something I've been saying I'll do.

Better a dry crust with peace and quiet than a house full of feasting with strife.

—PROVERBS 17:1

I read a story once about a woman who had raised her five children by herself without much money. Her children had survived with hand-me-down clothes, simple meals, few toys, and used books. Although finances were always tight in this house, there was a lot of love and the children had thrived, all graduating with honors from college, some from graduate school.

At some point in our lives many of us fall victim to the belief that money will buy happiness, and that if only we could buy ourselves or our children some particular thing, we or they would be content. But two cars in the garage, expensive gifts, exotic vacations, and new clothes aren't what bring lasting joy. Researchers consistently say that close relationships with those around us are what bring people the most joy and that having a warm, loving family environment is a good predictor of happiness and emotional stability.

If you are down because you believe that life isn't complete without certain possessions or your children will be emotionally stunted because your budget is limited, think instead about how you can make the relationships in your life richer through expenditures of your time and love. If you can put energy into strengthening the ties that bring contentment, you'll lessen the likelihood of depression and be able truly to see that a "dry crust with peace" is better than "feasting with strife."

The greatest pleasures are often the least expensive.

*Each woman is being made to feel it is her own cross to bear
if she can't be the perfect clone of the male superman and the
perfect clone of the feminine mystique.*

—BETTY FRIEDAN

From the time girls are little, we are bombarded with
messages that to be a successful woman we must be bright,
skinny, attractive, and ambitious. It's not enough to have a
satisfying job; we're expected to be perfect housekeepers,
nurturing mothers, and athletically fit, as well. Buying into
this misperception that it's possible to be this type of
Superwoman is believed to be a major factor contributing
to the high rates of depression among women.

Several authors have written persuasively in recent
years about how damaging American culture is to women
in developing their independence and self-esteem. For example, whenever a woman begins to make gains in business, the "ideal" woman suddenly becomes a childlike waif.
Advertising also conspires to make us feel as if we aren't
attractive unless we're slender, Caucasian, and under
twenty-five. If we buy into these beliefs, we're destined to
feel inadequate. If we refuse to allow the media to define
our self-worth, however, we stand a better chance of having
high self-confidence and of not succumbing to depression.

Be realistic about the expectations you have for yourself today. Read some books by feminist authors so that
you can develop a questioning mind and not take the "feminine" images around you at face value. The more you can
learn to define who you are and want to be on your own
terms, the less likely you'll be to base your happiness on
conforming to an unrealistic ideal.

I will not allow society to dictate my expectations for myself.

When a vision begins to form, everything changes.
—JEANE DIXON

Therapists often encourage clients with poor self-image to imagine themselves acting "as if" they had the qualities that they'd like to possess. For example, if we're timid in social gatherings, we need to imagine being outgoing and self-confident. And if we frequently lose our temper or fail to keep our word, it's a good idea to visualize ourselves being patient and trustworthy. As therapists know, and scientists have proven, the more our subconscious mind "believes" that we are doing something, the more likely it is that we'll carry out that behavior in reality.

A friend of mine who had a knack for dating selfish, unreliable men decided to try visualizing herself in a committed and loving relationship. Every day for ten minutes she vividly imagined being happy with a man who respected and cared for her. Gradually she stopped bringing home men who hurt her and began to attract more thoughtful, gentle people. My friend believes that by seeing herself as more contented and less needy probably changed how she came across to others.

Use the technique of visualization today to create a behavior or situation that will bring you more happiness. If compulsive eating is a problem, imagine yourself eating moderately, and if always giving into others' expectations depresses you, envision yourself being more assertive. If you can learn to create an inner picture of exactly what you want to be, you'll have the tools to change your life for the better.

I will visualize myself being joyful today.

I've been at the nadir of my life already. . . . It does give you a perspective.

—BRANDON TARTIKOFF

By the time we reach our late thirties or early forties most of us have weathered a crisis that has given us perspective on other aspects of our lives. For example, a friend of mine who was diagnosed with a serious illness in her early thirties said that everything that happened afterward seemed trivial in comparison to enduring months of hospitalization and invasive tests. "It's hard to be upset about being dumped by a guy when you thought you were going to die!" she now remarks.

Middle-aged friends of mine say something similar. As young newlyweds with an infant, they ran out of money one weekend in the midst of a blizzard. With only seventeen cents to their name—not enough to heat the house—they and their dog all huddled in one bed during the weekend, trying to stay warm. Their financial picture eventually brightened, but that depressing weekend is the touchstone against which they measure all of their other setbacks, none of which have seemed so bad in comparison.

Try to have some perspective on what's ailing you today. Are your woes the most difficult you've ever faced or is there something else you've weathered before that was more serious and depressing? If the latter is true, draw strength from having already come through difficult emotional times and survived. Call upon the same inner resources and support system that helped you then and remember that you are probably stronger and more resilient than you think.

This time in my life will pass.

When it is dark, we see the stars.

—RALPH WALDO EMERSON

Some friends of mine endured a heart-breaking loss several years ago when their unborn child suddenly died in the ninth month of pregnancy. Despite a trouble-free pregnancy, for unknown reasons the fetus strangled on the umbilical cord just days before she was to be born. The sorrowful couple had no choice but to deliver the baby, and after holding her and grieving for several days, they had a funeral service and tried to cope with their pain as best they could.

I was moved to tears when the father told me this story at a dinner gathering one night. Noticing my emotions, he hastened to comfort me by saying that the experience had been beneficial in some ways for him and his wife. Not only did they treasure each moment they had with their two healthy sons, but they were forced to deal with unhealthy addictions that had been exacerbated by the tragedy. After drinking heavily for months after the baby's death, the mother underwent successful treatment for alcoholism. The father, who had always submerged his troubles in work, learned through therapy how to express his needs in a healthier way.

Just as this story shows, times of darkness sometimes enable us to see stars that may have previously been obscured. Try not to be embittered by the unfair and difficult events life may bring us from time to time because these may be perfect opportunities to grow and strengthen ourselves.

I will find the stars in my world when I perceive nothing but darkness.

Sleep is the best meditation.

—Dalai Lama

When we're agitated and our minds are going in a million different directions it's almost impossible to sit down, clear our heads, and come up with creative ideas and solutions. At such times I find that my only relief comes at night when I am asleep. Unchained from the tension of the day, my mind wanders freely and I often dream solutions to problems that elude me during the day. I have even learned that if I ask to be shown a direction in dealing with something, I'll receive my answer that night. Sometimes I'm surprised by what I learn about myself in dreams, but usually I find that my gut instincts about someone or something are confirmed, giving me courage to follow my heart.

If you feel as if you're going in circles today, try to take a short nap, even ten to fifteen minutes, which will rejuvenate your brain and body. Or if it is closer to bedtime, resolve to use sleep as a period during which you will completely unwind and be receptive to new ideas about whatever is troubling you. Not only will the solutions you desire probably appear, but you'll be rested and fresher in the morning.

I will use my sleep to heal myself.

Life can only be understood backwards; but it must be lived forwards.

—SÖREN KIERKEGAARD

Once when I was in the midst of an emotional and financial upheaval, I frequently spent time alone on long walks, wondering how I had managed to get myself into such a difficult position. Although deep down I knew that I was bright, creative, and energetic, I was tortured with self-criticism and spent a lot of time being angry and exhausted.

Now that the worst is apparently behind me, I am able to understand why this dark period was important to my growth as a person. Prior to having so many bad things happen so swiftly, I had had many things go my way with little or no effort. Suddenly I learned that life wasn't always fair, and that reaching for worthy goals didn't guarantee success. As a result of gradually developing humility and compassion for myself, I also learned to have them for others.

Adversity is usually not understandable at the time it occurs, so you shouldn't waste too much time or energy asking, "Why me?" Instead, try to channel energy toward finding solutions, such as seeing a therapist or reading a self-help book, and wait for the passage of time to reveal the valuable lessons of what you have endured.

The more contentedly I can live my life forward, the sooner I'll be able to look backward with gratitude.

Laughter is a form of internal jogging. It moves your internal organs around. It enhances respiration. It is an igniter of great expectations.

—Norman Cousins

Probably everyone has heard the story about how the author of the above quote fought a life-threatening illness with unorthodox healing methods. One of his main resources was laughter, which he stimulated by watching every funny television show—particularly *Candid Camera*—he could find. Through laughter and other means he beat his illness into remission and went on to live a long and healthy life.

Although finding humor in life may be difficult when we're depressed, it's usually there if we look. There's always a television show we can chuckle at, a comic strip that tickles our funny bone, or a comedian we can listen to. And if we're really brave we can poke fun at our inability to sleep well or our feelings of hopelessness. Making a lighthearted comment about something that is causing us pain can be a way of facing a difficult subject and making it palatable.

Try to find the lighter side of whatever is troubling you today. If you can't do that, at least make an effort to seek out stimuli that might cheer you up. Losing your cares in laughter, at least temporarily, can be the physical and emotional lift you need to help you get over a difficult hump.

Keeping my sense of humor in hard times is a way to keep my sanity and health intact.

He who wants a rose must respect the thorn.

—Persian proverb

All her life Alexa dreamed of being a mother. She imagined the joy of being pregnant, having baby showers, decorating a nursery, and spending blissful days with her children. Within a year of getting married, Alexa had her wish and gave birth to a healthy baby boy. But instead of finding the joy she had imagined, Alexa discovered that the reality of motherhood was sleepless nights, little time for herself or her husband, and constant baby-sitting hassles. It wasn't long before she regretted rushing into motherhood and wished she had more carefully thought through her decision to have a baby.

There aren't many things in life that don't have a downside, so when we go after our own personal "roses" we need to remember that there will always be thorns to contend with. Motherhood is one such rose that is wonderful when we're ready for it, but it's horrendous if we're not. Similarly, if we want a high-powered career and the prestige and salary that accompany it, we have to remember that this "rose" probably means longer hours at work, being separated from our families through traveling, increased scrutiny from our peers, and not much time for ourselves.

If we want to be happy, we must not be naive about the trade-offs that accompany achieving some of our dreams. There is nothing wrong with setting our goals high and looking for fulfillment, but remember that being savvy about the "thorns" we'll encounter is what will make the "roses" enjoyable.

I will mind the downsides that accompany my achievements.

The urge to write one's autobiography, so I have been told, overtakes everyone sooner or later.

—AGATHA CHRISTIE

In most addiction treatment centers, the therapeutic tool of composing an autobiography is used to help put people in touch with their feelings and innermost secrets. After writing the autobiography, patients usually read them to their peers for feedback about what themes and problems have emerged. People who complete this exercise almost always find it illuminating, cleansing, and very motivating for change.

My first published book was my autobiography so I unknowingly reaped the benefits of this therapeutic exercise. Feelings I thought I had dealt with years earlier came roaring back while I was writing, and happy memories that I had almost forgotten came alive again. Not only did I understand myself and my motives better when I finished, but I liked myself better, as well. Seeing my life in a framework helped me to understand why I had been self-destructive, and I was able finally to forgive myself for things that had haunted me for years.

If you had to write about your life, where would you start and what would you say? Who has been influential and how have you matured thus far? Try to write about these and related topics for ten minutes every morning in a journal and don't worry about punctuation or perfection. The more you allow your inner thoughts to flow unimpeded, the healthier and happier you'll be.

I will examine myself on paper today.

It is not death that a man should fear, but he should fear never beginning to live.

—MARCUS AURELIUS

One of the things I often hear women voice is their inability to live fully until they can stand up for what they believe in and do the things that bring them pleasure, not just the things they feel obliged to do. For some this occurs after their children grow up and leave home, for some it's when they move away from their parents, and for others it is when they feel proficient in their jobs. Many women, however, never reach this point trying instead to please others all their lives and never living for themselves.

Assertiveness training is always a part of the treatment given women for depression because when depressed, we're likely to defer to those around us. If we always go to the restaurant that someone else wants to eat at, see movies our husbands want to see, or buy clothes our mothers think we should wear, we'll never have our own lives. Learning what we want to do, how to speak up for ourselves, and what gives us the warmest feelings of accomplishment are lessons in trial and error, but they are necessary to achieve happiness and self-confidence.

Are you afraid of having your own life today because you're so wrapped up in fulfilling others' expectations? Can you stand up to others who disappoint you or put unnecessary expectations on you? If you cannot, the inevitable result will be repressed anger and depression, which will prevent you from enjoying the life you were placed on earth to live in the very short period we are here.

I will not be fearful about living the life I want to live.

Suffering, once accepted, loses its edge, for the terror of it lessens, and what remains is generally far more manageable than we had imagined.

—LESLEY HAZLETON

I once read a story about a man who lost his arm to cancer and whose wife became deeply depressed as a result of suddenly becoming his full-time nurse in addition to being his wife and the mother of their children. As the burdens on her mounted, she told her husband that she needed to talk to a therapist about her depression because she was having trouble getting out of bed and thinking positively. He forbade her from seeking treatment, saying, "Pull yourself up by your bootstraps like I have. I can provide all the support you need."

Only after a friend intervened and explained the importance of getting therapy in the early stages of depression did the man relent and permit his wife to get help. Later he admitted that he had been frightened of the stigma of having a wife in therapy. Through individual and joint sessions, the couple's lives improved and the wife recovered from depression.

If you know you need help for depression today and someone's opinion is preventing you from getting counseling, perhaps a friend could intervene, as one did for the couple above. Suffering in silence because of some perceived "stigma" or fear of what depression actually is only ensures that your misery will continue unabated and that you'll postpone taking control of your life and mental health.

I will share my suffering with others today so that I don't have to shoulder my pain alone.

In our civilization, men are afraid that they will not be men enough and women are afraid that they might be considered only women.

—THEODOR REIK

Recently, I spoke with a high-school friend about how our lives are unfolding, how happy we are with our choices, and what our ambitions are. She and I have taken very different paths; I've chosen to combine motherhood with a writing career and she has chosen to stay home with her daughters while her husband pursues a career that requires a lot of travel. Although she has a full day from dawn to dusk and does a variety of volunteer activities, my friend is "so embarrassed" about "just being a mom" that she won't write to our school's alumnae magazine to inform them of her activities.

One of the results of the women's movement has been to give us the freedom to choose from a variety of professions, and if we have chosen to make motherhood a full-time career, we need to start by taking pride in our decision, not being ashamed of it.

It's important to remember that some people look down on stay-at-home moms because they don't know how much work and creativity the job entails; others are jealous that they can't do the same. In the long run, however, our happiness must be independent of what others think of us or of our choices, so learn to ignore other people's opinions and acknowledge with certainty that you've done what's right for you.

I will follow a path that brings me happiness regardless of what others might think.

If our faith delivers us from worry, then worry is an insult flung in the face of God.

—ROBERT RUNCIE

I know a woman who is always looking for the downside to anything she's engaged in. If she's going boating she worries about drowning. If her children have colds she worries that they'll blossom into tropical viruses. And when she makes a business decision she spends days obsessing about what could go wrong.

Studies have shown that about 15 percent of the population are chronic worriers who spend at least eight hours each day obsessing about things that are mostly out of their control. This worrying results in insomnia and depression, not to mention lost productivity. People who've been instructed to take half an hour each day to write down their worries have been found to reduce the levels of worry and stress in their lives by one-third to one-half. Throughout the day, whenever they found themselves beginning to worry, they were taught to shut the thought off immediately with the admonition, "I'll think about that during my worry period."

If you find that the better part of each day is devoted to your darkest fears, buy a "worry journal" and focus such thoughts into one block of time. If you can teach yourself to be an efficient worrier and stop frittering away the day on nameless doubts and obsessions, you'll not only be a more productive person, but you'll undoubtedly be happier, as well.

I will limit my negative thinking today.

The most intense conflicts, if overcome, leave behind a sense of security and calm which is not easily disturbed.
—CARL JUNG

I have some friends who have a very rocky marriage and whose hostility is always simmering toward each other. Despite their animosity and obvious unhappiness, their marriage continues, partly because they won't discuss how they feel. I asked the wife one day why they didn't just have a big argument and vent their emotions. "Oh, we never argue," she said. "It's not healthy for the children to hear us yelling at each other."

Whenever we are miserable about something but don't voice our emotions, depression is the inevitable result. It's more unhealthy to keep rage, sadness, and anxiety within than it is to let it out safely—regardless of how the children or anyone else might react. Similarly, if we allow ourselves to cry, scream, or explode about something that's upsetting us, the calm we feel is comparable to the stillness after a huge storm.

Intense conflicts—either within ourselves or with others—are not enjoyable, but sometimes they're what's necessary for us to deal with something and then move on. If you are avoiding a conflict because you're afraid of confrontation, remember that keeping your emotions inside will only hurt and depress you while solving nothing.

My soul always finds a safe port after a storm.

If there were any justice in the world, people would be able to fly over pigeons for a change.

—ANONYMOUS

Sometimes we hear or read about something that is so awful we wonder if there is truly any justice in the world. For example, one day I watched four sets of parents talk about their efforts to come to grips with the senseless rape and violent murders of their daughters. These men and women were all struggling with depression and a feeling that life is unfair because innocent people can suffer so.

Although this is an extreme example, we all experience moments of grief or depression because something very unfair has happened to us. Examples could include being fired because of corporate downsizing, losing our home to a fire or flood, or becoming seriously injured through someone else's negligence. A therapist who specializes in grief counseling says that venting our feelings of injustice, embracing our pain and rage, and allowing time to pass are the only ways to cope with a depression caused by this type of suffering. It's imperative to express and feel this sort of pain fully in order to process it and move ahead with our lives.

If you are depressed because you've been unfairly victimized, expect to take some time to recover from your pain and sadness. Some forms of depression can be helped effectively in a short period of time but when sadness has injustice as its root, it's going to be harder to bounce back. Don't try to make sense of your feelings and don't run from the intensity of them because it's only by living through them that you find peace and happiness again.

I will accept the injustices in my life with strength and courage.

Nobody is ever met at the airport when beginning a new adventure. It's just not done.

—ELIZABETH WARNOCK FERNEA

In most societies the passage into adulthood is celebrated with an elaborate set of rituals. As part of a typical initiation, the boy or girl is separated from the culture and sent off on a "vision quest" to learn or experience something profound, during which the soul dies and is reborn. After returning to society, the child is treated in a more mature way and is given a new set of responsibilities to honor this passage into adulthood.

Depression is like a major initiation but it's one we'll probably go through many times, not just once. As in the solitary "vision quest," we'll probably endure most of our sadness alone. Although we can always enlist the aid of friends, family, and therapists, the deepest and most profound changes will only come about when we wrestle with ourselves in silence. If our soul successfully dies and is reborn, however, our return from depression can mark a move into greater wisdom, empowerment, and responsibility.

Try to view your depression today as an initiation into a greater level of awareness. Like the adventurer who isn't met at the airport, keep in mind that the greatest travels into enlightenment are often solitary journeys of inward transformation and that having a companion would only dilute the power of the trip.

The greatest adventures of the soul are taken alone.

It is sacred work that women are doing as they reclaim their bodies for health rather than victimization, reclaim their bodies for creativity rather than destruction, reclaim their bodies for life.

—LAUREEN SMITH

In New York City a group of women have been meeting with a mission. They are people who have been on countless diets throughout their lives but who have been unsuccessful at reaching and maintaining their goal weights. Now they are joining together to "take their lives back" and ban diets forever. If they can learn to love themselves at whatever weight they're at, they believe, they won't spend so much time hating themselves and being depressed about their bodies.

This movement parallels the way women have recently begun to fight back after being raped or sexually abused. Traditionally women didn't press charges after being molested, often because they were embarrassed or ashamed that they had "done something" to lead the attacker on—a surefire way to guarantee depression. Now more and more women are identifying themselves as rape "survivors" who are putting the blame where it belongs and saying that they have nothing to be ashamed of.

If you are depressed because you feel that your body has been a battleground—either sexually or emotionally—it's time to reclaim it as your own. Support groups and counseling can help redefine your body as precious property, and self-defense classes can empower you to take control of your boundaries. Whatever you do, it's important not to cede control of your bodies to any outside force because only through being your own masters can you really have a life.

I will reclaim my body today.

Midway life's journey I was made aware
That I had strayed into a dark forest,
And the right path appeared not anywhere.

—DANTE ALIGHIERI

When Dante wrote these opening lines of the *Inferno* in 1300, he was thirty-five years old and describing his own midlife crisis of how he wanted a political position but could not obtain it. Several centuries later, midlife crises still exist and cause us heartache, confusion, and depression about roads we may have wanted to take at one time but that now are impossible for one reason or another.

Although the middle of life is statistically about age thirty-seven, people have been known to have crises as early as their twenties and as late as their sixties. Whenever we start to worry about the future, regret the past, and wonder what the meaning of life is, and what our role in it is, we are having a midlife crisis. One person I know used this period to enter therapy, get a divorce, and change to a profession that better suited her talents. Another dove into extramarital affairs to prove to herself that she "still had it." The first one, after several difficult years, entered what she called her "golden age." The second is still looking for happiness.

All of us will at some time hit a bump when we experience confusion, fear, and sadness about our lives. Although you may feel overwhelmed and unable to cope at times, remember that midlife crises have been around for centuries and that therapy, self-help books, a sense of humor, the companionship of friends in similar straits, and the perspective of Dante can all eventually help us survive intact.

I will use my midlife crisis to pave the way for my golden years.

I am never upset for the reason I think.
                          —*A Course in Miracles*

Often when we are upset we are quick to assign the blame for our feelings to something superficial. For example, we may explode at a colleague for something trivial when we are *really* angry because our mother was short with us last week. Or we can assign our depression to not feeling well or not having enough money when, in fact, other factors are causing the world to look bleak.

Whenever I probe the reasons for my depression I inevitably find that my feelings stem from anger and fear. If I have a string of days in which I don't feel creative and my writing doesn't flow, I become depressed. When I examine my feelings I find that I'm really afraid that I'm not intelligent enough to be a writer and that I can't make enough money to support myself doing something I love. Identifying these roots gives me more ammunition to fight my blues and enables me to address what's really bothering me.

If you are down today, try to look beyond the obvious for the reasons behind your feelings. Are you attributing your sadness to being low on money when the main issue is that you don't like appearing needy and vulnerable? Or do you think you're depressed because a relationship ended when what's really bothering you are fears of abandonment? When we carefully examine our feelings we might be surprised to find that old fears and resentments are responsible for making us blue, and that addressing them is what will help return peacefulness and joy to our lives.

I will dig deep to uproot the main causes for my depression.

The only unnatural sexual behavior is none at all.
—SIGMUND FREUD

Lots of my friends bemoan the lack of fireworks in their sexual lives. They complain that several years of sameness with one person has dulled their interest in that man or woman, and that they've settled into boring sexual routines that exclude spice and variety. At this point a number of them either consider having an affair or they actually do it, convinced that nothing they do can improve the situation with their partner.

Amanda is a woman who refuses to let years of marriage to the same man ruin her sexual life. Every month she books a room in a hotel, sends her children to her sister's house for the weekend, and meets her husband in the hotel lobby in a glamorous outfit. The weekend recharges both of them and keeps them interested in each other. Another middle-aged woman I know writes her husband sexy notes and slips them in his briefcase, promising to be available that evening for "fun and games."

Sometimes we have to work at making things we enjoy happen. Spontaneous sex is wonderful but when you have a busy life it's unlikely that it will just happen. Put some energy today into bringing greater satisfaction to your sex life, either through taking a risk, talking to a sex therapist, or having a frank talk with your partner. Learning to create sexual pleasure—or any other kind of joy—on a regular basis instead of hoping it will just fall into your lap guarantees that you'll always have some control over your happiness.

I will put some energy into creating my own joy today.

Art is the window to man's soul. Without it, he would never be able to see beyond his immediate world; nor could the world see the man within.

—LADY BIRD JOHNSON

One weekend I took a trip to see an exhibit of Greek art from the fifth century B.C. that featured statues, friezes, and other works from the Acropolis and surrounding areas. During the two hours spent observing these items, I was completely transported to another time and emerged feeling energized and peaceful. For several days afterward I lived in a bubble of happiness and contemplation, and found that the timelessness of the exquisite pieces had helped put the world and my travails into a better perspective.

Some of my friends enjoy looking at photography, some like abstract painting, and others find relics from certain periods to be their favorites. But no matter what type of exhibit moves you, taking the time to go to a museum and wander around in a peaceful and reflective environment is good for the soul.

Take a trip to a museum today or as soon as you can if you're feeling frazzled and down. Also, keep in mind that city parks and town centers often feature fountains and statues that can serve the same purpose as a visit to a museum. Appreciating works of art will not only provide a peaceful interlude in a busy world, it may stimulate your creativity, yielding a new outlet for self-expression.

When I create or enjoy art, I bathe my soul with love.

*And now we come to the magic of words. A word, also, just
like an idea, a thought, has the effect of reality upon undiffer-
entiated minds.*

—EMMA JUNG

Top athletes all have a habit in common: they pump
themselves up to perform well by talking aloud, saying
things like "You can do it!" "Don't give up now!" and
"Good shot!" This self-talk isn't just helpful to athletes,
however; psychologists say that using positive affirmations
can turn a poor self-image into one of confidence and vitality.

Chances are most of us talk to ourselves already, but
we may say the wrong kinds of things. For example, behav-
ioral experts say that losers often fall into a trap of saying,
"I can't," "I'm no good," and "I'll never win"—negative
expectations that usually fulfill themselves and breed depression. Instead we need to learn to say helpful, uplifting
things like "You'll do better next time" or "I'm proud I
took a risk."

Try to carry on a conversation with yourself today that
makes you feel good about yourself, particularly if you're
depressed and feeling cynical. You can start with "You're
special" or "You look nice today," and then go on to congratulate yourself about taking a risk, making an uncomfortable phone call, or being loving with your children. The
more you can learn to create positive expectations that you
can verbalize, the more likely they will turn into reality.

I will carry on positive conversations with myself today.

Discouragement seizes us only when we can no longer count on chance.

—GEORGE SAND

One day I was fretting to a friend that I was short on money, between jobs, and uncertain of how to proceed with my life. She laughed and reminded me that I'd said similar things to her many times over the years, but that I'd always been "saved" with some type of answer or windfall when I was most desperate and about to give up hope. When I thought about it I had to agree; in every seemingly hopeless and depressing situation, a "door" has always opened just when I thought there were no options left.

Many of us find that in certain predicaments, although we do everything at our disposal to solve a problem, nothing seems to work. Then, just as discouragement sets in, a "miracle" occurs that lifts our spirits. For example, a single friend of mine who was despondent about not being married went to play tennis by himself after attending a wedding. On the court he met an attractive young woman who was practicing alone. Within three months they were married, and they still marvel about the circumstances that brought them together.

If you are depressed because your efforts in solving something have come to naught, try not to give up. If you can retain a hope—albeit slender—that the tide is going to turn your way despite a bleak forecast, you might be surprised to find that you get the relief you need right at the critical moment.

I won't give up hope today.

Children are not born knowing the many opportunities that are theirs for the taking. Someone who does know must tell them.

—Ruth Hill Viguers

It was once thought that depression only occurred among older teenagers and adults. That view has changed in the last decade, however, when it was discovered that children as young as five can be clinically depressed. It's also been found that eight to nine percent of children from ten to thirteen experience a major depression in the course of a year, with the average bout lasting eleven months. By the age of sixteen, 16 percent of girls have suffered a major depression. Experiencing depression as a child increases the risk of adult depression by 75 percent.

If you are a depressed adult, think back to your childhood for signs that you were at emotional risk. Did you suffer from insomnia or lethargy or experience trouble making friends and developing social skills? Did you have low self-esteem, trouble concentrating or feelings of hopelessness? Depressed children and teenagers are often unable to discuss their sadness, and display it as crankiness, irritability, impatience, and anger, especially toward their parents.

After-school classes that teach social skills, cognitive restructuring, and self-esteem have had remarkable success with children and teenagers, and certain medications are beneficial, too. Use your experiences and wisdom today to help a younger person know what opportunities are available, and your efforts will increase that person's chances of happiness as an adult.

I will help a younger person find resources to overcome depression.

If it ain't broke, don't fix it.

—Anonymous

One day a close friend of mine called to say that she had decided to go off her antidepressant. I was taken aback, particularly because this woman had changed tremendously for the better during the three years she had been on medication. While taking medication she had been stable and happy, whereas before she had been depressed and prone to wild mood swings.

In an embarrassed voice she said that her mother had encouraged her to go off the medication because she thought her daughter would do just fine without it. Her mother didn't like the idea of my friend being "on drugs" and she preferred to think that she could be "normal" without them. I and others convinced my friend that she had become a much healthier person while taking the antidepressant and after several days she decided to stick with the medication. The decision probably didn't please her mother but it was clearly the correct one for my friend.

It's very hard to accept the idea that we may be prone to a biological imbalance that can be corrected with medication, but feeling "normal" for some can only be achieved with the help of antidepressants. If you are feeling "bad" about needing medication or someone else is pressuring you to get off antidepressants, ask yourself what is truly in your best interests, because learning what you must do to enjoy mental equilibrium—and then actually doing it—is the most important step you can take toward feeling better.

Whatever steps I need to take to be happy, vital, and optimistic are the right ones for me.

Marriage is our last, best chance to grow up.

—JOSEPH BARTH

In the last few decades, the length of the average marriage has shrunk from seven to four years. Therapists say that this is partly the result of having a generation who has grown up with divorce and experience this as an acceptable way of life, and partly it is because we have a society that demands quick fixes. If we hurt in our marriages and we don't want to exert time and energy working out our problems, we're more likely to head for divorce court than we are to go to a marriage counselor.

I don't know anyone who has a perfect, hassle-free marriage. Everyone I know has had rough patches where one or both members were jobless, sex was unsatisfying, money was tight, tragedy had struck, or the hassles of child-rearing had come between them. Most of the couples have worked through their problems and remain married but some have divorced without really giving the marriage a shot. They've either gotten involved with someone else, decided that the lack of a "spark" meant the marriage was dead, or become so distanced that a break was inevitable.

If you're feeling depressed about a rocky relationship today, remember that it's normal to have down times with someone you love. Instead of running away, decide that you will make every effort to rekindle the love and respect you once had for this person through counseling or other avenues. While the marriage may not survive, if you give it your best shot before you throw in the towel, you'll walk away with greater self-esteem and the knowledge that you didn't just quit when the going got tough.

Difficult times in a relationship are opportunities for growth.

Addition by subtraction.

—BRANCH RICKEY

In team sports it's essential that everyone function together as a unit for the team to succeed. If there is a troublesome player—someone who doesn't try his or her hardest, who complains a lot, or who backstabs others—it affects the morale of the other players, lessening their chances of success. When such a player is traded, to the team's benefit, this is known as "addition by subtraction."

This is a useful analogy for our personal lives. In order to function as healthy, happy individuals, we must live and work in a harmonious atmosphere where all parts of our lives complement the others. When this balance is upset by a self-destructive addiction, negative thinking, an abusive relationship, or poor health, we must eliminate this area in order to restore harmony.

Is there something you can subtract from your life today that is troublesome and contributing toward depression? If you regarded the people in your life as a team, is there someone you'd be better off "trading" for another person who will enrich your life? Is there an addiction, such as an eating disorder or alcoholism, that you'd benefit from eliminating? Keep in mind that paring people and situations from our lives doesn't have to be a negative or depressing experience because doing some judicious "trading" can bring us more happiness.

I will add to my life by subtracting something that brings me no joy.

We are going to have to find a way to immunize people against the kind of thinking that leads to self-devastation.

—JONAS SALK

One day I read a magazine article called "How to Get Undepressed Fast." Being a driven, type-A person, I liked the idea that someone could lick depression fast, especially in light of the fact that I recently had a bout that lasted for many months. So I bought the magazine and took it home, determined to learn something to help me when the blues struck again.

The article discussed the strides that have been made with cognitive therapy, the premise of which is that because we often think ourselves into depression, we should be able to think ourselves out, too. The author said he'd routinely disparaged himself for years whenever he'd attempted something new, thinking, "You'll never succeed," "You're stupid," or "No one likes you." In short-term therapy he learned to replace irrational thoughts and negative perceptions with more accurate ones. Doing this enabled him to distinguish reality from unreality, and to reinterpret events in a positive, self-enhancing way.

Cognitive therapy can be completed in twelve sessions, and studies show that for some people it is as effective as drug therapy or conventional talk therapy. If you feel this would be beneficial, seek out a therapist who can help you get on the path of clear thinking. And if not, just remember that the premise of cognitive therapy—how we interpret stressful events leads to depression, not the events themselves—is something that can help us process any event in our lives that is adversely affecting us.

I will send myself positive, loving messages today.

Comparisons do oft-time great grievance.

—JOHN LYDGATE

One day I was reading a letter to the editor in a depression-support newsletter that gave voice to a problem many people with a chronic illness face. "I'm unable to accept the fact that I have a lifelong problem that will require medication," the woman wrote. "I'm embarrassed and I feel stigmatized by society at large, so I resist taking the pills that I know make me feel 'normal' and part of the rest of the world. This tears me apart on a daily basis."

Although many people who struggle with depression don't need to take antidepressants throughout their lives, there are others who do. A friend of mine who suffers from manic depression feels wonderful when she takes lithium, but at least once a year she considers stopping her medication because she doesn't want to be "a lifer." Another friend who has a family history of mood disorders resisted taking antidepressants because she felt "stigmatized" until her doctor gave her an ultimatum to do something about her worsening mental condition. Both of these women feel well and function beautifully on their respective medications, and because of their family histories will probably need to stay on them for the rest of their lives.

If we come from a genetic background that includes a history of depression, it's more than likely that we'll need medication to control our moods for the foreseeable future. Instead of unfavorably comparing ourselves to others who don't have this same situation, it's wise to seek out support groups and medical professionals who can provide encouragement and remind us that being different doesn't mean we're inferior.

I won't compare myself to anyone else today.

Blessed are they who heal us of self-despisings. Of all services which can be done to man, I know of none more precious.
—WILLIAM HALE WHITE

When LaTasha was growing up, she attended a prep school where she was the only African American in her class. Because of her privileged upbringing and ease among her white classmates, her African American friends called her an "Oreo." Stung by their rejection she learned to socialize mainly with her white friends and eventually married a European businessman. A lifetime of feeling "different" has left her with low self-esteem and confusion about her identity.

LaTasha's situation is not unique. Therapists say that minority groups are at high risk for depression because of the discrimination they face. In therapy, LaTasha realized that her depression had begun in her teens. She started shoplifting because the thrill of stealing helped her bury her confusing emotions. Now she frequently reminds herself that her self-worth is independent of her skin color, and that she doesn't have to behave a certain way or socialize with certain people in order to feel good about herself.

If you are a member of a minority group struggling with depression, consider whether your feelings are tied to low self-esteem caused by discrimination. Therapists can help identify and address this destructive emotion, but anyone who does this valuable service—a friend, a pastor, or a parent—is, indeed, "precious."

I can learn to love myself irrespective of how others treat me.

All birth ends in death.
All creation ends in dissolution.
All accumulation ends in dispersion.
All that appears real is transitory.
. . . Come
Drink the elixir of fearlessness!

—Nagarjuna

At my tenth college reunion, I struck up a conversation with a man who had spent the decade since our graduation accumulating degrees, honors, and high-paying jobs. During a sabbatical from his law firm, he'd worked in a low-income area helping people start their own businesses, a job that he found to be much more fulfilling than his legal work. As a result, he was wrestling with whether to stay put and continue in his safe, financially secure, legal job, or whether he should throw caution to the wind and do something that brought him more satisfaction. His depression at being unable to move forward confidently was obvious.

Quite often we get stuck in ruts with careers, people, and routines that are safe but that don't make us happy. Some people accept this because they're afraid of making changes in the status quo, and their misery continues unabated. Others, however, summon up the courage to go after whatever it is that they *do* want, and they don't allow their fears to prevent them from taking action.

Drink the elixir of fearlessness today if vacillating is depressing you. Not only will you feel empowered by being assertive, you may go down a new path that leads to greater happiness and satisfaction than you can imagine.

I will boldly pursue something that I want to do but that frightens me.

Nothing fixes a thing so intensely in the memory as the wish to forget it.

—MICHEL DE MONTAIGNE

One of the most pervasive crimes against young women is sexual abuse, which often occurs as incest perpetrated by a father or other trusted male family member. Because it is so traumatic the child often develops two personalities: one that functions normally and one that takes over during the abuse. In some cases the victim even develops a number of personalities, known as multiple personality disorder, to cope with the trauma. The victim usually suppresses all conscious memory of the abuse until later in life when flashbacks begin.

I know a number of people who in their late twenties and early thirties suddenly started to experience memories of childhood sexual abuse. All of them had periods of intense depression and self-destructive behavior prior to the flashbacks, as well as a significant lack of childhood memories. Each began to have the flashbacks in unexpected ways; one woman remembered her abuse when her daughter reached the age at which her own abuse had started, and another was unexpectedly confronted with her memories during a session of hypnosis in her therapist's office.

If you are struggling with feelings of unworthiness, depression, or self-destructive behavior, consider the possibility of having repressed memories of abuse that could be the key to your recovery. Make sure that you explore these memories in a safe, supportive environment, but take comfort in the fact that the subconscious usually only releases what we have the strength to work through.

My mind protects me and can be used to heal me.

The most painful death in all the world is the death of a child.
—Thomas H. Kean

I know several people who have outlived their children, and the grief they live with every day is indescribable. One woman whose son has been dead for almost thirty years lapses into a depression every year around his birthday. Another woman drank so much when she lost her newborn that she now needs many drinks each night just to sleep. And another woman who watched her three-year-old daughter die from a brain tumor gained fifty pounds, and therefore looking in the mirror is a constant reminder of her sorrow.

Time is one of the biggest aids in overcoming major crises like the death of a child, but reaching out and sharing your pain can help ease sorrow, as well. Talk as much as possible about your feelings with understanding friends and family. Start a "grief" journal and even compose letters to the deceased child. Or, attend meetings of other parents who have lost children; one friend flies to another city for these meetings because they've been so helpful to her.

As wounded and saddened as you may feel now, try to remember that you'll need to incorporate laughter and fun into your life again at some point if you are truly to heal, and that the finest tribute you can pay to someone you've lost is to remember them with joy.

Losing someone dear to me doesn't mean I have to give up happiness forever.

Man may work from sun to sun,
But women's work is never done.

—Anonymous

Studies have shown that one of the main reasons women say they're unhappy with married life is because of the unequal division of housework. Although many say their partners want to help, the fact is that most don't, even when the wife works full-time. And the problem tends to escalate after the birth of a child, when many women opt to stay at home but resent the extra housework they're expected to do. When these issues aren't resolved they can bubble over into anger and depression.

Psychologists who have studied this phenomenon say that the basic problem is that women often feel unappreciated for what they do, particularly if that work goes unrecognized and unrewarded. "My husband feels work is valuable only if you're paid for it," one woman laments. Another says that she's furious that her husband is advancing rapidly in his career while she stays home with their baby but she feels selfish about saying anything.

One way to get your partner's attention when you feel unappreciated is to do the unexpected. For example, don't wash the dishes, vacuum, or cook for a week. Taking away services that they have come to expect can make them pay attention to what you do. Also, don't be shy about stating a need for more validation for your efforts because until you can ask for what you need, resentment about the work that's "never done" will probably increase.

My burdens are lighter when I feel appreciated for my efforts.

If you want a place in the sun, prepare to put up with a few blisters.

—ABIGAIL VAN BUREN

When I wrote my first book and it started to receive a lot of publicity, I eagerly ate it up. I loved the fact that reporters were calling me for quotes, TV stations wanted me on the news, and letters were streaming in by the bushelful. It wasn't long, however, before I learned there was a downside to being somewhat well known. Some people hated my book and felt no compunction about telling me so, a few friends resented my higher profile, and areas of my life I had thought were private were suddenly open for public scrutiny.

Whenever we strive to stand out in any way—at work, in our families, or among our friends—we won't always get the responses we desire. There will be some people whose toes we step on and those who are jealous of our efforts or successes. It's a human tendency to take shots at people when they're on the top but it's never easy to accept when the detractors are friends or family members whose support we may have counted on.

Keep in mind today the saying about how the monkey who climbs the highest has the most exposed backside. Also be aware of the fact that achieving your goals may make you the target of others' anger, envy, and pettiness. Instead of being depressed about it, resolve to stay on course and surround yourself only with those who want the best for you.

When I want to pick a rose I have to remember that there are usually a few thorns underneath.

Rather light a candle than complain about the darkness.
—CHINESE PROVERB

I think the world can often be divided into people who complain about things and people who actually do something about them. For example, I have a friend who is suffering from several signs of depression—frequent crying spells, a change in eating habits, and feelings of hopelessness about her future—but she refuses to seek counseling. I also know someone who saw an internist and then a therapist at the first sign of postpartum depression so that she'd have the tools to cope with this debilitating but very treatable illness.

Depression strikes millions of women every year but instead of seeking the appropriate help, a lot just complain about their lethargy and lack of interest in life and never get the proper care. Sometimes this is due to a failure in understanding their depression, but often it's because complaining about something is easier than actually doing something about it. Confronting a problem head-on is frightening because it forces us to look hard at ourselves and take stock of changes we need to make in our lives.

Choose to light a candle today instead of just complaining about the darkness. Taking action through education, seeking the advice of a professional, or just acknowledging that it's time to make a change can be the empowering step you need to take to bring light back into your life.

I will light a candle in my life today.

Life is a process of becoming, a combination of states we have to go through. Where people fail is that they wish to elect a state and remain in it. This is a kind of death.

—ANAIS NIN

One morning I read an obituary about one of the pioneers of the "hang ten" concept of surfing in the 1960s whose blond good looks had epitomized the lazy, good life of the California "beach bum." The man's ex-wife said that he had never been able to adapt to such responsibilities as fatherhood, and that his desperate desire to recapture his sixties lifestyle had tormented him and driven him to kill himself with alcohol.

Whenever we go through a transitional phase, we probably feel sad about the past and want to hang on to it or what it represented to us. This can happen when we outgrow our first love, watch our children become independent, or see our parents become elderly and infirm. All of these sorts of occasions will induce a type of melancholy, which is normal; it's when we go to great lengths to keep the past alive and refuse to accept change that we hurt ourselves and become prey to depression.

Try to welcome the transitional phases in your life despite the fact that they will probably make you feel blue initially. "Growing pains" don't just occur when our bodies change; they occur when our lives change, too, and both situations require that we push through the hurt in order to grow up and successfully take on the challenges of life.

I will greet the next stage of my life with anticipation and optimism.

Money-giving is a very good criterion . . . of a person's mental health. Generous people are rarely mentally ill people.
—KARL A. MENNINGER

One day I was talking to a friend of mine who is battling an incurable physical disease that has severely limited where she can go and how she lives her life. Despite all of her health problems and the costs she's incurred dealing with them, she remains one of the most generous people I know. She's the first to call when you're feeling down, she's quick to give her money to worthy causes or needy friends, and she cares more about bringing happiness to others than spending money on herself. I'm convinced that this generous attitude is partly why she's able to deal so well with an illness that would devastate most others.

I contrast this woman's charitable behavior with the attitude of a wealthy acquaintance who feels entitled to every penny he has earned and who refuses to part with any of it without a fight. Instead of giving his relatives love, he measures their worth in monetary terms, withholding birthday and holiday checks if they have displeased him. It's not surprising that despite his money he's a miserable, lonely man whom few people enjoy being around.

Today, find a charity or cause that you believe in and try to give a check—small or large—on a regular basis. Although this may hurt financially or you may feel awkward at first, it will definitely train you to think about the welfare of others—a surefire way to help beat depression.

A generous act will improve my mental well-being.

Remember that a kick in the ass is a step forward.
                                                    —ANONYMOUS

One of the hardest things to live through is having a very public failure or embarrassment. Almost everyone I know, myself included, has been fired from a job at one time or another, or been humiliated in front of coworkers by a boss. How we respond to these very painful whacks in the rear says a lot about how we'll bounce back from similar indignities in the future.

Lily wanted to work in marketing but took a less attractive job in banking to be near a man with whom she was in love. When the relationship ended she wished she hadn't made a career decision based on her emotions. A few months later, Lily was let go in a cutback. After brooding over her two losses for a few weeks, Lily decided to put the best face on the situation and focus on finding the kind of job she had initially wanted but not pursued. Now she has a position for which she is well suited and she's grateful she was let go from the bank.

If you are brooding because you've been kicked in the rear, take some time to analyze the ramifications of what has happened to you. Is it possible that the boss who dressed you down also made some good points about how your work could improve? Is the job you lost one you really loved, or is there something else you'd like to pursue? Learning the fine art of turning your typhoons into tail winds can make these sorts of challenges work for you instead of against you and can put you several steps ahead of where you'd be if it had never happened at all.

Adversity is an opportunity to challenge my assumptions about what's right for me.

The sorrow which has no vent in tears may make other organs weep.

—FRANCIS J. BRACELAND

In my late twenties I endured a seemingly endless series of hardships, and disappointments. Although I thought I was handling the adversity well, others began to comment on my haggard appearance. I also made steady pilgrimages to my doctor's office with low-grade fevers and frequent infections. But worst of all, I awoke one morning with abdominal pain so severe I was taken to an emergency room and diagnosed with a bleeding ulcer. That day I realized I had to make some changes to protect my physical and emotional health.

Therapy helped me recognize that I had buried my emotions and troubles, assuming that no one would want to hear about my trials. Instead of processing my mood swings and grief in a healthy way, I had kept much of it bottled up inside and replayed my miseries endlessly in my head. Once I was in that trap it was very difficult to reach out and ask someone to help me, but seeing a therapist, talking with friends, acknowledging my pain, and using antidepressants helped return my mind and health to normal.

Take advantage of opportunities to vent your sadness today. Screaming, crying, throwing things, writing in a journal, exercising, and seeing a therapist are some helpful ways not just to vent the pain, but to keep your body from "weeping."

I won't repress my tears today.

I do not say a proverb is amiss when aptly and reasonably applied, but to be forever discharging them, right or wrong, hit or miss, renders conversation insipid and vulgar.
—MIGUEL DE CERVANTES

Well-meaning friends can say the most infuriating things during difficult times: "At least you have your health," "It's always darkest before the dawn," or "It can't get any worse than it is now." When life *does* get worse or the dawn seems to be further and further away, these bromides can have the effect of upsetting us more than helping us.

To be fair, inspirational quotations and proverbs can often have a beneficial effect on our moods and attitudes. But if we hear the same ones over and over again, they become meaningless and begin to trivialize how we feel. In fact, one friend who was having financial trouble told me that after countless people said, "At least you have your health," she snapped, "Yeah, but my health can't pay the bills!"

Try to be understanding if people are throwing proverbs at you in an effort to cheer you up; it may be the only response they can think of. If it angers you, though, explain that you'd prefer to talk specifically about what's bothering you without hearing a clichéd response. Although it may stop the conversation dead in its tracks, it might also open the door to a more helpful and meaningful dialogue with someone who cares about you but doesn't know what to say.

I will be assertive when the "help" others offer me isn't helpful.

The world is too dangerous for anything but truth and too small for anything but love.

—WILLIAM SLOAN COFFIN

I watched a fascinating show one day about near-death survivors who had all experienced the same vision after being declared clinically dead. Each one said they had left their bodies, gone through a long tunnel at top speed, and then met a being of light that most chose to call Jesus Christ. In this presence they relived their lives, re-experiencing everything they had ever done in two ways—how it had affected them as well as how it had affected those around them. Before returning to their bodies they had learned the lesson that the purpose of life was to love and to do so was our noblest challenge as humans.

Radiating love is one of the hardest things to do if we're depressed because we're usually self-centered, angry, and hurtful. Choosing to express and demonstrate love, however, has the capacity to turn our days around if we allow it. By opening our hearts to feel compassion for others, we allow that same emotion to permeate our defenses and we encourage a positive change in our attitude.

Try to choose love, not anger or hatred today. Keep in mind that your behavior doesn't just affect yourself, but that it impacts on countless others, as well. And if there is, indeed, a life review at the time of your death, you'll want to take care that your actions and attitude today are as loving as possible.

I will express love toward myself and others today.

Over the years our bodies become walking autobiographies, telling friends and strangers alike of the minor and major stresses of our lives.

—MARILYN FERGUSON

One expert in treating depression has written that anyone who endures physical or sexual abuse is guaranteed to become depressed and that our bodies carry a memory of that abuse deep in the tissue. Because our bodies "remember" the abuse, she encourages her patients to act out the pain physically so that it doesn't continue to hurt them either consciously or subconsciously.

One of the therapist's favorite techniques for dealing with abuse is called the Pumpkin Project. The patient gets a pumpkin to represent the abuser and then draws a symbolic face on it. The top is cut open and the seeds pulled out as if they were the abuser's guts; the patient throws and stomps on them as desired. Finally, the pumpkin is destroyed in whatever method is most appealing. Many of her patients like to mangle the pumpkin with their bare hands, allowing all the old feelings of rage, shame, and fear to wash over them. Some women finish off the exercise by microwaving the remains of the pumpkin or burying it.

Allow your depression to be vented in a very physical manner today. If you can't find a pumpkin use a cantaloupe, watermelon, or other similar item that you can safely destroy. Or try ripping up a phonebook, tearing it page by page. Whatever you do, make sure that your body is involved in the exercise because until the source of depression is destroyed, it may come back to haunt your mind and body in the future.

I heal my mind when I heal my body.

We take our bearings, daily, from others. To be sane is, to a great extent, to be sociable.

—JOHN UPDIKE

One of the lowest points in my life was when I moved to the country and found myself surrounded by beautiful scenery and lots of cows, but no friends. Because I was completing a book at the time, I was alone for long stretches of time with only a baby to occupy me. The more isolated I felt, the more depressed I became. And the more depressed I became, the harder it was to force myself to get out. The highlight of many days was just having a conversation with another adult at the grocery store, gas station, or dry cleaner's.

Mothers of small children are particularly vulnerable to becoming isolated and depressed. So are women who are laid off from jobs and afraid to let others know of their "failure." One of my friends told me that as a result of giving birth to her son in the winter she became house-bound and lonely. Medication and joining a new mothers group were what restored her sanity.

Has depression sapped your desire to be sociable? Have you let friendships slide because of work or other responsibilities? If the answer is yes, make a point of getting out among people today, preferably with a friend. Not only will you temporarily forget about yourself, but you'll find that the stimulation of being with other people can be a terrific antidote to the blues.

I will not isolate myself today.

Any time is the time to make a poem.

—GERTRUDE STEIN

For several years I have published a newsletter that helps people learn how to heal from the pain of eating disorders and the depression that accompanies them. Nearly every week I receive poems for publication from readers who say that writing verse has been the most healing thing they have done in processing their emotions and dealing with the mood swings.

Anyone can write a poem. There is no format that is considered "correct"; the only correct poem is the one that you connect with. Try your hand at writing a few lines about how you are feeling and allow the emotions to create the lines and the punctuation. The process of letting your feelings spill onto the page unedited is one of the most time-tested ways of fostering and maintaining emotional health, and it's one that we can use at any time and in any setting.

Poetry is the voice of my soul.

You think you have a handle on God, the Universe and the Great White Light until you go home for Thanksgiving.
—SHIRLEY MACLAINE

My friend Janice is a very mature and insightful mother of two grown children. During most of the year she handles daily life and its minor hassles with aplomb and good humor. She is a great sounding-board for friends and her priorities are in order. But all of her self-esteem and poise vanish like clockwork each Thanksgiving when she visits her parents, and she inevitably returns home depressed, vowing never to make the trip again.

For many of us, holidays are a time to relinquish our maturity temporarily because we find ourselves—often unconsciously—imitating childhood behaviors that no longer serve us well. For example, the moment Janice arrives at her parents' house she starts to compete with her older brother for their approval. Then her mother usually finds something disparaging to say about Janice's appearance, and the mother-daughter battles of many years earlier are reignited. Janice starts to sulk, thinks of similar incidents that have occurred throughout her life, and then leaves in a huff.

Because of relentless advertising messages that the holidays are a joyous and warm time, it's easy to forget that they can also be very difficult, particularly for women. Consider solutions such as staying home to create your own holiday traditions if family togetherness is a problem, and remember that whatever keeps you serene and grateful is always going to be the wisest course.

I will be especially gentle with myself during the emotional swirl of holidays.

*Why do you spend your money for that which is not bread,
and your labor for that which does not satisfy?*
—ISAIAH 55:2

I am acquainted with a person who grew up in poverty
and rose to be the head of a large company with hundreds
of employees. He is a millionaire many times over and has
a house that is like a museum, yet he is an unhappy man
who is forever scrambling to find something that will satisfy
him. When money didn't work for him he began to collect
cars and boats, and when that didn't do the trick, he divorced his wife and now drinks heavily to ease the pain of
loneliness and depression.

Most of us will never be millionaires, but the lesson of
this story is still pertinent to our lives. All of us at some
time buy things—like clothes, jewelry, and trinkets—in the
mistaken belief that they will make us happy. It is the same
longing that leads us to become workaholics or hedonists,
which doesn't necessarily make us better people. Lasting
happiness never comes from external situations; it only
comes when we are transformed from within.

Do an honest analysis today of where your time and
money go and what percent of it is devoted to meaningful
pursuits. If you discover that most of your energy is going
toward elevating yourself in ways that are unhealthy or superficial, try to redirect your priorities to include more time
for spiritual and charitable work. You'll often find that
whenever you can put the welfare of others before your
own, the inner emptiness that used to be sated with external trappings will exude joy, not depression.

I will labor toward something that brings me lasting joy.

Maturity is coming to terms with that other part of yourself."
—RUTH TIFFANY BARNHOUSE

I have several friends who suffer from compulsive behavior that has in the past made their lives almost unlivable. One friend pulled out so much of her hair that she occasionally had to wear hats and scarves to hide the gaps. Another felt compelled to make exhaustive to-do lists for every member of her family that kept her awake most nights past midnight.

Such behavior is often called obsessive-compulsive disorder ("OCD") and can be controlled effectively with medication and therapy. Although people with OCD often feel that their rituals are what keep them sane and that omitting them will result in harm, they are also often depressed and embarrassed by the strange compulsiveness of their actions. Through therapy, gradual exposure to what the sufferers fear most, and medication, those with OCD can gradually eliminate their obsessive behavior and find peace and serenity.

If you think you have OCD, see a medical professional for a diagnosis. Not only is it depressing to feel that you have no control over your behavior and activities, but extreme compulsiveness often prevents a person from doing the activities she most enjoys. Taking the first step toward getting help for this very treatable illness will play a large role in returning hope and happiness to your life.

I will not allow unhealthy obsessions and compulsions to rule my life today.

Touch . . . is ten times stronger than verbal or emotional contact and it affects damn near everything we do.
—SAUL SCHANBERG

Anthropologists who have studied certain tribes in Latin America report that the children rarely cry or fuss, they don't need to be disciplined, and they usually grow up with high self-esteem and optimism. The reason for this, the experts say, is that these cultures feature a lot of touching and hugging, and that children are held, caressed, and made to feel special starting at a young age.

In our society we don't encourage personal contact. Infants sleep in cribs instead of with their parents, and when a baby cries we're told that comforting them will "spoil" them. As adults we are often uncomfortable being touched or hugged because our society often frowns on public displays of affection. But research has shown that touch is one of the key things that promotes self-esteem and happiness. For example, patients who are touched by their hospital caregivers heal faster than those who are only spoken to, and people who are briefly touched by supermarket cashiers report higher levels of contentment and happiness than those who aren't.

One effective way to fight depression is to bring touch into your life. Whether it is reaching out to touch someone today, asking for hugs from friends or family members, or visiting a massage therapist, you will be giving your emotions a boost. Depression often breeds isolation, but if you can fight that tendency by making physical contact with another person today, you'll have taken an important step toward lifting that cloud of sadness.

I will give or get a hug today.

Not everyone grows to be old, but everyone has been younger than he is now.

—EVELYN WAUGH

How we react to bad times varies tremendously from person to person. I know some people who actually thrive on difficulties, only feeling alive and purposeful when they have a crisis to manage. Others respond in opposite ways; they become sick, cynical, and look as if they are carrying the weight of the world on their shoulders, as a result of their problems.

Of all of the American presidents of recent memory, Ronald Reagan is the only one who refused to allow the various burdens of his position to visibly age and harden him. Most of the men who hold this office have ended their tenure looking markedly older than when they were elected, but Reagan's sunny personality, optimism, and spiritual faith were cited by friends as some of the reasons why his eight years in power didn't make him look so old.

Remember today that no matter how bad you feel or what you're going through, you can decide that depression will not age you physically and emotionally. Regular meditation has been shown to be an effective way of dealing with stress and depression, as well as serving to lower the amount of aging hormones in the body. So today take some time just to relax and breathe if life seems overwhelming. Not only will you improve your mental health, you'll enjoy the side effect of not wearing your troubles on your face.

I will not grow to be old before my time.

When we yield to discouragement it is usually because we give too much thought to the past and to the future.

—Saint Teresa of Lisieux

Diana was forty-eight when her husband of eleven years announced that he was in love with another woman and that he wanted a divorce. In short order, Diana's husband moved out, fired her from the business they had co-founded, and Diana began a descent into depression. "I'm old, unemployed, and unlovable," she thought to herself every day when she looked in the mirror. "I have nothing to look forward to."

Gradually Diana got back on her feet. She started jogging, entered a new career, and began to date. Her forward progress, however, was slowed by mournful reminiscences of what she'd lost, and many days she was paralyzed with fear about her future. After one rocky and tearful day Diana suddenly realized that there wasn't anything she could do about the past, and that her emotional survival depended on doing her best one day at a time. It was only after this pragmatic assessment that Diana made peace with her situation and recovered from depression.

Although it can sound trite to ask us to take life one day at a time, frequently that's what we must do if we're discouraged about where we've come from or we're frightened about the future. Try to focus on today only and cut off your mental wanderings if they start to overtake your thinking. If you can keep your mind only on what you can accomplish in the next twenty-four hours, it will be easier to see the world and your life in a hopeful, optimistic way.

I will live in day-tight compartments.

Living with a saint is more grueling than being one.
                                                  —ROBERT NEVILLE

One day I was talking with a friend who was depressed about the difficulty of juggling her business and personal lives. She was upset because at work she was facing a number of pressing deadlines while at home her children were demanding more energy than she possessed. "I never feel adequate in any area of my life anymore," she lamented, adding, "My husband is so much better at this juggling act than I am."

I've heard this complaint from countless women over the years. Whenever we feel deficient in one area, we compare ourselves to someone we feel is doing a better job and we elevate them to sainthood. Once we've set up this unfair comparison ("My husband is calmer with the children than I am," or "He's more organized than me,"), we are sure to feel depressed and inferior around them, regardless of whether our views are accurate.

Remember today that there are no saints or perfect people to whom you should compare yourself. Sure, some may handle things better at times, but that doesn't mean you need to put yourself down or forget about your own special qualities. Learn positive skills from those you admire but keep your own unique talents and assets in perspective, particularly when a negative frame of mind tempts you to believe that you don't have any.

I am as "perfect" as the next person.

Hatred is self-punishment.

—HOSEA BALLOU

A famous political strategist spent much of his career attacking opponents and devising political campaigns that eviscerated the personal lives of the men his candidates ran against. He often cheerfully admitted that hatred and a desire to "win" were his chief sources of motivation. Years later as he lay in bed dying a prolonged and painful death, he renounced his life's work, saying that living with hatred had reaped nothing but depression about how many people's lives he'd hurt.

Hating people never brings happiness. Psychologists say that hatred is usually an indication of unhappiness with something in ourselves and that when we express rage verbally or physically, the real victim is us. It takes energy to carry around hate for someone and when that is our main emotion, there's no room for love, forgiveness, or joy.

If you are depressed, ask yourself if your feelings stem from unexpressed anger about something that happened long ago. Were you physically or emotionally abused? Ridiculed in your childhood for your beliefs or looks? Humiliated at work? Dumped by a boyfriend? Any one of these situations has the potential to create long-standing feelings of unworthiness and hatred, and until you can view your *bête noire* with compassion and acceptance, you'll only punish yourself with depression.

I won't allow thoughts of hatred to possess my mind today.

Since you are like no other being ever created since the beginning of Time, you are incomparable.

—BRENDA VELAND

Several years ago when a certain antidepressant hit the market it was hailed as the greatest, most wonderful thing ever discovered for people suffering from depression, phobias, and addictions. Adoring articles told of the millions of Americans whose lives had been changed for the better after taking it. As a result, I tried it to help me get through a very hard time. Unfortunately the medication made me sick and I had to stop taking it, which only made me feel like more of a failure since the world's greatest antidepressant helped everyone but me. Luckily, another medication did the trick.

The lesson I learned from my experience was that there are many ways to recover from depression and that subscribing to a particular viewpoint or medication because it has worked for someone else may be detrimental to my emotional and physical health. For example, one person may find relief through exercise and therapy, while someone else may prosper with antidepressants and a certain diet.

Be flexible today about how you cope with your blues. Just because a particular therapist, course of treatment, or activity has worked for a friend doesn't mean it'll work for you. Instead, seek out answers that mesh with your beliefs, life-style, and chemistry and don't be discouraged if you have to try several solutions before discovering what works for you.

There are always different strokes for different folks when it comes to finding what's effective.

Each friend represents a world in us, a world possibly not born until they arrive, and it is only by this meeting that a new world is born.

—ANAIS NIN

So often we hear about men taking off a night a week with "the boys" during which they drink, play poker, and reminisce about shared experiences. It's rarer to see women taking time to get together with their female friends and hash out their problems, share a meal, or laugh about things they've done together. But more and more I'm hearing stories about female friends going to great lengths to preserve their relationships in spite of their jobs, their marriages, and the pressures of motherhood.

One such group calls themselves the Moms. These five women met during Lamaze class and now get together once a month at someone's house to share potluck dinners and stories of childcare and lazy husbands. Another group calls themselves the Lunch Bunch. These four professionals meet every few weeks for lunch at a restaurant to share stories about their lives and offer encouragement to each other.

Try to find time to gather with female friends who will help you through troubled times and relive some past pleasures. Although it may seem impossible to squeeze one more thing into your schedule, experiencing the richness of female kinship through a book club or a leisurely meal is a sure way to have fun, beat the blues, and put your well-being high on your priority list.

I am not too busy to share my life with my female friends.

God gave burdens, also shoulders.

—Yiddish proverb

I read in the paper one morning about a woman who'd given birth to a handicapped child when she was in her early twenties. The woman recalled that she'd been totally unprepared for anything but a perfect child and that she'd become deeply depressed over how she would care for him. As time went on, though, she surprised herself by coping resourcefully and even became a well-known crusader for the rights of the handicapped. In fact, she was so successful in changing laws and regulations at the local level that she was selected to oversee national policies pertaining to discrimination of the physically impaired.

If we think about it, we have also probably been faced with a seemingly insurmountable problem, but managed to somehow overcome. A friend said that in the beginning of her first pregnancy she'd learned that her mother was dying of lymphoma. Although she often felt overwhelmed by the pressures of trying to care for herself and spend as much time as possible with her mother, she managed both with grace. She credits her husband, her friends, and her faith for giving her comfort and support when she was most depressed.

Don't forget today that while God does indeed give us burdens, we are provided with shoulders to carry them, too. You may feel crushed and dispirited by some event, but by reaching out for help and believing in yourself, you'll find that coping is easier than you think.

I am capable of dealing with whatever comes into my life.

I am a woman first of all.

—ANAIS NIN

Men and women are different creatures, and one of the ways we differ from men is in our hormonal make-up. The word *hormone* comes from the Greek meaning "stir up," which is exactly what female hormones do from time to time—stir us up in various ways. To deny that this occurs or to pretend that we are similar to men in every single way is contrary to biological evidence.

One of the ways our hormones influence us is right before our menstrual periods when some of us suffer from premenstrual syndrome (PMS). People who are affected by PMS say that they are alternately depressed, irritable, and hungry several days out of each month, and every woman who has ever had a baby knows that the "baby blues" are all but inevitable within a week of delivery. For the majority of women these types of depression clear up of their own accord, but for others the severity can be so disabling that professional help or medication could be necessary.

Be aware today of how your female nature could be contributing to your mood swings. If you are prone to depression every month, take care to prevent yourself from unnecessary suffering by avoiding food or drinks that may exacerbate the problem and making sure you get enough exercise. And if you've suffered from postpartum depression before, make sure you have some therapeutic resources available after your next baby. Our unique biology may have inconveniences at times, but with planning and education we can weather whatever our hormones stir up in us.

I am proud of what makes me a woman.

In a way winter is the real spring, the time when the inner thing happens, the resurge of nature.

—EDNA O'BRIEN

For many years I have been a winter-hater because I can't stand the cold, the ice, and the snow. Trees without leaves depress me, I can't stand wearing layers upon layers of clothes, and the amount of time spent outdoors is minimal, at least in my part of the country. An acupuncturist, however, has converted me to thinking that winter is not just a season to be endured but an important time to retreat inward, replenishing and redirecting my energy.

In the Eastern system of medicine winter is a yang season during which the body needs warm root-type foods and the spirit should plant inner "seeds" that will sprout in the spring. These "seeds" can include analyzing one's direction in life and making necessary corrections, beginning a spiritual journey, or starting a diet and exercise program. But whatever the choice, the purpose is to still the mind, listen to one's body, and heed whatever message comes.

Instead of resenting the limitations of winter, focus on the critical inner tasks you can do during this time. Getting in tune with yourself can not only help you address imbalances that may be contributing to your depression, but it can teach you how to use the rhythms of nature to heal yourself.

I will use the coming months to heal and redirect my spirit.

You know what happens to scar tissue. It's the strongest part of your skin.

—MICHAEL R. MANTELL

Depression never leaves us unscarred. The days, weeks, or months we deal with lethargy, hopelessness, insomnia, eating changes, and self-destructive behavior can't help but fundamentally alter us and the way we see the world. If we receive the proper help and allow this emotional wound to close, the experience can leave us stronger, wiser, and more compassionate. If, however, the depression drags on and we do nothing to make ourselves feel better, the wound will never heal and we'll never grow that resilient scar tissue.

If your depression is making you feel battered and broken today, try to remember that a deep cut feels awful at first, but once it heals properly it leaves you with stronger emotional "skin." With the proper assistance, self-love, and the healing passage of time, your emotional "break" may become your greatest strength.

The unscarred person is the one who's never discovered her own strength.

Silence is the cheapest therapy in the world.

—JONATHAN FOUST

Every morning I go out for a walk or jog, and often I take along a portable tape player so that I can listen to whatever strikes my fancy in the way of books or music. On the mornings when I choose silence, however, I inevitably have more creative thoughts and breakthroughs with personal and professional problems. Letting my thoughts flow uninterrupted seems to leave me feeling more insightful and balanced than when I indulge in being entertained.

Silence has long been recognized as one of the quickest and easiest ways to access inner knowledge. Religious traditions usually involve enforced periods of silence as ways to attain spiritual knowledge. Although I know people who visit monasteries and other healing retreats for weekends, others find silence by simply having a quiet time every day when they unplug the phone, turn the television off, and let their minds roam uninterrupted.

Isolation is not the same as silence. When we're depressed, we tend to avoid others and replay negative messages in our heads. The silence that heals is a deliberately structured period in which we communicate with our inner selves, ask for guidance, and listen to what comes up. Not only will we feel more balanced, when we submerge ourselves in silence, but we'll foster a spiritual connection that helps us cope with every challenge that confronts us.

I will nourish the silences in my day.

Give a woman a job and she grows balls.

—JACK GELBER

Some of the most astonishing transformations I have seen in terms of self-esteem are among women who have decided to leave home and take a job in the working world. Whether this has been done out of necessity or out of choice, women who enter the working world with low self-esteem usually discover that accomplishing tasks on deadline, working well with colleagues, and receiving a paycheck gives them more confidence than staying at home and not getting paid or being intellectually challenged.

This type of transformation occurred in an older friend of mine who had to go back to work when money became tight. Although she was terrified to reenter the job force after more than a decade of being at home, she overcame her fears and landed an assistant's position at a radio station. Within several years she was a different person. Instead of being completely wrapped up in her children's lives, she grants them more independence and has a healthier relationship with them. She is now more willing to take risks and learn new things, and she exerts more of an effort to dress up and look attractive every morning, which makes her feel better about herself.

If you suffer from low self-esteem and you don't work outside the home, consider taking on some volunteer activities or a part-time job. The more you can assign yourself tasks that allow you to stretch and grow as an intelligent, creative person, the more fulfillment, excitement, and joy will be in your life.

I will add a job or an activity to my life that will help me grow in self-confidence.

I see adult sexuality more as an expression of emotional attitude than as a function of anatomy.

—RUTH BERKELEY

A middle-aged friend of mine, Rita, began therapy in her forties because she was depressed about never having formed a lasting, intimate relationship with a man. The therapist helped Rita see that her father's comments about her ugliness as a child had caused her to internalize that belief, leading Rita to reject all femininity by starving herself into a boyish shape and never wearing flattering clothes. Although she appears to others to be a trim, attractive woman, Rita doesn't see herself that way and thus behaves in ways that deflect interest from men.

One of the therapist's first assignments to Rita to help change her self-image was to go to a lingerie store and buy a sexy outfit. Rita, however, was so upset by visiting this store, that she walked in and out quickly, nearly bursting into tears. This assignment helped Rita learn that by shutting off the sexual, feminine part of herself for all these years she had also cut off the ability to feel playful, joyous, or spontaneous. These emotions are just starting to return as she works on visualizing herself as a sensual and vibrant woman.

Be aware of the messages you send yourself today about being a woman. Although depression normally brings about a loss in libido and self-esteem, ask yourself if you've internalized inaccurate messages about your femininity that could be causing the dark moods. If so, learning to discover, or rediscover, the joys and pleasures of being female can take us on some of the most exciting rides of our adult life.

I am a vibrant, healthy, and desirable woman.

Without wood a fire goes out; without gossip a quarrel dies down.

—Proverbs 26:14

I know a woman who is continually depressed about the relationships she has with her husband's sisters. She often complains that they treat her cruelly, and she's obsessed with the fact that they completely ignored her prior to her wedding. Despite the fact that a great deal of time has passed since the original hurt and she rarely sees her sisters-in-law, my friend replays the drama constantly, keeping the feud going through her own thoughts and actions.

Sometimes when we've had arguments we feel compelled to tell everyone about it in an effort to justify our position and ameliorate our bad feelings about the situation. Whenever we do this, however, we make no headway in feeling better. Instead, we just keep the battle alive through our obsession with being right. But, by taking the high road and addressing our differences in a more mature way, we're bound to feel better than if we just continue throwing wood on the dying embers of the argument.

If you're depressed because an old quarrel with someone is still alive and burning within you, ask yourself if your own behavior might have something to do with your emotions. Continually rehashing a past disagreement won't help you; it will only keep you unhappy and angry. Try to learn to channel your energy toward creating harmony, not enmity, and you'll find that not only will the fires of anger be extinguished, but it will be easier to find happiness in your relationships with others.

I will not throw wood on old fires today.

Evidently Christmas was an unmitigated joy only for the people who inhabited department store brochures and seasonal television specials. For everyone else the day seemed to be a trip across a minefield seeded with resurrected family feuds, exacerbated loneliness, emotional excess, and the inevitable disappointments that arise when expectations fall far short of reality.

—Joyce Rebeta-Burditt

In the two weeks preceding Christmas, calls to depression hotlines usually skyrocket because people—overwhelmingly female—feel stressed, sad, and lonely. One therapist says that between Thanksgiving and Christmas her female patients set unrealistic standards for themselves to create perfect meals, perfect parties, and perfect decorations.

There are several ways to combat the "holiday blues." We can set budgets to avoid overspending on gifts so that we don't get depressed about being strapped when the bills come in. We must set limits on eating and drinking because too much of either creates negative moods. Finally, we have to remember that our mothers and grandmothers didn't have the same time demands placed on them that we do today, so even if they baked pies from scratch or sewed new holiday dresses, our lives may be happier and simpler with store-bought items.

Once we can learn to choose activities, surroundings, and people that bring us happiness instead of misery, we can generate genuine holiday cheer.

I will not create unrealistic expectations for myself during the holidays.

Blaming mother is just a negative way of clinging to her still.
—NANCY FRIDAY

When Janet was growing up, her mother often made fun of her budding sexuality with such comments as, "It doesn't matter if you wear a bra or not because there'll never be much there." Janet's mother also flirted outrageously with her boyfriends, and when Janet became a playwright, her mother refused to attend the performances or she showed up drunk. Partly as a result of her dysfunctional relationship with her mother, Janet suffers from low self-esteem, depression, and an inability to sustain rewarding female friendships.

How we interacted with our mothers while we were growing up is a key indicator of whether we'll be happy, well-adjusted adults. Clashes are common in the teenage years as mothers are threatened by their daughters' desire for independence, but when mothers continually try to upstage or put down their daughters, they cause lasting wounds. Continuing to blame our mothers for our problems in adulthood without doing anything to address those challenges, however, will only perpetuate this unhealthy relationship.

Instead of blaming your mother today, try to understand her and have compassion for her efforts to do her best for you. Once you can move out of the role of victim and into the role of survivor, you'll not only be free from childhood pain, but you'll have better tools to pass along to your own children.

When I accept and affirm my mother, I love and respect myself.

A reservoir of rage exists in each person, waiting to burst out.
—REX JULIAN BEABER

When I am at my most depressed, I am often at my angriest. I find that my rage erupts over silly things: losing a parking space, a child's misbehavior, or a stranger's actions. I am usually surprised at such crazy responses to minor irritations, but depression is not a rational condition and anger is not an uncommon side effect.

Most therapists believe that depression is a mask for a deeply buried anger that must be vented in order for the person to overcome depression. There are many safe ways to express anger; smashing ice cubes, pounding pillows, and screaming in the car, are just a few. Women often find these types of exercises difficult and embarrassing because of the deeply ingrained belief that showing anger is un-feminine, so find a private spot where you can completely express your feelings without worrying about being seen or overheard.

Don't be frightened of your rage if it starts to spill out today. Not only is anger a sign that you are very close to uncovering some core issues, but when it is released appropriately, it can give you a sense of happiness and well-being.

My anger helps me understand myself and why I respond to people and situations the way I do.

*The thing that makes you exceptional, if you are at all, is
inevitably that which must also make you lonely.*
                                         —LORRAINE HANSBERRY

There was a girl in my high school who was so brilliant
at such a young age that it was discouraging to be in the
same class with her. She was doing math and science projects at a college level in ninth grade and she was continually selected for academic honors. Being in the same class
with her meant that you'd never have the top grade, no
matter how hard you tried. Because no one could match
her, jealousy inevitably created cruelty, and people made
fun of her instead of realizing that she couldn't help the
fact that she was born gifted and that being very intelligent
came as naturally to her as breathing.

Whenever we stand out in some way we are going to
feel lonely. This is true of stunning models who are
shunned by jealous girlfriends, of ambitious people who are
back-stabbed by their business associate, and of handicapped people who are surrounded by others who don't
know how to relate to them. If we are different in any way
and we decide not to conform to the expectations of others,
we threaten those who prefer to be part of the crowd and
their discomfort will leave us feeling isolated.

If you are depressed and lonely today, consider that
you might be exceptional in a way that makes others un-
easy. Instead of being sad and trying to fit in, work harder
to find people who share your interests and who accept you
just as you are. Although it can be lonely to be yourself, it
would be more depressing to compromise yourself and try
to be like everyone else.

I will seek out people who appreciate my uniqueness today.

I felt like writing about a time when I was probably, and I think all of us are, the happiest in our lives—before the obligations start in.

—NEIL SIMON

As we get older, our burdens get heavier. We amass bills, our children cause us concern, and our friends and parents suffer from serious illnesses. The carefree nature of childhood—when we are cared for by our parents—dissolves into years of worrying about paying our bills on time, sustaining important relationships, and having peace of mind.

One of the heaviest obligations that face many women today is the simultaneous caring for both their children and their aging parents. The number of women who have this double duty has grown so large that researchers have dubbed them the "Sandwich Generation," and have noted that depression and stress-related illnesses are common to them. One woman I know holds down a full-time job, goes home to feed her children, and then goes to her mother's home at night to cook her meals and do her errands. She laments that she has no quality time for herself or her family, but guilt and lack of money prohibit her from putting her mother in a nursing home or getting extra help.

If you are feeling overwhelmed and depressed by your burdens today, try to take some steps to simplify your life. Seek out the support of people who are in similar binds, try to arrange a sharing of duties, and investigate options like adult day-care. Above all be gentle and realistic about how much you're doing, and allow time to experience the very human emotions of anger, self-pity, and sadness that accompany being so many things to so many people.

I will meet my obligations with courage and the support of those who can understand them.

Never mistake motion for action.

—ERNEST HEMINGWAY

A friend of mine who was depressed about her husband's drinking and abusive behavior toward her and her daughter is a classic case of someone who mistook motion for action. Amy talked endlessly about her situation, enlisted the sympathy of family and friends, gathered lists of potential alcoholism treatment centers, yet did nothing concrete—like scheduling an intervention or attending a support group—to help change the situation. As she filled her time with more and more busywork yet failed to confront her husband or his problems directly, her fatigue and depression deepened.

Too often when we're sad about something we postpone taking action because we're fearful of the outcome. Amy knew exactly what was troubling her, but she confused her "busywork" with genuine progress. I, too, am guilty of this tendency. For example, if I'm depressed about "writer's block," I'll often sharpen pencils, clean my computer, or do unnecessary research instead of just sitting down and trying to write.

If you are depressed, try to take concrete steps toward finding ways to feel happy. Instead of talking about needing a therapist, pick up the phone and make an appointment with someone. If you're upset about a troubling situation, confront it head-on instead of just gathering information about it. The more specific actions you take to counteract depression, the more likely you'll be to find solutions to what ails you.

I will take action today.

How many are the things I can do without!

—SOCRATES

Having problems making ends meet dramatically increases the likelihood of suffering from depression. And as females we are particularly vulnerable to having the financial problems that lead to depression; as single and divorced women with children to raise we often live beneath the poverty level and we still earn less than our male peers.

My friend Celia became severely depressed when her husband left her for another woman, refused to pay child support for their sons, and stuck her with his credit card bills. Within months she went from living a comfortable life to falling behind on mortgage payments. Scrutinizing every purchase and living hand-to-mouth for several years until she got back on her feet left Celia feeling anxious and upset all the time. It was only after having a number of sessions with her parish priest that Celia began to see that her situation wasn't completely hopeless; her setback taught her to be thrifty, she developed feelings of self-sufficiency, and the children forged a relationship they wouldn't have had otherwise.

Although it's very difficult, try not to allow financial hardship to overwhelm you and cloud your hope for the future. Increase your resourcefulness by seeking out second-hand stores and yard sales and improve your marketability through education and training. Although being female does increase the odds of being poor, with thriftiness, optimism and the assistance of others, you can often get back on your feet and enjoy the happiness that financial stability can provide.

I will not allow a lack of money to overshadow what happiness I do have in life.

*Is it sufficient that you have learned to drive the car, or shall
we look and see what is under the hood? Most people go
through life without ever knowing.*

—JUNE SINGER

Making the decision to go into therapy is difficult because most of us don't want to think that we need help
negotiating the rough passages of life. For most of our lives
we've probably been able to muddle through unaided, so
when something big threatens our emotional well-being, we
may hesitate before calling in a professional for guidance.
We may also have misconceptions about what therapy involves, or we might think it frivolous to pay someone to
talk about ourselves.

Despite universal misgivings and fears, everyone I
know who has gone into therapy has been happy with the
results. Whether they have been in counseling for four
weeks or four years, the process of setting aside time for
appointments, investing money in themselves, and seeing
the results of being introspective and proactive has been
gratifying and life changing. Therapy is hard work, but
sticking with it when the going gets tough can give us self-
esteem, courage, and a belief in our ability to survive hard
times.

Ask yourself today whether knowing how "to drive the
car" is sufficient to get you through life or whether it's time
to see a mechanic who will help you understand what is
under the hood. Although we may think we understand
ourselves, an unbiased professional is probably better at
dealing with something as important as our mental health.

*When I fearlessly look under my "hood," I am able to drive
through life with purpose.*

We call this Friday good.

—Thomas H. Eliot

Although Loreen doesn't suffer from bouts of depression that render her incapable of eating or sleeping properly, or of seeing the world in a hopeless way, she habitually feels depressed every Monday morning upon awakening. Research has shown that she isn't alone; people tend to be most depressed on Monday mornings when the workweek looms ahead and to be happiest on Fridays because the possibility of a relaxing and enjoyable weekend is at hand.

Therapists advise that to minimize these feelings of depression we should try to keep to as normal a schedule as possible on weekends. For example, staying up late several nights in a row and eating poorly can cause feelings of lethargy on Monday mornings. So it's wise to avoid bingeing and to try to go to bed as close to our normal time as possible on weekends. And not expecting our weekends to be magical times can help avoid feelings of letdown when Monday rolls around and our high expectations for the weekend haven't been met.

If Monday morning is traditionally a down time for you, try to think of ways to make it more pleasant. Perhaps scheduling a treat—like lunch with a friend—can make Monday less ominous, as can going to bed on Sunday night at a reasonable hour. While Mondays may never bring the same sense of anticipation that the end of the workweek does, it's good to know that the solution to these types of blues is always just four days away.

I won't let the Monday blues drag down my week.

Two things a man should never be angry at: What he can help, and what he cannot help.

—Thomas Fuller

Leslie grew up in a physically and emotionally abusive household. Her father often singled her out for beatings when he had had a bad day and her mother gave her frequent tongue-lashings about how fat, lazy, stupid, and thoughtless she was. As an adult Leslie has had a hard time thinking of herself in positive terms, and whenever something goes wrong in her life she becomes extremely depressed and mulls for days about her childhood trauma and how much it has contributed to her low self-esteem.

While it is true that Leslie has suffered greatly and that the abuse has definitely affected the way she feels about herself, it's also true that there is nothing she can do to alter the past. It is her choice to dwell on these misfortunes and to blame her childhood for her problems instead of trying to find ways to heal herself. Many resources exist to help people like Leslie recover; books on dysfunctional families, self-help groups, and motivational speakers are just some of the options.

There are many things we cannot change including painful situations that occurred in childhood. If you are dwelling on something that ended long ago, make the decision to close that chapter of your life. The sooner you can stop obsessing about something you cannot change and direct your mental energy toward creating an attitude of hopefulness and change, the greater are your chances of finding the happiness that may feel so elusive now.

I will accept the things I cannot change and not allow them to dictate my behavior today.

Of course I don't always enjoy being a mother. At those times my husband and I hole up somewhere in the wine country, eat, drink, make mad love, and pretend we were born sterile and raise poodles.

—DOROTHY DeBOLT

One morning I was jogging with a friend who said she had a confession to make that she felt guilty about: She didn't always enjoy staying home with her children. "It's so hard to admit it, and so depressing to know I feel that way, but if I don't talk about it, I'm going to go crazy!"

I, too, have to confess to having the same emotions at times. As much as I love my children and cherish being with them, I need some time every day when I can be alone and gather my thoughts. When I don't get this period I begin to lose my emotional balance and become depressed. My solution has been to have regular childcare—even when money is tight and I have to forgo another pleasure— so that I can do something that reminds me I'm more than just a mom. This action benefits everyone; I'm saner, my children are exposed to other people and to learning situations, and our time together is that much more precious.

Virginia Woolf once wrote that every woman needs a "room of one's own" if she is to be happy. Work today to make sure that you have a "room" of some kind—whether it's an actual room, a block of time, or a solitary activity— that allows you to do something relaxing and empowering. And keep in mind that unless you stake out this important piece of sanity, no one else is going to do it for you.

I will find my own "room" today.

Being a good psychoanalyst, in short, has the same disadvantage as being a good parent: The children desert one as they grow up.

—MORTON M. HUNT

I know someone who has been seeing the same therapist for over seven years on a regular basis. Although she has worked through a divorce, changed jobs, improved her disposition, and become a more diverse and outgoing person, she is still dependent on her therapist to help her through every major and minor crisis she faces. Once she was offered a stimulating position at a higher pay in another state but turned it down, saying that she couldn't bear to be parted from the therapist she relied so heavily on.

If we are seeing a therapist, we will naturally become somewhat dependent on that person for a while, particularly if we are in crisis. But once we've dealt with the major issues and learned coping skills, it's imperative that we leave the "nest" to try and fly on our own. For some people this may take as little as a few months; for others, depending on the complexity of issues, it could be years. But any good therapist will encourage us, after the appropriate period of time, to rely on ourselves and not use the therapist as a crutch to solve every problem that comes our way.

If you are in therapy, take stock of your progress today. Is every session a learning experience or has therapy just become a comfortable haven from life? It feels scary to strike out on our own whenever we've been dependent on someone or something, but if we're hindering our growth because we're frightened of being self-sufficient, then it's probably time to face our fears and learn to fly solo.

Outgrowing my therapist is a sign of progress.

Ah! it is well for the unfortunate to be resigned, but for the guilty there is no peace.

—MARY SHELLEY

Victoria is depressed and feels guilty. Despite having had a first baby with relative ease, she and her husband have unsuccessfully struggled for more than five years to have another child—a condition called "secondary infertility." "I'm glad I already have one perfect child, but that doesn't erase the fact that the past few years have been filled with unmet expectations and sadness because we can't give our son a brother or sister," she says.

There doesn't have to be a "right" reason for being depressed. If something is causing us to feel dispirited, we must take steps to cope with that problem instead of judging ourselves harshly for having the emotions in the first place. Victoria finally found a support group for mothers like herself, which helped her cope with her feelings of sadness, anger and inadequacy. "These women understand how unhelpful it is to be told that we 'should' be happy with one child. They help me see that my grieving is normal," she says.

Don't add to the already heavy burden of depression by feeling guilty. Depression can result from a variety of factors—including environmental, situational and chemical. So instead of telling ourselves that our feelings aren't valid, we need to seek out counseling, medication or other sources of support. Until we can learn that depression isn't a matter of willing ourselves to feel a certain way, we will have "no peace."

I will not judge or blame myself for depression.

Thinking gets you nowhere. It may be a fine and noble aid in academic studies, but you can't think your way out of emotional difficulties.

—ETTY HILLESUM

One of the most effective ways to stop ruminating on your troubles (which only worsens them) is to engage in a task that requires concentration. Television-watching and other passive activities don't count. Below are some ideas to stimulate your brain juices:

1. Do the Sunday crossword puzzle.
2. Get an early start on your taxes.
3. Begin to learn a computer program.
4. Balance your checkbook.
5. Do a jigsaw puzzle.
6. Read the biography of someone you admire.
7. Listen to a tape that teaches a foreign language.
8. Go to a lecture at a museum.
9. Plan your dream vacation, complete with lodging and driving routes.
10. Put together a piece of furniture from a do-it-yourself store.

These are just suggestions; you should do whatever distracts you most successfully to take your mind off your troubles.

A stimulated mind is a happy mind.

God allows us to experience the low points of life in order to teach us lessons we could not learn in any other way. The way we learn those lessons is not to deny the feelings but to find the meanings underlying them.

—STANLEY LINDQUIST

When Miriam's infant son died in her arms she was catapulted into what she calls "the dark emotions" that led to her greatest spiritual breakthrough. She explains, "The day of my son's funeral was the clearest day of my life. I felt his eyes radiating throughout the sky, his life-force intensified a thousandfold, and I recognized for the first time that there is a purpose in life and that purpose is to love the world as if it were your own child."

When we are immersed in darkness the ensuing spiritual breakthroughs can be the most formative events of our lives. These are the times when our concept of God actually becomes our knowledge of God, and we discover that through mourning and emptiness we allow a new type of fullness and love to fill us up. The theologian Matthew Fox has written that this is not a salvation from pain, but a salvation *through* pain.

If you are in your "dark night of the soul," try not to fight the grieving and despair. The process of spiritual rebirth includes going through a torturous period of doubt and turmoil, but once a part of you inside has died, you are free to usher in a new chapter of spiritual flowering and joy.

The low points in life often bring the spiritual high points.

Each morning sees some task begun,
Each evening sees its close.
Something attempted, something done,
Has earned a night's repose.
                    —HENRY WADSWORTH LONGFELLOW

Every year Fran experiences the blues the day after Christmas: she's sad that the hoopla in anticipation of the holiday is over, she's exhausted from all the work she's done to prepare for Christmas, and she's usually unhappy that her grand expectations for the day weren't met. Therapists call this "letdown" depression because it's common to experience sadness when an important occasion has just come and gone.

If you have "letdown" days after holidays, birthdays and special occasions—like weddings—it's wise to prepare ahead for the inevitable blues. One effective technique is to schedule the "letdown" day with activities so that you don't have time to nurse your depression. For example, on the day after Christmas Fran shops the sales all day long. Another friend treats herself to a manicure or massage the day after her wedding anniversary, which gives her something to look forward to if her husband hasn't remembered the occasion.

Don't allow "letdown" days to take you by surprise. If you've always been emotional after special days you've eagerly anticipated, plan ahead so you don't have time to brood. Schedule a weekend getaway, a matinee at the theater, or lunch with a close friend, and do as much as you can to keep your mind and hands occupied. With some planning, there won't be any dispiriting days following your bright ones.

I will finish a set of tasks to keep me from feeling down.

If we admit our depression openly and freely, those around us get from it an experience of freedom rather than the depression itself.

—ROLLO MAY

A university in the city where I live holds an annual symposium on depression and related illnesses every spring, and a well-known person is invited to give the key-note speech about how they survived their own bout with depression. The speakers have ranged from famous writers, to television journalists, to a Hollywood celebrity, but the result has always been the same: a famous person disclosing their bout with depression results in a flood of publicity and prompts large numbers of people to seek help for their depression for the first time.

In my own circle of friends I've found that disclosing my periodic depression has enabled others to open up to me about their own episodes. Not only do we always learn something from each other, but I always feel better when I find out that someone else has experienced the same type of situation before and survived. Above all, it's helpful for us to realize that we don't have to appear perfect or flawless.

Don't underestimate the power of confession if you're feeling alone in your depression. I believe that a problem shared is a problem half-solved, so try to shed your inhibitions and confide your fears and anxieties in those closest to you. Not only will you help yourself, but such candor may be a spark for someone else to begin the healing process.

I free myself and others from expectations when I am honest about how I feel.

The capacity for passion is both cruel and divine.
—GEORGE SAND

One night I was at a party when a person I didn't know well finished a glass of wine and announced to me that she was unhappy and wanted to have an affair with a friend because she no longer felt any passion for her husband. She also was seeing more lines in her thirty-five-year-old face, she said with a sigh, and unless she took advantage of this dangerous opportunity she feared she'd never feel sexy, desirable, or exciting again.

I'm not sure whether this woman ever acted on her desires but I do know that unless she found another way to generate the feeling of passion in her life, she was bound to be unhappy for a long time. Everyone has an activity or person in their lives who can stimulate those emotions; for artists it is their work, for mothers it is often their children, and for literary types it is a good book. While these activities are admittedly more mundane than illicit sex, the enjoyment we receive from them often has the ability to lift us from depression.

Be aware of the power and danger of passion today. We must make sure that we have enough of this potent emotion for happiness, but not so much that it runs away with our sanity. Good, safe passion will uplift and satisfy us; dangerous passion may feel wonderful for a short period of time, but it will ultimately only drain us and leave us longing for more of what can never satisfy us in the long run.

I will indulge myself with "safe" passions today.

Guilt: the gift that keeps on giving.

—ERMA BOMBECK

Ever since becoming a mother, I've had to fight feelings of guilt because of a chronic lack of time in my life. It sometimes seems as if no matter how much effort I put into my marriage, my work, or my children, there aren't enough hours to do a "good enough" job and I get down on myself for being imperfect. But more and more I've begun to fight back because I recognize that much of my guilt comes from having unrealistic expectations for myself and my busy life.

For example, someone once commented to me that she'd "never" allow her children to watch anything but Sesame Street, which made me feel awful because I permit a wider variety of shows, particularly when I'm busy and need time to myself. Upon reflection I realized that my friend has live-in help and doesn't work outside the home, which makes this type of restriction far easier to enforce. Another friend is active in countless charities and fund-raising drives, which can make me feel guilty, until I remember that she's unmarried and childless and has far more free time than I do.

As busy women we can really torture ourselves with guilt, but we must learn how to stop or we'll always be depressed about our perceived "deficiencies." Try to focus on what you've done well today—like fixing a nutritious meal—and tell yourself that you've done a good job. If you can learn how to ease up and see yourself in a more generous light, you won't need to torture yourself with "the gift that keeps giving."

I am "good enough" just as I am today.

Words are the physicians of a mind diseased.

—AESCHYLUS

Sally has a very low opinion of herself and is often depressed about what she perceives as her "failings": She insists that she doesn't have friends, isn't attractive, and can't succeed at whatever new activity she tries. To combat these misperceptions, Sally's therapist told her to start a journal and record every positive comment she received and every feeling of satisfaction about herself she felt. In a short period Sally was able to see that her convictions didn't match how others perceived her and her outlook over time became more positive about herself.

Whenever we're depressed we tend to see ourselves—and the world—in a bleak way and we selectively focus on negative information. If we can put nice things in a journal —like receiving a compliment on our appearance or feeling proud after completing a project at work—then we'll have something concrete to refer to when we feel low. Therapists say that whenever we read positive things about ourselves we are distracted from negative thoughts and receive mental feedback that is incompatible with depression.

If your mind is feeling "diseased" today, use the power of words to heal it. Write down every nice thing that happens to you and review it at the end of each day. If you can use concrete events to create positive emotions about yourself, you'll eventually drown out the negativity that you've become accustomed to.

I will use words to heal my mind today.

The greatest and most important problems of life are all fundamentally insoluble. They can never be solved but only outgrown.

—CARL JUNG

There are certain passages in life that are inevitable and, usually, depressing: having loved ones die, watching our children grow up and leave us, getting older, having a painful love affair, or discovering that our bodies can't do things they once did so easily. Although most of us will experience these phases with varying amounts of sadness and wistfulness, there's no real solution to this type of pain except to learn that life has bittersweet moments that we'll never be able to erase, only outgrow.

Jacqueline has had trouble dealing with her parents' declining health. Every time she visits their house and notices how forgetful her mother has become, or how difficult it is for her father to walk, she goes home depressed. "I know there isn't anything I can do to make them young and vital again, but it's still hard for me to admit to myself that they can't take care of me if I need them. Now *I'm* the one who has to take care of *them*," she says regretfully.

Be patient with yourself if you're depressed about normal passages of life. You will hurt for a while and be awash in nostalgia, but with time and support from friends, these are phases that you will eventually outgrow.

Even if I can't solve my sadness, I can outgrow it at times.

Index

A

Abuse, Oct. 6
Acceptance, Feb. 11, Aug.
    13, Sept. 5, Sept. 12,
    Sept. 26, Dec. 20
Aggressiveness, July 8, July
    26
Aging, Jan. 16, Apr. 27,
    July 19, Oct. 26, Dec. 15
Alcohol, Apr. 1
Alternative Therapy, Aug.
    23, Nov. 20, Dec. 23
Amends, June 2
Angels, Mar. 3, Aug. 5
Anger, Feb. 19, Mar. 10,
    Aug. 24, Oct. 22, Dec.
    13
Artistic Temperament, Feb.
    26
Assertiveness, Apr. 13,
    June 27, Aug. 4, Oct. 18

B

Balance, Apr. 7, June 18,
    Sept. 27, Nov. 4
Body Language, Aug. 26
Burning Bridges, Apr. 8

C

Caffeine, Mar. 14
Calendar Blues, Jan. 26,
    Dec. 19, Dec. 26
Cancer, June 28
Change, Mar. 5, Nov. 14
Chaos, Sept. 13
Childhood, Feb. 7
Childlike, Mar. 15
Chocolate, Apr. 26
Common Sense, Feb. 15
Compulsive Shopping, July
    14
Coping Skills, May 30
Creating a Vacuum, Jan.
    12, July 20
Creativity, Apr. 18
Criticism, Feb. 2, Sept. 14
Crying, Apr. 11
Cynicism, Apr. 24

D

Dancing, June 14
Dark Side, Sept. 29
Daydreaming, Jan. 22
Death, June 6, Nov. 10
Decision-Making, Mar. 6

Delusions, Aug. 14
Detachment, May 13, Sept. 11
Determination, June 13
Discrimination, Mar. 29, Nov. 7
Divorce, Mar. 19
Domestic Abuse, Apr. 15, Aug. 18

E
Education About Depression, June 8
Electroconvulsive Therapy, June 26
Emotions, July 1
Envy, Aug. 30, Nov. 12
Exercise, May 12, Sept. 23, Oct. 5
External Appearance, May 6

F
Failure, Mar. 20
Faith, Apr. 19
Family Problems, Jan. 10, Mar. 11, Aug. 1, Sept. 17
Fear, May 20, June 4, Nov. 8
Feminine Mystique, Jan. 23, Oct. 9
Food, Mar. 2, Aug. 21
Forgiveness, June 23, Oct. 1, Dec. 10

Friendship, Jan. 20, Apr. 10, May 29, July 17, Aug. 11, Dec. 2

G
Gardening, Apr. 28
Genetic History, Feb. 9, Aug. 27
Giving, Jan. 9, May 8, Nov. 15
Goals, Jan. 1, May 7, Aug. 6, Sept. 4
Gratification, Feb. 22
Gratitude, June 17
Group Support, Feb. 12
Growth, Apr. 30, Oct. 24, Dec. 5
Guilt, June 7, June 30, Aug. 25, Sept. 22, Dec. 29

H
Happiness, Mar. 31, May 31, June 20, July 7
Hatred, Nov. 30
Healing, Jan. 27
Helping Others, June 9
Hiding, Feb. 10
Hitting Bottom, Mar. 30
Holidays, Nov. 23, Dec. 11
Honesty, Jan. 25
Hopefulness, Oct. 31
Hormones, Mar. 8, Dec. 4
Housework, Nov. 11

Humility, June 25
Humor, June 10, July 12, Oct. 15

I
Imagination, Sept. 30
Imagined Ugliness Disorder, May 17
Injustice, Oct. 23
Inner Child, Apr. 4
Inner Peace, Jan. 8
Isolating, Feb. 1, June 16, Nov. 17, Nov. 21

J
Job Stress, Jan. 6, Oct. 3
Joy, Sept. 9
Juggling Roles, Jan. 15

L
Learning from Mistakes, Mar. 24, June 11, Aug. 9, Sept. 24, Nov. 16
Learning to Receive, Feb. 8
Listening, Mar. 27
Living in the Moment, Jan. 21, July 25
Living Fully, Feb. 17
Loneliness, July 10, Sept. 10, Dec. 14
Love, Nov. 19
Lying, Mar. 1

M
Manifestation of Depression, May 9, July 2, Sept. 25, Nov. 1, Feb. 5, June 19, Oct. 8, Nov. 24
Medication, Jan. 4, July 5, Aug. 8, Nov. 2, Nov. 6
Memory, July 21, Nov. 9
Miscarriage, Aug. 12, Oct. 12
Money, Dec. 17
Mood, Aug. 10
Motherhood, Feb. 20, May 19, June 3, July 9, July 13, Aug. 2, Dec. 21
Mothers, May 10, Sept. 2, Dec. 12

N
Nature, May 3, May 14, Sept. 7, Sept. 19
Nutrition, Apr. 23

O
Obsession with Body, Mar. 18
Obsessive Compulsive Disorder, Nov. 25
One Day at a Time, Jan. 7, Nov. 28
Optimism, Feb. 24

P

Panic Attacks, Jan. 30, Sept. 6
Passion, Dec. 28
Patience, Oct. 14, Dec. 31
Perfectionism, May 15
Personal Power, Aug. 7, Sept. 8, Oct. 25
Perspective, May 5, July 3, July 16, Sept. 15, Oct. 11
Pets, Mar. 26
Playing, May 1
Pleasure, Mar. 17, Apr. 5, Oct. 29
Popularity, Aug. 29
Positive Thinking, Feb. 28, Apr. 20, May 4, Sept. 1
Post-Partum, Feb. 16
Power of Fabric, Mar. 23
Power of Scent, Jan. 19, July 23
Power of Touch, Nov. 26
Power of Words, Jan. 11, Nov. 18, Dec. 30
Prayer, May 26, July 6
Pregnancy, Mar. 16, July 30

R

Reaching Out, Jan. 5
Realism, May 2, Oct. 16
Recovery, May 25
Relationships, May 23, Nov. 3

Relaxation, Aug. 15, Nov. 27
Remorse, June 15
Resiliency, Apr. 22
Resourcefulness, Apr. 6
Responsibility, Mar. 28
Retirement, Aug. 17
Risk-Taking, June 1, July 11, Aug. 3
Rituals, May 16
Rootedness, May 24

S

Sanity, Jan. 31
Seasonal Affective Disorder, Sept. 20
Secondary Infertility, Dec. 23
Self-Confidence, Feb. 21, July 22
Self-Deception, Feb. 25
Self-Esteem, June 22, Nov. 29, Dec. 8
Self-Image, Mar. 7, Dec. 9
Self-Pity, Jan. 2
Self-Scrutiny, Aug. 16, Sept. 21, Oct. 27
Self-Talk, Oct. 4, Oct. 30
Separating from Children, Apr. 14
Sequencing, Mar. 12
Setting Limits, May 18, July 28

Sex, Apr. 9, July 18, Oct. 28

Sexual Desire, Jan. 17, Feb. 3

Sharing, Feb. 14, Mar. 4, Mar. 13, Dec. 27

Showing Up for Life, Mar. 25, Sept. 28

Silence, Jan. 14, Apr. 16, Dec. 7

Sleep, Oct. 13

Sleep Deprivation, Feb. 6, Mar. 21, Oct. 20

Smiling, June 24

Smoking, Jan. 24

Solitude, Feb. 29, July 4

Soothing Rituals, Mar. 22, July 24

Sorrow, June 21

Soul, Mar. 9

Spiritual Growth, Feb. 13, Dec. 25

Spiritual Strength, Apr. 29, June 29

Spirituality, Apr. 3, May 11, May 21, July 15, July 29, Aug. 20, Sept. 16

Stress, May 28, Aug. 31

Suffering, Jan. 18, Sept. 3

Suicide, Jan. 13, Aug. 19

Summer Doldrums, July 31

Support, April 25

Surviving, Feb. 23, Oct. 2, Dec. 3, Dec. 6

T

Taking Action, Sept. 18, Oct. 7, Nov. 13, Dec. 16

Tea, Apr. 12

Therapists, Feb. 18

Therapy, July 27, Oct. 19, Nov. 5, Dec. 18, Dec. 22

Thinking, Dec. 24

Thoughtfulness, June 12

Time, May 22

Tranquilizers, May 27

U

Understanding Depression, Aug. 22

Unemployment, Apr. 17

Uniqueness, Apr. 2, Dec. 1

V

Victimization, Feb. 27

Visualization, Oct. 10

W

Weight, Jan. 28, June 5

Workaholism, Feb. 4

Worrying, Jan. 29, Oct. 21

Writing, Aug. 28, Oct. 17, Nov. 22

(Photo by Alain Jaramillo, Ironlight Studios)

CAROLINE ADAMS MILLER is the author of *My Name Is Caroline* and *Feeding the Soul,* as well as a contributor to *Full Lives: Women Who Have Freed Themselves from Food and Weight Obsession.* In 1988 she started The Foundation for Education about Eating Disorders (F.E.E.D.), a nonprofit organization that provides information about eating disorders and consults with schools and other organizations about how to cope with and prevent the spread of anorexia, bulimia and binge-eating disorder. Ms. Miller is a frequent guest on television and radio shows, as well as a noted public speaker. A *magna cum laude* graduate of Harvard University, Ms. Miller lives in Bethesda, Maryland with her husband and two children.